# A HISTORY OF THAILAND

by

**RONG SYAMANANDA,** M.A. (Cantab)

Professor of History

Chulalongkorn University

*Eighth edition 1993*
*2,000 copies*
**ISBN 974-08-0591-4**

**CHULALONGKORN UNIVERSITY**

 **THAI WATANA PANICH CO., LTD.**

599 Maitrichit Road, Bangkok, Thailand          **230.-**

# AUTHOR'S PREFACE TO THE THIRD EDITION

Probably the contents, the style and the form of the second edition of this book have appealed to the readers. That is why it has been selling rather well and so it is now out of print. Its success has encouraged me to pick up a pen and revise it, while preserving the arrangements as in the previous edition. In doing so, I have brought the story of the book up to the present by adding a few pages to the last chapter on " Democracy in Thailand", for which a great deal of material is in my hands. In this connection, there are two schools of thought. The conservative school asserts that a reliable history of any nation should be terminated at a period approximately one generation or thirty years before the present time, since some of those who have played a part in it are still alive and their records are normally not open to the public, and therefore it would be rather difficult to produce a true picture of the period. On the other hand, the contemporary school aims at including all the important events up to the present in such a history, although some of the documents bearing on it may not be accessible or available, and this will assist those who live in the present generation to acquire at least a grasp of what has been happening around them. I myself subscribe to the view of the contemporary school.

Once again I confirm my responsibility for the publication of the present edition. As a matter of fact, I have since the appearance of the first edition, been waiting for any comment or opinion, directly delivered to me, but none has reached me. I therefore assume that all is well for my "History of Thailand." Frankly speaking, I still welcome any advice, suggestion or comments for its improvement.

*Rong Syamananda*

*July 30, 1976*

## AUTHOR'S PREFACE
## TO THE SECOND EDITION

It is gratifying to note that the sale of the first edition of this book which was printed in January 1971 was exhausted in about one year. I have, since then, been receiving inquiries as to when the second edition will be issued. This dovetails with my desire, since I wish to revise the book so as to bring it up to date and make it a better one. In the revision of the volume, I made some additions and deletions and put in some pictures and maps for the sake of accuracy and greater clarification. For this task, my colleagues in the Faculty of Arts, Chulalongkorn University, willingly gave me their full co-operation, for which I thank them sincerely on this occasion.

I wish to repeat, however, that I am responsible for everything that is printed in the present volume. Should it appear to be incorrect, I shall be grateful to any person who draws my attention to it, so that it will be put right afterwards.

*Rong Syamananda*
October 2, 1972

# AUTHOR'S PREFACE TO THE FIRST EDITION

In my student days in England, I came across an old English proverb: "Nought venter nought have," written by John Heywood in the sixteenth century. I now wish to apply the proverb to this book. It has always been my unalterable ambition to write a history of Thailand in English so as to present a Thai point of view to foreign readers. To the best of my knowledge, there have, so far, been only two such versions of Thai history, while the rest have been produced by foreign scholars. The reason why there is a dearth of books on Thai history in English, though some Thai scholars are capable of doing such a kind of work, is that they lack self-confidence or they say that they do not possess sufficient knowledge of English for this purpose nor do they have time to devote to the writing. Moreover, they do not apparently like to be subject to criticisms of an unkind sort. In this connection, there is an aspect that is unsavoury. A book may be 99.90 percent perfect, but if a slip or slight mistake is found, an outcry would be raised against it as if a serious crime has been committed. I still believe in the value of the above mentioned proverb which encourages me to take up the challenge and to put the material which I have been collecting for many years into book form.

There are two kinds of history — simple history and complex or advanced history. The book which is before you is a simple history. That is why I have dispensed with footnotes. Some people agree with me that a footnote which sometimes occupies more than half a page not only interrupts continuous reading but it also interferes with concentration. A bibliography of books, journals and articles which I have consulted or utilized is given at the end of the present volume.

I would like to stress the fact that I accept the sole responsibility for the subject matter and opinion expressed in it. Should any slip or mistake crop up in it, I willingly crave pardon for it. Corrections will be gratefully acknowledged and made use of in a future edition, if there is a sufficient demand for it to be printed. In conclusion, I thank Mr. William Warren, a senior lecturer in English and my colleagues in the Department of Geography and History and the Department of Library Science, Faculty of Arts, Chulalongkorn University, for their generous assistance and co-operation in the perusal and proof-reading as well as for the offer of useful suggestions for the improvement of the book.

*Rong Syamananda*
January 8, 1971

# CONTENTS

# CONTENTS

# INTRODUCTION

The present volume of the history of Thailand begins with the adoption of the Tri-Rong flag as the Thai national flag and also of the name of Thailand for the country — Muang Thai.

NATIONAL FLAG. Before Rama II's reign (1809-1824), the Thai national flag was plain red. As far as it can be traced, no one knows when this flag came into use. However, the ship carrying the Upaliwong Buddhist mission to Ceylon in 1753 hoisted the red flag. Presumably the red flag must have been widely used from time immemorial. The exact reason for adopting red as the colour of the flag must remain a matter of conjecture. It might have represented "blood" which would in turn signify bravery, as the Thais had already shown themselves as valiant warriors who never shrank from any impending danger. Noteworthy instances of such famous deeds are many - Queen Suriyotai's death in combat on her elephant in 1549, King Naresuan's assault of a Burmese camp by climbing the wooden stockade with the blunt side of a sabre held in his mouth in 1586, and Phya Pijai, "the Broken Sword," for his daredevil fight with the enemy in 1773. Good fortune favoured Rama II with three white elephants. The first one was found at Battambong in 1812, and was a perfect male specimen. The second one, another perfect example of a male white elephant, was presented to him by the Prince of Chiang Mai in 1816, and the third one, also a male elephant, was a gift from the Prince of Nan. In his "Lords of Life," Prince Chula Chakrabongse stated that "According to Brahmanic belief, if a monarch possessed one or more white elephants, it was a glorious and happy sign. These noble animals were not exactly white and in the Thai language they are not called white but albino. They had pale yellow eyes and white nails, any hair on the head or body was white, and the hard rough skin was either pink all over or had pink patches on the head, trunk or forelegs." The possession of these white elephants constituted a glorious reflection on his reign and gave him much delight. In order to celebrate this auspicious event, he caused the symbol of a white elephant surrounded by a chakra or wheel to be put in the middle of the red flag. The royal sailing ships then showed the new flag in the countries where they traded, and thus it became a familiar sight in the foreign waters. In later reigns, the chakra was quietly removed, and the red flag, with the white elephant symbol, continued to be the national flag until 1917.

**NATIONAL FLAG OF THAILAND UNTIL 1917**

On September 28, 1917, Rama VI(1910-1925)changed the national flag to be the Tri-Rong one, consisting of five horizontal bands of, from the top, red, white, double dark blue, white, and red, since the white elephant flag often had a shabby look when it was flown abroad. Siam joined the Allies in the First World War and it is most likely that the King wished to show a modern looking flag to the world. The red background of the flag would in all probability bode ill for a monarchy in view of fact that the Bolsheviks were at that time using the red flag. The preamble of the Law on the National Flag emphasized the fact that the old national flag was not imposing enough for the country. There should be three colours in the new national flag corresponding to those that were normally found in the flags of the Allies of Siam. For the benefit of the people, a statement was issued to clarify the significance of the three colours. Red, white, and blue represent the Thai nation, Buddhism and monarchy respectively. Such is the red, white and blue Thai flag, as is well known everywhere and in design and colour, it is on a par with any other national flag.

NATIONAL FLAG OF THAILAND

SIAM OR THAILAND. What does Siam or SAYAM in Thai language mean? According to M. de La Loubère's "A New Historical Relation of the Kingdom of Siam," "The Name of Siam is unknown to the Siamese. It is one of those words which the Portuguese of the Indies do use, and of which it is very difficult to discover the Original.........In a word, those that understand Portuguese do well know that according to their Orthography Siam and Siaom are the same thing, and that by the Similitude of our Language to theirs, we ought to say the Sions, and not the Siams: for when they write in Latin, they call them Siones."

"The Siamese give to themselves the Name of Tai, or Free, as the word now signifies in their Language: and thus, they flatter themselves with bearing the Name of Francs, which our Ancestors assumed when they resolved to deliver the Gauls from the Roman Power. And those that understand the Language of Pegu, affirm that Siam in that Tongue signifies Free." Etienne Aymonier stated in his " LE SIAM ANCIEN " that "Ces Siamois qui n'ont jamais-point essentiel à noter - perdu le contact de leurs frères de race, s'appellent eux-même les Petits Thais ou les Thais Méridionaux, par opposition aux Grands Thais ou Thais du Nord. Mais leur véritable nom technique est celui de SYAM, qui paraît pour la première fois, à notre connaissance du moins, dans une inscription en langue vulgaire du CHAMPA, vers 1050 A.D., puis reparaît au XII siècle dans la galerie des bas - reliefs d'Angkor Wat." In 1924, Prince Damrong Rajanubhab gave a series of lectures on the history of Thailand at Chulalongkorn University in which he pointed out that "The name Siam arose in the Sukhothai period, but it was used by foreigners. The Thai people themselves did not call their country Siam, but they named it Muang Thai or the Kingdom of Sukhothai." As a matter of fact, Siam is a Sanskrit word. This therefore shows that the Indians must have been the first to call the country by this name. China and other nations only copied it and called it accordingly. The meaning of Siam, when translated, is twofold. Firstly it means swarthy. Secondly it means gold. If the word Siam is applied to people, the meaning will be swarthy people. If applied to the country, it will be a gold bearing one. Most of the foreign scholars of archaeology have considered that the word Siam which arose in those days applied to the Thais who had settled down in the south. The Great Thais (Ngiou) who made their home in the Burmese territory have therefore been called Shans on the understanding that originally Shan was the same word as Siam. With the lapse of time, it has been pronounced differently and has become Shan. However, the writers of another school have objected to this consideration on the ground that the Great Thais and the Little Thais have a fairer complexion than the Laotians and the Khmers. It would not be proper to call them swarthy people. Their own consideration is that Siam should mean an area where there is a gold mine, because the country really has a gold mine. This dovetails with the religious history which says that Asoka the Great entrusted his missionaries with the establishment of Buddhism in the Suvarnabhumi. Pallegoix also stated in his "Description du Royaume Thai ou Siam" that Sayam meant the dark race. Prince Wan Waithayakorn accepted Prince Damrong's opinion concerning the Indian origin and the Sanskrit meaning of Sayam. In his "Research Work on the Thai Race," Luang Vichitra Vadhakarn wrote thus: "It is certain that Sayam is a Khmer word. It may be translated as black, swarthy or gold. There is now a general consensus of opinion that the name Sayam was first adopted for use in the eleventh century and that it means swarthy, gold colour or gold."

Before the Thai people migrated southwards from China, the Menam valley, corresponding to the north and the centre of the Indo-Chinese Peninsula, was under the Khmer rule from about 1000 A.D. and was divided into the northern and the southern region. The Khmer governor of the northern region lived in the city of Sayam which later became known as Sukhothai, and it was the Thais who changed the name. Lavo, now known as Lop Buri, was the governor's seat of the southern region. The Chinese who had been trading in Indo-China before that time combined the names of Sayam and Lavo or Lohoh together and called the country of the Thais "Sien-Lo Kok", "Sien-Lo", "Hsien", or "Hsien-Lo" as appearing in some Chinese chronicles. Marco Polo (1254-1324), a Venetian traveller, who spent about seventeen years in the service of the Emperor Kublai Khan of China, made use of the Chinese material when he wrote a book on the countries in the Far East. He called the country of the Thais "Locac" a strange version of Siam. His book "Travels of Marco Polo" was widely read and translated into many Western languages. Thus the Europeans began to take great interest in China which was supposed to be an exceptionally rich country and also to refer to the country of the Thais as Siam with some variations after the Chinese, long before the arrival of the Portuguese at Ayutthaya in 1511. During the reign of the Ming dynasty (1368-1644), Thailand with the name "Hsien-Lo" had, in fact, been a firmly established foreign nation with the Chinese. Odoric de Pordenone (1286-1331) wrote in his book of travels as follows: "Trente lieues par delà Malaca, on trouve le Cap de Sincapara, et l'ayant doublé on rase à main gauche les royaumes de Pan, et de Patane, qui appartient aussi au Roy de Sian." The Portuguese, however, came on the Thai scene as the first Europeans who set foot on the Thai soil, and coined different names for the country such as Sarnau, Xarnauz, Sion, and Ciama. Castanheda favoured Siao for it, while Correa gave the name of Siam to it. The word "Siam" was used by Sir James Lancaster in his first voyage to the Far East in 1592. Other names of Sayam were Siyam, Ansean and Asian. By the seventeenth century, Siam became the generally accepted name of the country among the Europeans, as witnessed by Mr. de La Loubère's book on Siam (French version) which was printed at Paris in 1691 and its English version which was issued at London in 1693. The Mons and the Khmers named the Thai country Sayam, while the Burmese favoured the name Jodia instead. However, Sayam in Thai language did not appeal to the Thais who preferred to call their country by the official name of the current capital. When Sukhothai was the capital from 1238 to 1378, the country was known as the Kingdom of Sukhothai. With Ayutthaya as the capital (1350-1767), it was the Kingdom of Ayutthaya. At the beginning of the Bangkok period, it was known as Muang Thai or Krung Thai (Thai State), as witnessed in the Burney Treaty of 1826. Sayam or Siam became the official name of the country only in the reign of the fourth monarch of the Chakri Dynasty — King Mongkut (1851-1868). When he signed the treaty with Great Britain on April 18, 1855, Muang Thai was still used, but in the ratification of the said treaty on April 5, 1856, Siam was substituted for Muang Thai for the first time and continued to be used till June 24, 1939 — a period of less than one hundred years.

Still the popular name of the country has been Muang Thai from ancient times. It appears on the stone inscriptions of the Sukhothai period and in the treaty with Great Britain in 1826. In his book on Siam, Kaempfer called the country "Muang Thai." Muang corresponds to "land" and Thai is "free." Muang Thai then means the Land of the Free. Luang Vichitra Vadhakarn put forward a theory that "Thai" signified great in the Sukhothai period and acquired the meaning of free at the beginning of the Ayutthaya period. Slavery was unknown among Thai citizens in the Kingdom of Sukhothai and the first few kings of Ayutthaya adopted it from the Khmers. A slave who succeeded in fleeing from Ayutthaya into Sukhothai became a freeman at once. For this reason, the meaning of the word "Thai" is "great' in respect of the race and "free" as regards the status of a person in the Kingdom of Ayutthaya. It has been suggested by De La Loubère that the Thais should be proud to call themselves the Franks of the East. His book, *A New Historical Relation of the Kingdom of Siam*, states that "The Siamese give to themselves the Name of Tai, or Free, as the word now signifies in their Language : And thus they flatter themselves with bearing the Name of Francs."

After the revolution of 1932, the leaders of the new government became increasingly nationalistic-minded. When the Pibulsonggram government took office at the end of 1938, it embarked on a programme of national reconstruction. With regard to the name Siam, it did away with it both in Thai and European languages. In Thai, Prades Sayam was changed to Prades Thai, and in English the name was Thailand with the equivalent form in other languages. This change was clearly stated in the State Convention Number One, which was issued by the Thai Government on June 24, 1939. The reason given was that the new name conformed to the racial origins and the popular practice of Thai people. It was another step in the propagation of nationalism, which won popular support among the Thais. Among the foreign countries, Japan was the most enthusiastic in using Thailand. An article appeared in the Osaka Mainichi and the Tokyo Nichi Nichi on December 25, 1939, saying that "Thailand no longer dealt with myths concerning the white elephant and Buddhist monks. Now the Thais were doing everything they could in developing their country into a powerful one." At the outbreak of the European war which later engulfed the whole world as the Second World War, the British and the French continued to cling to the name of Siam. At the end of the war, Thailand found herself in a dilemma. She was neither a defeated country nor a liberated one. After the Pearl Harbor attack on December 8, 1941, the Japanese troops passed through the country, and as a result of the alliance made with Japan, Thailand declared war on the United States of America and Great Britain on January 25, 1942. Luckily for the Thai people, Mr. James Byrnes, who was the American State Secretary in August 1945, announced the Thai declaration of war null and void, since it was against their will. The Allied troops then moved into Bangkok in order to disarm and repatriate the Japanese soldiers to their homeland. The Thai Government deemed it a necessity to please the Allies, and therefore reverted to the old name of Siam towards the end of 1945, much to the satisfaction of a small circle of conservative-minded Thais.

Field Marshal Pibulsonggram became Prime Minister again six months after the coup d'état of November 8, 1947. He gradually paved the way to restore the name of Thailand, and on the Wesak or Visakha Puja Day,May 11, 1949, an announcement was made that Thailand would be henceforth the official name of the country. It is right and proper that this should be so, since it is the correct translation of Muang Thai, and the Thai people are generally pleased with it. Nevertheless articles have so far appeared every ten years or so in the Bangkok newspapers, proposing or urging the reversal of Thailand to Siam. In the drafting of the constitution which was proclaimed in 1968, the Constituent Assembly in 1961 engaged in a lively discussion on the question as to whether the name of Thailand should be retained or changed back to Siam, and finally resolved the point in favour of the present name of the country. So Thailand is on all maps, no matter where they are printed.

# CHAPTER I
# ORIGINS AND MIGRATIONS OF THE THAIS

ORIGINS OF THE THAIS. The Thais are one of the great and progressive races who inhabit the Indo-Chinese Peninsula. At one time conflicting theories and opinions prevailed as to the origins of the Thais. According to Khun Vichitmatra's "Lakh Thai" (Thai background), "no one knows exactly where the Thai people originated. Broadly speaking, they had their original home in the vicinity of the Altai mountains where the Mongols to which they belonged originated. Afterwards they spread towards the south where they established their great settlement in the valley of the Yellow river........ This happened at least 6,000 years ago." His theory does not seem to hold water now. In Professor Wiens' book on *China's March Towards the Tropics*, "In the headwaters area of the Yang-tzu, we come to a branch of the T'ai family known variously as Lao, Ailao or Ngailao. Tradition places their home at the intersection of Ho-nan, Hu-pei, and An-hui provinces from whence they extended westward along the Chia-lung Mountains. Chinese historians also mention a T'ai tribe called the 'Great Mung' inhabiting the western part of Ssu-ch'uan during the period over B.C. 2000. Lacouperie said that they were obviously of the same (T'ai) race and may have been the progenitors of Shans of Tongking called by the same name at the present time. Two other T'ai tribes of Ssu-ch'uan, the Lung and the Pa, are mentioned around B.C. 1971, said Cochrane. It may be that the Chiu-Llung Mountains take their name from the former." This passage reveals the original home as being somewhere in Szechuan and is corroborated by the following historians and writers. Likhit Hoontrakul wrote a book on *The Historical Records of the Siamese-Chinese Relations* in which he quoted Chinese evidence to show that in the fifteenth reign of the Chou dynasty (696-682 B.C.) there occurred the removal of Tai people of Lo State from Ki-Kiang (Hupeh) across the Yangtze-Kiang river to Ping-Kiang (Hunan). Professor Phya Anuman Rajdhon expressed his view in *The Cultures of Thailand* that "The Thai tribes in their early days some two thousand years or more had their home probably in the north-west corner of China which is now the province of Shen-Si." Prince Dhani Nivat wrote *An Outline of Siamese Cultural History* in which he merely said that "The Siamese form a section of the great Thai which people an extensive territory stretching from the valley of the Yang Tse to the seaboard of southeastern Asia." In *The Thai Peoples* written by Erik Seidenfaden, "the Thai originated in western central Asia from where they trekked eastwards and populated vast tracts of China prior to the advent of the Bak people, the later Chinese." Dr. W.C. Dodd stated in *The Tai Race* that "The first mention of him (Tai) cited by Professor Lacouperie occurs in the time of the Great Yu, who began to reign in B.C. 2208........ In a geographical survey which goes under the name of this ancient ruler we hear of the Ta Mung, i.e. the Great Mung, in what is now the northwestern part of Sze-chuan Province, or western central China. Now the name Mung does not sound much like Lao or Tai or Shan. Yet it is as truly one of the race-names as any of these." According to Cochrane's *The Shans*, the Chinese seem to have come in touch with a Shan tribe called 'Great Mung,' at the time of the geographical survey which goes under the name of the Great Yu. The western part of Sze-Chuan is given as their habitat, and the time is put at more than two thousand years B.C. M. Terrien (de Lacouperie) says that they are 'obviously of the same (Shan) race,' and they may be the progenitors of the Shans of Tonking called by the same name at the present time. Two other Shan tribes of Sze-chuan are mentioned a little later (1917 B.C.), the Lung and the Pa. It may be from the former that the Kui-lung range of mountains takes its name. Kui is a Shan word that might even now be very properly used of a mountainous wilderness, and the name may mean the Wilderness of the Lung or the Lung Wilderness. Still another branch of the Shan family (or another name for the same branch), the Lao, has already been mentioned. If these Shans had their early home at the intersection of Honan, Hupeh and An-hui provinces, and later extended westward in the Kui-lung range, it would give us a belt of Shans (Mung, Lung, Pa, Pang and Lao) on the left bank of the Yangtze reaching from western Szechuan almost to the sea, ending in Kiangsu, where we started in our linguistic survey. The Lao mountains may have taken their name from this latter Shan tribe." In a History of Thailand, approved by the Thai Ministry of Education for use as a school text-book sometime ago, "originally the Thais were a great race which had its own language and separated itself from the Mongols in the same way as the Chinese. Their original home was in what is now the north-western part of Szechuan, more than four thousand years ago," while in K.P. Landon's *Siam in Transition*, "the Siamese are a branch of the Thai people, who formerly lived north of the Yangtze River in the comparatively small area which today constitutes Szechuan Province in western China." Wood's *History of Siam* says that "in the year 585 B.C. the Chinese Empire did not extend farther south than the great River Yangtze-kiang. The region of the barbarians then included all the Provinces lying south of that stream. Who were these babarians? Doubtless many and various tribes were included among them; but most of them were Tai people, the ancestors of the Siamese, Laos and Shans of to-day." In Hall's *History of South-East Asia*, "the Shans, the Laotians and the Siamese are all descended from a parent racial group, cognate to the Chinese, which is thought to have made its first historical appearance in the sixth century B.C. From that time onwards Chinese records make frequent references to them as barbarians south of the Yangtze-kiang."

In view of the above mentioned theories and opinions, which, it is believed, are based on Chinese records, it may be summarised with a degree of certainty that the Thais originated in western or northwestern Szechuan 4500 or 5000 years ago. Yet the latest comment on this matter, as appearing in *Thailand's Cultural Heritage* by Eugene H.C. Wang in the Journal of the Institute of Cultural Research, 1967, is that "The ancestors of the Thais moved down to the plain of the Indo-China peninsula in the thirteenth century from Yunnan, south-west part of China, and much earlier than that, perhaps from the southern area of the Yangtze river. Their earliest history and cultural tradition are not well recorded in spite of fragmentary accounts in the Chinese annals."

MIGRATIONS OF THE THAIS. The Thais then spread out, according to their inclination, in a fan-like manner along the Yangtze valley in order to seek a better livelihood. When they came into contact with the Chinese, they were already a great old race, but they did not unite themselves into a nation. They were divided into tribes or groups, each tribe or group having its own prince or chieftain. The Chinese called them by the proper names of Mung, Lung and Pa, but the Thais called themselves Ailao. As time wore on, however, the

Thais organized the territories where they lived, into the kingdoms of Lung and Pa. The kingdom of Lung was situated somewhere north of the Yangtze river, but it did not enjoy a long existence. About 936 B.C. the Tartars began to invade the western part of the land under the Chinese and soon harassed the kingdom of Lung. Unable to resist their pressure, the Thais of Lung moved towards Szechuan where they joined themselves with the Pa. Another group of the Thais established another kingdom at Ngiou which, according to the available evidence, occupied a territory south of the Yangtze somewhere round the present city of Changsha. The Thais and the Chinese belong to the Mongolian stock, as is shown by the physical resemblance between them and the affinity of their languages. However, the Chinese apparently regarded themselves as being superior to the Thais after the commencement of their intercourse. From the sixth century B.C. onwards Chinese annals make frequent references to them as the "barbarians" south of the Yangtze. This is no surprise to anybody well acquainted with Chinese history. The Europeans who reached the shores of Chinese in the sixteenth century A.D. received a similar treatment, as they were also called barbarians. The Thais found it impossible to settle down permanently along the banks of the Yangtze since the Chinese began to make gradual encroachments on their livelihood.

In the meantime, the Chinese emperor, Wu Wang (1122-1115 B.C.), had rewarded his victorious generals with land parcelled out to them and they ruled as chiefs of vassal states. Owing to their expansionist ambition, they engaged in internecine wars among themselves with a result that the inhabitants suffered badly and, finding that they could not pursue their occupations peacefully, they moved to the Thai territories.

On the assumption of power in China about two centuries before the Christain era, the Ch'in dynasty sent an army to subdue the kingdom of Pa. It was natural that being a small kingdom, the Pa surrendered after putting up some resistance against the Chinese. Meeting with a similar fate, the Ngiou territory was annexed by China under Shih Huang Ti (247-210 B.C.), who, having achieved the unification of the country, proclaimed himself as emperor or Huang Ti.

Some Thais had to submit to the Chinese rule and were eventually absorbed by them, while others made attempts to preserve their independence. In order to attain their objective, they started their southward migrations gradually and intermittently, as they could collect their people who were prepared to face hardships and danger. They came to call themselves Thai during their migrations which occurred at the beginning of the Christian era. According to Luang Vichitra Vadhakarn again, "In 69 B.C. the Thais began to migrate towards the Indo-Chinese peninsula." However hard they tried, they could not escape being harassed by the Chinese. They were attacked by the Chinese General Kong Beng who played an important part during the age of the Three Kingdoms, and they were forced to submit to the Emperor of Szechuan in A.D. 225. Still they never ceased to move down towards the Indo-Chinese peninsula and their migrations took hundreds of years. In Cady's *Southeast Asia : Its Historical Development*, "The Shan or Thai people long occupied the watersheds between the headwaters of the Red River on the east, the upper Mekong Valley on the west, and the Yangtze River on the North. Much of the area was brought under Han China's control by Emperor Wu Ti in A.D. 109." However, some Thais who set up small principalities or towns in Yunnan were independent of their powerful northern neighbour and also of each other. Realizing their limited strength, they formed themselves into the kingdom of Ailao in 122 B.C. Again the new kingdom was by no means a match for China, though it vowed peace as its policy. In his quest for the true teachings of the Lord Buddha, Emperor Wu Ti (140-86 B.C.) who was beginning to lose interest in Taoism decided to send a mission to India, but the Thais refused to grant to it permission for free passage through their Ailao country on the ground that it might include espionage as part of its assignments. The Ailao kingdom which had not been long in existence was still afraid of China's interference in its internal affairs. The refusal naturally brought about the wrath of the Chinese emperor who did not want his plan to be thwarted by the Ailao and therefore ordered his troops to march against them. Raising a stiff and stubborn resistance against the enemy, they fought for more than ten years, and in the end, they capitulated in 87 B.C., due to exhaustion of all resources. A Chinese commissioner was appointed to govern the Ailao with his headquarters at their capital.

Seizing a unique opportunity which cropped up due to the change of the dynasties in China, the Ailao Thais rose against the Chinese emperor in A.D. 9. With the assistance of the Empress Dowager, the Chief Minister, Wang Mang, got rid of the young Emperor, aged five, and proclaimed himself emperor of the new Hsin dynasty (A.D.9-23), but he was not accepted by the people who rebelled against him. After the rising, the Thais executed the Chinese commissioner, the symbol of Chinese authority, and recovered their independence. Unfortunately they could not preserve it for a long time. Falling prey to the cunning persuasion of a Chinese representative which caused their volte-face in A.D. 50, they paid homage to the Chinese emperor who then allowed them to govern themselves under the surveillance of a commissioner until they were deprived of their free status in A.D. 225.

# CHAPTER II

## MOVEMENTS OF THE THAIS TOWARDS THE INDO-CHINESE PENINSULA

The constant pressure which the Chinese exercised on the Thais caused them to migrate towards the south, since lacking unity, some of them could not organize an effective resistance to the Chinese and were eventually absorbed by them, while others made attempts to preserve their independence. However the Thais who decided to remain in spite of innumerable difficulties in maintaining their precarious existence joined their forces together under the leadership of Sinulo who established the Kingdom of Nanchao (Southern principality) which covered west and north west Yunnan in 651. The capital of Nanchao stood somewhere near Wating. The question as to whether Nanchao was really a Thai kingdom has occurred among historians time and again. One suggestion is that on the ground of linguistic and racial evidences, it should not be regarded as a Thai kingdom. With regard to the people in Yunnan, for instance, the Thai race was not the principal one and much smaller in number than the Yi race or the Lolo and the white race or Minchia. The controversy concerning the exact nature of Nanchao could easily create an endless series of discussions. Nevertheless it should be borne in mind that the Sinulo dynasty continued to rule the Kingdom until 902. During that period, the Kingdom retained the Thai characteristics, and at the end of the dynasty, it became increasingly sinicized, due to the unceasing infiltration and penetration of Chinese influences into it, until it was overthrown by Kublai Khan's army in 1253.

Only the main events of the Sinulo dynasty are dealt with here. Sinulo himself consolidated his rule through the conclusion of a treaty of friendship with Kaotsong of the Tang dynasty. In 674, he was succeeded by his son, Lo Sheng-Yen (674-712), who paid two visits to China during his reign in order to strengthen cordial relations with the Emperor. On the demise of Lo Sheng-Yen, his son, Sheng Lo-Pi (712-728), and his grandson, Pi Lo-Koh (728-748), ruled Nanchao in succession. Apparently Pi Lo-Koh felt that his power did not pervade the whole of Nanchao which included five other independent principalities, created by Sinulo, for the pacification of the land. Sinulo himself had appointed his relatives to rule them, but they had executed a volte-face by declaring independence. Pi Lo-Koh therefore determined to dispose of them through trickery so as to achieve his plan to unite Nanchao. The five rulers were invited to participate in a sacrificial ceremony to their ancestors. Being suspicious of Pi Lo-Koh's intentions, one of them refused to attend. After a grand feast, the four rulers were burnt to death in 731, thus affording the opportunity to him to overrun their principalities. Soon after the ruler who declined the invitation to the ceremony presumably suffered the same fate. Thus Pi Lo-Koh had all Yunnan under his sway, where he built the towns of Taiho and Tali. He also rendered valuable services to China, helping her in the attack on Tibet and in crushing a rebellion, and in 745, during the reign of the Emperor Mingti (the sixth of the Tang dynasty), he made a new treaty of friendship with the country.

The next king of Nanchao was Koh Lo-Feng, Pi Lo Koh's son, who commenced his reign in 748. A Nanchao inscription of 766 praised him for three reasons. He treated his children fairly, adopted a right attitude towards his retainers and maintained correct relations with his brothers and sisters. Probably in conformity with his policy to usher in a new era, he moved his capital from Wating to Talifu, known to the Thais as Nongsae. At first he followed his father's policy in maintaining friendly relations with China which he visited some years later. However, after his return to Talifu, he turned against that country, owing to the misconduct of a Chinese prefect who seemed to have seduced his wife, and to the impossibility of representing the matter to the emperor by the reason of the corrupt action of the palace eunuchs. He declared war and proceeded to seize a number of Chinese towns. Seeing that Nanchao would not be able to resist the might of China by itself, he made an alliance with the King of Tibet, and this policy proved to be the right one for him. The Chinese tried to subdue him several times, but they met with no success, and finally, the outbreak of a pestilence forced them to beat a retreat. His reign lasted thirty years, and his successor was I Moh-Sun (778-808), who was his own grandson. In conjunction with the Tibetans, the new king made a raid into what is now modern Szechuan. The Chinese realized the importance of Tibet as an ally of Nanchao. Li Mih, the Chinese general, who had suffered a defeat from its army therefore advised the Chinese emperor to make conciliatory advances to I Moh-Sun with a view to effecting the isolation of the Tibetan power. In 794, I Moh-Sun broke with the Tibetans, won a battle with them and was consequently rewarded by the Chinese with a gold seal and title of king. He continued the war against the Tibetans as an ally of China until his death in 808. As time wore on, Nanchao and China became enemies again and engaged in intermittent wars.

Among the six kings of the same dynasty who succeeded I Moh-Sun was Lung Shun, generally known as Fah or Fa. This name would probably correspond to the old Thai or Burmese title Payah or Phya, as suggested by E.H. Parker's *The Old Thai Empire*. During his reign (877-897), he made peace with China, and his son married a daughter of the Emperor. He met a violent death, as he was assassinated by one of his eunuchs. His son, Shun Wa Cheng, who ascended the throne after him, managed to preserve the dynasty intact for five years before it terminated in 902. Thenceforward for a considerable period, little mention was made of them (Nanchao kings) by the Chinese dynastic histories. The kingdom of Nanchao ended with its conquest by Kublai Khan in 1253.

The Chinese annals, as translated into Thai by the National Library of Thailand, show that Nanchao was a progressive kingdom. The king was undoubtedly an absolute monarch. In the administration of the kingdom, he was assisted by the ministers of Defence, Justice, Public Works, Finance, Foreign Affairs, Commerce, the Interior, the Royal Ceremonies, and the Census, as well as by the heads of the departments of Granaries, Horses and Oxen and also of the Secret Records' office. There were four classes of provincial governors, and town officials belonged either to the secretarial section or to the judicial section. Besides these officials, he was served by his personal advisers, and land was apportioned to them according to rank.

Rice cultivation was the most important occupation of the people, and after it came the silk rearing and the silk and cloth weaving. Being free from the corvée or forced labour to the State, people paid their taxes in kind such as rice and served in the army. If they had horses of their own, they were assigned to the cavalry; otherwise they were attached to the infantry. Horses and oxen were probably in good supply, as was indicated by the Departments of Horses and Oxen. As regards minerals, Nanchao could boast of gold which was found in the sand and on the mountains.

The Thais could no longer brook the strong pressure of the Chinese and looked towards the south for their safety. As was natural with peoples in ancient times such as the Egyptians and the Babylonians, who depended on the rivers for their livelihood, they followed the river valleys in making their trails southwards and then extended themselves in both eastern and western directions. In the words of Louis Finot, who was at one time the Director of the "Ecole Française d'Extrême-Orient," "the march of this strange race (the Thais), being supple and fluid like water, insinuating itself with the same force, taking the colour of all the skies and the form of all the river banks, but keeping the essential identity of its character and language under different aspects, has spread out like an immense sheet from south China, Tongking, Laos, Siam to Burma and Assam." The western group of the Thais descended along the Salween river where they became Shans or Great Thais. They established principalities such as the Thai state of Mogaung, which was founded north of Bhamo in upper Burma in 1215. The Shans or Great Thais will be referred to again in the later periods of Thai history during which they played an important role.

Meanwhile some of these Shans had proceeded west and set up the Ahom kingdom in eastern Assam in 1229. The historical knowledge about the Ahom Thais has largely been derived from their annals known as the "Buranjis." They succeeded in maintaining their independence for a period of more than six hundred years, in spite of the fact that they encountered the native tribesmen of Assam, the Muslims, the Hindus, and the British as their enemies. Towards the end of the Ahom kingdom, they began to lose their language and culture, as they were gradually absorbed by the Hindus who made settlements in an ever increasing number in their land. Even their kings adopted such a Hindu name as Gaurinath Singh (1780-1794) instead of such Ahom titles as Sukafa or Supinfa. Finally, since the all powerful British ruled India, the Ahom Thais accepted their protection, and their country was annexed to it. Such was the end of the Ahom kingdom in 1842.

Choosing the Mekong valley as their home, the eastern group of the Thais spread its ramifications to Tongking, and constituted the ancestry of the Laotians whose land King Fagnum (1353-1371) united into a powerful state for the first time and the extent of his country was probably the biggest ever known in Lao history. The middle group emigrated into the Menam valley. These last two groups were at one time referred to as the Little Thais.

# CHAPTER III

# THE INDO-CHINESE PENINSULA
# AND THAI PRINCIPALITIES

Long before the conquest of Nanchao by Kublai Khan's army, the Thais had seeped through the Indo-Chinese peninsula where they found the land to be fertile with an abundant supply of water and thus suitable for an agricultural life and so they settled down. Professor D.G.E. Hall stated in *A History of South-East Asia* that "Kublai Khan's conquest of the kingdom of Nanchao in 1253 caused an even stronger 'effervescence' among the T'ais. Coedès thinks that the prodigious epic of the Mongol conquest struck their imagination and inspired them to great achievements. Whether this be so or not, the Mongols adopted the traditional Chinese policy of 'fragmentation' and favoured the establishment of a series of T'ai states at the expense of the older states. And what happened was not a mass displacement of population in the areas affected but the seizure of power by a T'ai governing class." The Indo-Chinese peninsula must have been known to the Indians by the Sanskrit name of Suvarnabhumi. The fall of Nanchao forced the Thais to move southwards in a much larger number than before, thus increasing their own people in the Menam valley in particular. However, for some reason or other, some of them remained in south China. Even to-day scattered in Yunnan, Kwangsi, Kwantung and Hainan are many Thai groups, bearing their specific names.

Such stone implements as axes, arrow-heads and utensils have been dug up in various parts of the Indo-Chinese peninsula, thus indicating that the earliest inhabitants must have been primitive people who lived in caves during the neolithic age about 4000-5000 years ago. George Coedès *Les Etats Hinduisés d' Indochine et d'Indonesie* says that "On peut donc sans grande exagération dire que les populations de l'Inde extérieure étaient encore en pleine civilisation néolithique tardive lorsque la culture brahmanobuddhique de l' Inde est arrivée à leur contact." The Thai-Danish Pre-historic Expedition which carried out the excavations in the valley of the Kwae Noi (small tributary) and the Kwae Yai (big tributary) of the Meklong river in the province of Kanchanaburi from November 1960 to March 1962 made extremely interesting discoveries such as skeletons, stone axes, decorative beads, and potteries, thus enhancing the arduous work of past historians. In fact, such old relics have been found scattered from Tongking to Udon Thani, Lop Buri, Kanchanaburi and down to Perak, proving again the neolithic civilization of the Indo-Chinese peninsula. Next came the Negritos whose "arrival, probably from India, must go back to the dim past, perhaps many thousand years before the birth of Christ," according to Seidenfaden's *The Thai peoples*. The Mons, the Khmers and the Lawas then made their appearance. As they were more civilized than the Negritos, they gradually replaced them and pushed them down to the Malay peninsula where the remnants of their progeny, known as the Semang, are still found in a small number in the south of Thailand. The Semang are nicknamed Ngo by the Thais because of their curly hair which is like a rambutan. They are dwarfs or pigmies; the men reach only a height of 150 centimetres and their women less than this. They are hunters and food gatherers and are skilful in the use of a blow pipe. Some years ago the writer had an opportunity to travel to the province of Yala in the south of Thailand, where he stopped at a self-help settlement in the Tharnto district and interviewed a Semang who was quite civilized, wearing a shirt and trousers. The Semang had already visited Bangkok with its tall buildings and wide roads which impressed him immensely. He then showed how adept he was with a blow pipe, with which he hit a tiny flag on the top of a bus.

The Mons and the Khmers were non-Thai peoples and were ethnologically akin to one another. There is a belief that the Mons came from the mountains of south China and the Khmers were a branch of the Mons, of which the Lawas formed a group of the Mon-Khmers. These people made their home in the Indo-Chinese peninsula before the Thais came into contact with them. The Mons who were later known as the Talaings of Pegu set themselves up by the Salween river where they extended themselves to the south of the Irrawaddy river, while the Khmers whose direct descendants are the Cambodians built up their homeland in the lower part of the Mekong river which is now Cambodia. The Lawas, flanked by the Mons on one side and by the Khmers on the other side, spread themselves lengthwise from the north to the south of the Menam valley. They all adopted the Indian culture and religions. Most of the Indians who arrived in the Indo-Chinese peninsula came in successive waves from south India, while the rest left their homeland in the other ports of India even as far as the centre and the north for South-East Asia. The Indian emigration must have started before the third century B.C. and continued until the first few centuries of the Christian era. At the same time the Indo-Chinese peninsula must have been a familiar name with the Indians; otherwise the Mauryan emperor Asoka (274-236 B.C.) would not have appointed his missionaries, Sona and Uttara, to proceed to Suvarnabhumi, where their mission was to establish Buddhism, and this was successfully accomplished.

Suvarnabhumi, meaning the land of gold, was known to the Romans as "Chryse Chersonesus." It must have been located somewhere in Indo-China and especially within the boundaries of present day Thailand, where gold has been discovered; some of it was at one time collected from the alluvial soil at Kamnerdnophakun in the Bang Saphan district of the province of Prachuap Khiri Khan, while gold mining was operated at Toh Moh in Narathiwat, and the metal has been found by geologists in Kabin Buri in Prachin Buri. There has been a difference of opinion among some archaeologists and historians as to the exact centre of Suvarnabhumi. Would it be Thaton in south Burma, Chaiya in south Thailand, or Nakhon Pathom or Suphan Buri in the central plain of Thailand? On account of many relics typifying the age of Asoka such as a wheel of law, a deer statue and a stupa built in the same style as the one at Sanchi in India, it has been established that the area extending from Nakhon Pathom to Suphan Buri constituted the centre of Suvarnabhumi.

Besides Buddhism, Brahminism was introduced by the Indians into Indo-China, but it did not thrive very well like Buddhism. The Indians primarily engaged in trade, seeking such luxury articles as gold, spices, scented woods and perfumed resins from Indo-China as exports to their country which in turn sold them to Persia and Rome. They imparted their knowledge in various fields to the natives such as rice cultivation. According to B.P.Groslier's article on *Our Knowledge of Khmer Civilization. —A Re-appraisal*, "For plains, in south Indochina, then meant swampy deltas or flooded alluviums which could not be cultivated without extensive drainage or the water control system. But the Indians themselves

AERIAL VIEW OF PRA PATHOM CHEDI AT NAKHON PATHOM

were past masters in these techniques, as is clearly shown by their works in the Pallava country of Ceylon. And they very probably used them for their own food production in Southeast Asia, thus teaching the art to the local populations and giving them a basis on which to construct a fixed society and an advanced civilization." The Indians intermarried with the natives and in the Indo-Chinese peninsula, they mixed with the Mons, the Khmers and the Lawas who were attracted to Brahminism as well as Buddhism and finally they embraced them. Possessed of a better knowledge than the natives as has already been mentioned, their descendants began, in due course, to wield considerable power in the various kingdoms which were founded, namely, Funan, Dvaravati, Chenla, Champa, Srikshetra, Sudhammavati and Srivijai.

Regarding the political division of the Indo-Chinese peninsula, Funan was the first state which came into existence in the first century of the Christian era. The knowledge concerning this kingdom has been derived from the Chinese chronicles which a French professor, Paul Pelliot, translated into French, since no historic ruins or stone inscriptions are extant. This is found in *Le Fou-nan*, an article by this French professor in the "Bulletin d' Extrême-Orient," Tome III, 1903. Presumably wood structures which constituted living quarters fell into decrepitude with the lapse of time. At first Funan covered South Cambodia and South Vietnam with its capital standing somewhere below Pnom-Penh, and then it embarked on its aggrandizement. At its zenith in the reign of Jayavarman who ruled the land in the fifth century, it extended its boundaries not only to the lower part of the Menam valley but also to the upper part of the Malay peninsula. A French professor, Jean Boisselier, who carried out excavations at Utong in the province of Suphan Buri in 1966, has proposed a new theory concerning the original centre of Funan which, he believes, should be situated in that area, basing his belief on the similarity of metal decorations, beads and pieces of pottery found there and at Oc Eo which, it is generally believed, was a sea port of the country. According to him, the kingdom expanded from westward to eastward. This theory should be corroborated by more historical evidence before it is accepted. Two Chinese envoys, Kang Tai and Tchou Ying, visited the kingdom in the third century probably with a view to seeking facilities for their vessels to call at the ports of Funan. Rudravarman, who succeeded his father, Jayavarman, continued to despatch embassies to China, while a Chinese embassy which reached the shores of Funan made a request for some Buddhist monks as well as Buddhist sutras to be brought back with it. In usurping the throne from the legal heir, the King sowed the seeds of disunity among the people, bringing in its train the patent weaknesses and thus encouraging the vassal states to throw off their yoke. In 550, Funan was overthrown by a feudatory state, Chenla, which was the predecessor of the Khmer empire.

Once independent, Chenla failed to achieve coherence, and after 706, the country was split up into two separate parts, namely, the Land Chenla or Upper Chenla and the Water Chenla or Lower Chenla. The Land Chenla occupied the Upper Mekong valley with its centre probably established at Thakhaek, while the Water Chenla covered the Lower Mekong valley and Cochin China, founding its capital at Sambhupura or Sambor. Due to marriage between the members of the two royal families about 857, Upper Chenla and Lower Chenla were re-united to form the Khmer kingdom which afterwards developed into the Khmer Empire.

Among the Mons and the Khmers, the Lawas were apparently the weakest and were gradually assimilated by their neighbours. With the disappearance of Funan, a vacuum occurred in the central part of the Menam valley, so the Mons moved in to fill it and created the Kingdom of Dvaravati with Nakhon Pathom, as its capital towards the end of the sixth century. Having discovered a copper plate bearing the name of Harshavarman and Isanavarman at Utong, Jean Boisselier suggested that the town might have served as his seat of government for a certain period. To-lo-po-ti was the name by which the Chinese designated Dvaravati, and according to a Chinese monk, Hiuan-Tsang, who travelled to India, it stood between Burma and the Khmer kingdom. It was a progressive and prosperous country up to the ninth century using flat round coins as its currency. In 1943, two such coins, made of silver, were discovered in a chedi near the Prepratone monastery in the province of Nakhon Pathom. They bear the Pallavan script which reads as follows: "Cridvaravati çvarapunya" meaning "Meritorious work of the King Cri Dvaravati." Decline then set in, leading subsequently to the submission of Dvaravati to the Khmers about 1007, and Dvaravati was incorporated in the Khmer Empire which then proceeded to grow from strength to strength until the whole of the Menam valley up to Haripunjaya (Lamphun) and beyond was under the rule of the Khmers by the end of the tenth century. Haripunjaya was a Mon kingdom which was founded in 654, having Princess Chamadevi of Lavo as its first ruler. Her husband was the viceroy ruling at Ramnakawn and later entered the Buddhist monkhood. She had two sons, twins, seven days after her arrival at Lamphun, Prince Mahantayot and Prince Anantayot were born. Faced with some difficulties in governing her new kingdom, due to the opposition of the local chieftains who were recorded in chronicles as uncivilized aborigines, she managed in the long run to smooth them out and ruled the land peacefully. Haripunjaya, however, was small in extent and was forced to accept the vassalage of the Khmers afterwards. With the recession of the Khmer might, King Mengrai, who subsequently established the Kingdom of Lannatai, began to make encroachments on it, and at last Lamphun fell to him in 1283.

With regard to the kingdoms of Champa, Srivijai, Sudhammavati and Srikshetra, their political fortune did not bear directly on the nation building of the Thais, so they are dealt with briefly. Champa was the kingdom which the Chams founded in the third century and came to a tragic end in 1471, owing to the constant attacks of the Annamese and the Khmers. It was situated approximately between what is now Tongking (North Vietnam) and Cochin China (South Vietnam). Since its loss of independence, it has become completely vietnamized. The kingdom of Srivijai, which was founded by the Sailendra dynasty in 683, at the height of its power extended from the Malay peninsula to Java, with its capital at Djambi near Palembang in Sumatra. The people worshipped Mahayanist Buddhism, as shown by the great Buddhist stupa, Borobudur, standing at some 30 kilometres north of Jogjakarta in south Java. With the lapse of time, Srivijai began to reveal signs of weakness, since the kings lacked ability and energy in ruling it. Eventually it had to fight a war on two fronts—one against King Ramkamhaeng of Sukhothai in the north and the other against King Wayam Wuruk of the Majpahit dynasty, ruling in Java in the south. Although it was simultaneously attacked in two different directions, it continued to resist stubbornly its enemies for eighteen years before its surrender. Srikshetra was a Pyu kingdom in what is now North Burma, while Sudhammavati was founded in South Burma by the Mons. Their origins are shrouded in mystery. The local chronicles say that these two kingdoms came into existence during the era of the Lord Buddha and lasted till the end of the eighth century.

Yasovarman I (889-900) who founded the first city of Angkor in the Khmer Empire is reputed to have been in control of the Mekong valley up to the borders of China and the Menam valley. But according to the Thai chronicles, the Khmers lost their sway temporarily over the Menam valley when King Anurudh or Anawrahta (1044-77), who first united Burma politically, attacked their empire and ruled over most of what is now Thailand. Having introduced Hinayanist Buddhism from Nakhon Pathom, he established it at Pagan or Pukam which was his capital. This religion developed into the so-called Pukam Hinayana Buddhism which then spread to the north of the Indo-Chinese peninsula. His domination over the Menam valley was of short duration and revealed signs of weakness, since Burma became disunited after the death of Anurudh. This paved the way for the Khmers to regain their might and the Menam valley was back firmly in their hands, especially at the time when Suryavarman II (1113-1150) was their most powerful king. His fame spread far and wide as a warrior and as a builder, since he conducted his campaigns against Champa and Annam as well as against the Mons and the Thais who had begun to infiltrate into the Menam valley and he first undertook the construction of Angkor Wat. The Khmers chose the city of Sayam, later known as Sukhothai, as the governor's seat of the northern region, while the governor of the southern region of the Menam valley lived at Lavo. Usually they erected temples as symbols of their mighty empire such as the three-spire Prang at Lop Buri (Lavo), a temple at Phimai which has just been reconstructed, and another one at Panomrung in the province of Buri Rum.

Concerning the question of Anawrahta's extension of his power to the Menam valley, it should be noted that according to Maung Htin Aung's *A History of Burma*, he did not himself proceed there nor did he adopt Hinayana Buddhism from Nakhon Pathom. What actually happened was that "Arawrahta must have demanded and received tribute from the kingdom of Dvaravati, which prompted its overlord, Udayadityavarman, to invade Tenesserim. But the Khmer empire was in the throes of mutinies and rebellions and Anawrahta did not consider the invasion important enough to warrant his going down to Lower Burma; he instead sent his four paladins, who easily repulsed the invader." With regard to Theravada or Hinayana Buddhism, Anawrahta was converted to it by a famous Mon monk by name of Shin Arahan.

The Thais who migrated from south China and reached the north of the Menam valley formed themselves into separate principalities which subsequently developed into kingdoms such as the Kingdom of Chieng Saen. According to the Singhanavati chronicles, a prince by this name led his followers to find a suitable site for his new city which he founded in 568. He was one of the sons of the prince of Nakorntes, and as was a generally accepted custom in those days when the principality was a small one, the sons were encouraged to move out from it and seek their fortune by taking possession of a new land. Singhanavati's city soon underwent a rapid development, becoming a principality and then a kingdom known as the Kingdom of Chieng Saen with its boundaries adjoining Nanchao in the north and Haripunjaya in the south. It is a matter of regret to note that Chieng Saen became an easy prey to the Khmer incursion, due to a series of weak kings who ruled over it and it capitulated, paying a tribute to the Khmers. Puncaraj, who was the 43rd king of Chieng Saen, was blessed with a son who was born in 1098 and assumed the name of Prohm. Prince Prohm grew up to be an exceptionally brave and capable leader who took charge of the training of his soldiers himself. As he conceived a plan to declare independence against the Khmers, he urged his father to stop the payment of the tribute to them, which advice he complied with. Failing to receive the tribute, the Khmers sent an army to crush Chieng Saen. With his army whom he could trust, he routed the Khmer forces and conquered their territory down to Jalieng.

Having extended his power as far as Lannatai, Luang Prabang, Wiengchan (Vientiane) and Lanchang, he founded the city of Fang (a district in the province of Chiang Mai) for himself to rule and named it Jaiprakarn, and in 1117, at the request of his son, Puncaraj moved out of his place of refuge at Wiengsituang and continued to rule Jonoknakorn or Jaiburi, the capital of Chieng Saen. Prohm should truly be praised as the first Thai king who deserved the title of the Great. By his victory over the Khmers, he certainly uplifted the morale of the Thais, destroying the myth of the invulnerability of the Khmers, and consequently Chieng Saen was really an independent kingdom. As regards the system of government, the king was an absolute monarch who ruled the land through the appointment of his sons or brothers to the governorship of big cities, while his relatives or officials who had rendered meritorious services were made governors of small or far away towns. In time of peace, the governors collected taxes from the local people for their benefit. Should a threat of war against the Kingdom loom on the horizon, they raised an army together with its victuals and led it to the battlefield. According to these arrangements, the governor of a big city was naturally supplied with a good amount of income and shouldered a military responsibility commensurate with it, while his counterpart in a small town enjoyed a proportionately smaller share.

Prohm died at the age of 79 in 1177, having ruled Jaiprakarn for 59 years, and the throne devolved upon his son, Jaisiri, who, after 11 years' rule, was confronted with a large

Mon army which invaded his city. Unable to resist it, he avoided the impending danger by moving out his people and led them towards the south where he found a deserted town, Pab, in the present province of Kamphaeng Phet. His people built temporary quarters there, but since the town was not suitable to serve as the seat of his government, he decided to move again in search of a more appropriate site for, at first at Traitruengs in Chai Nat and finally at Nakhon Pathom which was then designated as Nakhon Chaisi. Presumably his descendants were related to Prince U Thong who founded the Kingdom of Ayutthaya.

Jaiburi met with the same fate as Jaiprakarn at the hands of the Mons. The Prince was forced to lead his people towards the south where they built a city of Nakorn Thai in the eastern part of the present province of Phitsanulok. Other Thai principalities which had sprung up contemporaneously with Chiang Saen and afterwards were many such as Ngoenyang, Payao, Rad and Bangyang. The exact location of some of these cities is still a matter of conjecture. It has been suggested that Rad should be situated somewhere in the province of Phetchabun, while Bangyang might have occupied a site near Paknampo in Nakhon Sawan. Be that as it may, they realized their limited resources in men, money and military supplies, and therefore they yielded to the Khmers who then imposed upon them an obligation to provide them with a tribute in the form of water collected from various sacred places to be used in the royal ceremonies. The delivery of water as a tribute turned out to be a hardship for the Thais, because it was put in earthenware jars which were loaded on ox-carts, and these wares were subject to easy breakage during a long journey to Lavo or Angkor. A Thai legend says that a man by name of Ruang made a bamboo container to hold water which was despatched to the Khmers, and this aroused their suspicion of the independent attitude of the Thais. In fact, some of the Thai princes such as Khun Bang Klang Tao of Bangyang and Khun Pa Muang of Rad, who wielded considerable power, were already showing signs of independence towards the Khmers.

# CHAPTER IV
# THE RISE AND FALL OF THE KINGDOM
# OF SUKHOTHAI

SRI INTRATIT. Khun Bang Klang Tao and Khun Pa Muang joined their forces together and planned to overthrow the Khmer rule. As has already been mentioned, the former was the governor of Bang Yang, while the latter held the governorship of Rad, and the two towns were under the Khmer vassalage. In the execution of their plan, they refused to send any further tributes, including water, to the Khmers, so tradition says, and this was interpreted as a defiance of Khmer authority. In 1238, they attacked and defeated the Khmer commander at Sukhothai, the administrative centre for the northern part of the Khmer empire. Through the popular support of the Thais, Khun Bang Klang Tao was proclaimed king of Sukhothai. Khun Pa Muang was passed over in this matter probably because he was closely related to the Khmers or old Cambodians, his wife, Sikhara being a daughter of the Cambodian king. What does Sukhothai mean? It might signify "Happy Tai." If the name thus spelt is accepted as the phonetic form of the Pali "Sukho-daya," it means "Dawn of Happiness." Anyhow the people should have been happy, as is testified by a few lines of a stone inscription dated from about 1292. "This Sukhothai is good. In the water there is fish, in the field there is rice. The King does not levy a rate on his people...... Who wants to trade in elephants, trades. Who wants to trade in horses, trades. Who wants to trade in silver and gold, trades. The faces of the people shine bright." Khun Bang Klang Tao assumed the title or King Sri Intratit.

Meanwhile the Khmer kings could not subdue him, since they had weakened themselves in trying to carry on a vast building programme and to subjugate Champa. The construction of Angkor Wat which was begun by Suryavarman II (1113-1150) was completed by his successors. Jayavarman VII (1181-1215) built Angkor Thom and temples and conquered the kingdom of Champa. All these activities drained the Khmer Empire of men and money and the kings who succeeded Jayavarman VII were not of his calibre. The result was that much of his work perished soon after his death. Champa was evacuated and the Khmer power at Sukhothai was destroyed. Jayavarman VIII (1243-1295) was definitely a weak king as far as the relations with the Thais were concerned. He could not intercept the expansion of the Thai dominion, the extent of which covered the Menam valley and the Malay peninsula.

One further point that should be noted in this connection is that the Thais most probably had one unthought-of advantage over the Khmers as far as their physical condition was concerned. As they had moved down from south China where the climate was cold and invigorating for most of the year, they were full of virility and vitality, while the Khmers had, for centuries, been living in a hot land which gradually sapped their energy.

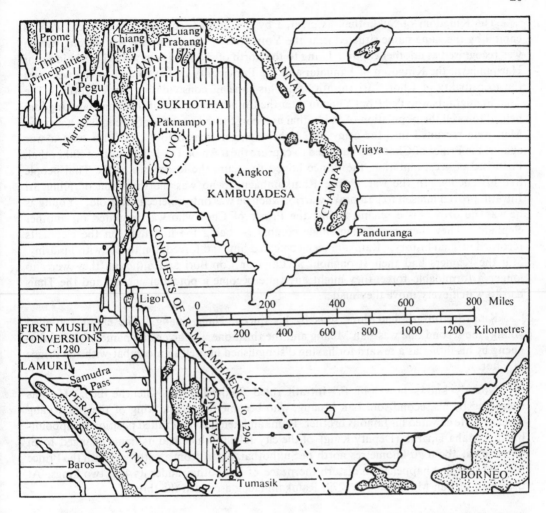

The victory of Sri Intratit over the Khmers at Sukhothai was an event of far-reaching importance, because it created a profound impression among the Thai people, who credited him with extraordinary ability and heroism. They humbly gave him the name of Pra Ruang meaning "Glorious Prince." The name of Pra Ruang is, in fact, conferred without discrimination upon all the kings of Sukhothai. The dynasty that ruled Sukhothai is thus known as the Pra Ruang dynasty, which, according to Coedès in his article on *Origins of the Sukhothai dynasty*, is recognised as "the first historical Thai dynasty. It has a double claim to this title, both because its cradle was precisely in the country designated by foreigners as Siam, and because it is this dynasty which, by freeing the Thai principalities from Cambodian yoke and by gradually extending its conquests as far as the Malay peninsula, paved the way for the formation of the Kingdom of Siam properly so-called. Its role in the history of Indo-Chinese arts and institutions is not less important than its political role; inheriting as it did the succession of the Khmer kingdom, which sank in part beneath the blows that it administered, it transmitted to the Siam of Ayutthaya a good number of Cambodian art-forms and institutions which still subsist in the Siam of to-day."

The Kingdom of Sukhothai, as created by Sri Intratit, covered a small area, with its capital by the same name situated near the Yom river. The other city was Jalieng, which was recognised as another capital. Lying to the north of the Kingdom were the Kingdom of Haripunjaya, the Kingdom of Lannatai and the Principality of Payao and to the west was the Principality of Chot. Sri Intratit spent his time in consolidating his kingdom. The Thai immigrants who fled from Yunnan after the Chinese conquest of the Nanchao kingdom helped to swell the population of Sukhothai and constituted a source of strength to his army. Men were recruited into the army in a larger number than before. He also won a war against the Prince of Chot who had tried to capture the town of Tak lying south of Sukhothai. Possessed of great ambition, the Prince hoped to secure the leadership of the Thai people like his enemy. In the war, Prince Ramkamhaeng, who was the third son of King Sri Intratit, proved himself to be a brave warrior when he was only nineteen years old. Young as he was, he drove his elephant against the Prince of Chot who was mounted on another elephant. They then engaged in single combat — being the first fight on the elephants recorded in Thai history. Ramkamhaeng defeated him and forced him to flee with his army. Still the Khmers had their stronghold at Lavo or Lop Buri and although they were no longer a formidable force, they might any time become a potential enemy, and the Thais had to watch every move they made.

King Sri Intratit had three sons by his queen, Nang Suang. The eldest son died young; the second one was Ban Muang and the third one was given the name of Ramkamhaeng by his father as a reward for having distinguished himself in a combat with the Prince of Chot.

Nobody knows how long Sri Intratit ruled Sukhothai and when he died. He was succeeded by his second son, Ban Muang, who became the second king of the Pra Ruang dynasty. He elevated his famous brother, Ramkamhaeng, to an exalted position by appointing him Maha Uparat (Deputy King) of the city Jalieng which had its name changed to Si Satchanalai about 70 kilometres north of Sukhothai. Apart from a petty war with the Prince of Chot, nothing happened to disturb the peace of Sukhothai under its first two kings. At the death of Ban Muang about 1279, Ramkamhaeng ascended the throne.

RAMKAMHAENG THE GREAT. There had up till then been only one Thai king who could be glorified as the Great. Would Prince Prohm be properly called the Great? According to the general conception of the Great, his outstanding exploit against the Khmers, as already mentioned, would evidently justify him for such a title. It is generally agreed that Ramkamhaeng was undoubtedly the second Thai king who really deserved the title of the Great. He was a valiant warrior, a wise statesman, a far-sighted scholar and a brilliant diplomat.

His attributes of a warrior were revealed long before his accession to the throne, beginning with his victory over the Prince of Chot. Since then, he had been busily enlarging his dominions and during his reign, Sukhothai was an extensive kingdom, bordering in the north on the kingdom of Lannatai at Lampang, including in the north-east Phrae, Nan and Luang Prabang and in the east Wiengchan (Vientiane) and covering in the south the towns in the Malay Peninsula and in the west Tenesserim, Tavoy, Martaban and Pegu (Hangsawati) up to the Bay of Bengal. These cities, towns and districts were either directly subject or tributary to him.

KING RAMA VI'S DRAWING OF
KING RAMKAMHAENG THE GREAT

Needless to say, the Kingdom of Sukhothai required a wise and skilful handling for its own safety and stability. Ramkamhaeng was an absolute monarch who organized the government of the realm along military lines. He was himself the head of the army and all the governors and officials in diminishing ranks in the cities and towns served under him in the following order: general, colonel, captain, sergeant, corporal and private. All the able bodied men must be soldiers; in peace time, they engaged in various occupations as civilians, and in war time, they were drafted into the army under the command of the King himself.

The capital of Sukhothai was the seat of government, while Si Satchanalai was the seat of the Deputy King. The near provincial towns were ruled directly by the King through officials sent from the capital. The officials were the governors representing him on the spot and had a hierachy of minor officials serving under them. Such towns were Tung Yhung, Bangyom, Song Kwae (Phitsanulok) and Sraluang (Phichit) in the east, Prabang (Nakhon Sawan) in the south, and Tak in the west. The outlying cities and towns were ruled by governors who were Thai princes or great officers, but they held office at the King's pleasure. Such cities and towns were Phrae, Phetchabun, Sri Thep, Praek (Sancaburi), Suphannaphum

(Utong), Ratchaburi, Phetchaburi and Tenesserim, and some of them were made up of a number of small towns. Each of the governors held the rank of a general, whose wartime duty it was to mobilize all the men to form a division for the defence of the Kingdom. On the borders were the vassal states or cities which had their own princes or governors, usually not of Thai race, such as Nan, Luang Prabang, Wiengchan, Wiengkham, Tavoy, and Nakhon Si Thammarat. The princes or governors, as the case may be, wielded unlimited power within their territory and had certain obligations to fulfill towards the King of Sukhothai. A tribute was periodically sent to him, and men were conscripted for him at the outbreak of a war. So the provincial administration would, in certain respects, resemble a kind of feudalism.

Ramkamhaeng governed with justice and magnaminity his own people as well as people of other nationalities who lived in his Kingdom, no matter whether they were Laotians, Khmers, Mons, Malays, Burmese or Chinese, so that they would enjoy peace and happiness in consonance with the name of Sukhothai. Their welfare received his unfailing attention. Whenever they wished to submit a complaint to him, they rang a bell which he caused to be hung at the palace gate. He would then grant them an audience so as to afford him an opportunity to find out by himself the causes of the complaint, and decided it according to its nature. The King could attend to the complaint himself because the population of Sukhothai was small. A custom then grew up, whereby a person who had suffered wrong or injury could appeal to the King, and it continued until the Bangkok period, beginning in 1782. He also showed considerable interest in the moral education of the people. He persuaded them to observe the simple Buddhist precepts, to make merit and give alms, and to attend a sermon regularly. He had a stone seat or Manangkasila throne, (now kept in Vihara Yod within the compound of the Temple of the Emerald Buddha), erected in the midst of a palmyra palm grove, where at his request, a monk preached a sermon on every Buddhist pre-sabbath day and Buddhist sabbath day and he conducted the affairs of the State on other days. Normally a Thai good Buddhist is expected to observe the five moral precepts:-

1. Do not destroy life.
2. Do not steal.
3. Do not tell a lie.
4. Do not commit adultery.
5. Do not take intoxicants.

In short, Ramkamhaeng's rule of Sukhothai had the characteristics of a paternal government and his people were happy, according to the stone inscription. Most of them engaged in agriculture and cultivated rice chiefly, while others carried on trade, which was greatly facilitated because no rate or tax was collected from those who engaged in it. In fact, he allowed free trade to spread throughout the land.

Ramkamhaeng has been credited with the introduction of "bullet coins" and cowrie shells. However, le May stated in his *Coinage of Siam* that "the northern folk adopted the bracelet, and later the kakim type of money because they traded entirely on land and through hilly country, and found this type of coinage convenient to carry about as bracelets or strung together. ......On the other hand, the more southern folk used the great river system of North-Central and Central Siam as their means of communication, and it was convenient for them to carry about coins of the "bullet" shape in bags which could be easily accommodated in their boats;" and he added that "the bullet type of coin did originate in some district in the North of Siam......and possibly in the eleventh century or earlier." Bullet coins were anyhow used by the people of Sukhothai who began to standardise them as baht, salung, fueng, etc.

The Thais had already embraced Buddhism by the time they settled down at Sukhothai. Like other peoples of South-East Asia, they were originally animists. Around them existed both benevolent and malevolent spirits. Every house, tree or hill, had a spirit. It was customary for the Thais to invoke their protection by offering them flowers, candles and incense sticks, food and rice wine. Later, during their southward migrations, they adopted Buddhism of the Mahayana sect which had already permeated China from India. About the end of the first century A.D., a Buddhist council was held under the patronage of King Kanishka of Gandhara, and it confirmed the division of Buddhism into the Mahayana sect or the "Great Vehicle" and the Hinayana sect or the "Small Vehicle." According to the Mahayana doctrine, one should not aim at becoming an Arahant, because one would attain to Nirvana or eternal bliss, which is of small help to others. One should, on the contrary, endeavour only to attain a Buddhabhumi or become a Bodhisattva in order to help others to get across the Wheel of Rebirth, or Sansara first, after which one would reach Nirvana. But a Hinayana Buddhist believes that one is able to attain to Nirvana by becoming a Buddha or an Arahant, and therefore Arahanship is one's goal.

Briefly stated, the Acariyavada or Mahayana school to-day constitutes the northern Buddhism and uses the Sanskrit language for its scripture, while the Theravada or Hinayana school represents the southern Buddhism which uses the Pali language for a similar purpose. Mahayana Buddhism is worshipped in China, Korea, Japan and Vietnam, and Hinayana Buddhism is followed in Ceylon, Burma, Laos, Cambodia and Thailand.

When the Thais emigrated into the Indo-Chinese Peninsula, they came into contact with the people who practised Hinayana Buddhism and Brahmanism. They became deeply devoted to the Hinayana sect which they adopted instead of the Mahayana sect, and they also took up the Brahmanic religion.

In the middle of the twelfth century, King Parakrama Bahu brought about a revival of the Hinayana Buddhism in Ceylon (Lanka) and his fame spread far and wide. Delegations of Mon, Thai and Khmer monks went there to study the newly revised Buddhist Scripture in order to bring back home what they had learned. On their return to the native land, the Thai monks preached Lanka Buddhism or Buddhism of the Sinhalese sect at Nakhon Si Thammarat. In the course of his tour of the Malay peninsula, King Ramkamhaeng visited that city, where he came to believe in the purified teachings of the Ceylonese school. With his support, a group of the monks of this school travelled to Sukhothai, where they established Lanka Buddhism. He exchanged his missions with Ceylon which then sent to him a Buddha image, Pra Buddha Sihing, through Nakhon Si Thammarat. This image has beautiful features and is highly venerated. Thus Ramkamhaeng became a devout Buddhist. Ruins of many monasteries or wats at old Sukhothai (the capital) to-day bear witness to the all pervading devotion of the kings and people to Hinayana Buddhism. According to the Jinakalamali Pakara, which was written in Pali by Pra Ratanapunya in 1517-1528 and translated into Thai by Mr. Sang Manavidura, Rocaraj, whom the translator identified as Sri Intratit, brought Pra Buddha Sihing to Sukhothai. Before this new information is accepted, however, further historical evidence should be forthcoming.

ONE SIDE OF SUKHOTHAI'S FIRST
STONE INSCRIPTION, SHOWING
THE THAI ALPHABET INVENTED
BY KING RAMKAMHAENG THE GREAT

Realizing the importance of the national language as a unifying force of his people as well as a symbol of their independence, he created in 1283 the first Thai alphabet, using as its basis the Mon and Khmer scripts which had, in turn, been derived from a south Indian script. He employed for the first time the new script in his inscription of 1292 at Sukhothai. All the consonants and vowels were written on the same lines. He was a scholar of Pali and neighbouring languages; otherwise he would not have been able to introduce such a script which has since his reign undergone some changes and is still in use now. It consists of 44 consonants, 32 vowels, and 5 tonal sounds. Evidently this monumental work testifies to his scholarship.

He proved his worth as a diplomat in cultivating cordial relations with King Mengrai of Lannatai, and Khun Ngam Muang, Prince of Payao, so that he could concentrate his attention on the Khmers who might at any moment be hostile to Sukhothai. In fact, these three princes developed close friendship in the early years, as they had studied under the same master. Ramkamhaeng never put an obstacle to the expansion of Lannatai. Early in his life, Mengrai built the town of Chiang Rai, where he ruled for several years. In 1283, he made a successful attack on Haripunjai or Lamphun, which had been under the Khmer vassalage, and he incorporated it in his kingdom. Ramkamhaeng and Ngam Muang willingly cooperated with him in choosing a suitable site for Chiang Mai which he founded as his capital in 1296. At the same time, he did not neglect Pegu or the Mon country in the west of his dominions. It was under the rule of his favourite, Makato or Mogado, who swore fealty to him, and in 1286 the Thai King conferred upon him the title of Chao Fa Rua or Wareru. Consequently Sukhothai was safeguarded in the west for a long time.

Ramkamhaeng opened direct political relations with China. After the conquest of Nanchao, Kublai Khan cast his longing eyes over Burma which, he thought, should come under his rule. Hearing of Ramkamhaeng's renown as a valiant king, he preferred Sukhothai to be neutral instead of joining Burma in fighting China, should there be an attack on her, and so in 1282, he sent an envoy, Ho Tzu Chih, to the Court of Sukhothai in order to negotiate a treaty of amity, but he died on the way. As Ramkamhaeng himself took account of the might of the Chinese Emperor, he reciprocated the Chinese mission by despatching an embassy to China for the first time in 1292. Other Thai embassies followed in 1294, 1297, 1300, 1314, 1319, 1321 and 1323. It is noteworthy that the embassy which travelled to that country in 1299 was led by an heir to the throne, on whom the Chinese Emperor bestowed a ceremonial coat of a gold design. Some of these embassies brought back Chinese artisans to improve the production of pottery wares known as Sungalok wares at Sukhothai and other towns where the kilns in ruins can still be seen to-day. In his book on *The Ceramic Wares of Siam*, Spinks said that "of even greater importance, however, is the fact that a ceramic centre of some significance had been in existence in the Kingdom of Sukhothai long before Chinese influences appeared. The Thais had traditionally employed earthenware utensils for household use and had known the art of producing such simple wares from earliest times." The wares were artistic in design and were beautifully made. There was a great demand for them not only in the country but also abroad. The Sungkalok wares, were exported as far as the Philippines, Java, Sumatra, Pegu, and India. The trade with China continued to be conducted by junks from the thirteenth century to the reign of Rama III or Nang Klao (1824-1851) in the nineteenth century. There was an exchange of envoys and missions from time to time, and every three years, Siam sent presents to the Chinese Emperor as a token of goodwill and gratitude, because her exports entered China duty free. However, such presents were regarded as a tribute by the Chinese who then took it for granted that Siam was a tributary or vassal state of their Emperor. There used to be a misconception of some Europeans about Siam as far as it concerned China. In fact, Siam has never at any time been a Chinese vassal state. She has from time immemorial been an independent country. No Chinese army has ever reached the confines of the Thai territory. At one time or another, some countries in South-East Asia felt the impact of the Chinese army on their people. When King Rama IV (Mongkut) ascended the throne in 1851, he decided to abolish the practice of sending presents to the Chinese Emperor.

Ramkamhaeng died about 1300. His friend, King Mengrai of Lannatai outlived him, while Prince Ngam Muang of Payao lived on until 1328. Ten years after his death, his principality was annexed to Chiang Mai. It was due to Ramkamhaeng's untiring efforts that Sukhothai reached its zenith, and it entered on a period of decline after his reign.

MAHATHAT MONASTERY,
LOCATED WITHIN THE COMPOUND
OF THE KING'S PALACE, AT SUKHOTHAI

In connection with the kings of Sukhothai, a stone inscription was discovered within the compound of Mahathat monastery during the reconstruction work of Sukhothai which was started under the auspices of Field Marshal P. Pibulsonggram, Prime Minister of Thailand, in 1956. It mentioned an oath which the grandfathers and grandsons of the Pra Ruang dynasty made together in 1392. The study of this inscription has led to the formulation of two schools of thought, one of which suggests that there should have been two more kings, namely, Saisonggram and Nguanamthom, while the other proposes the existence of one king, namely, Nguanamthom, on the ground that Saisonggram carried no title of a Payah. Now the general tendency is to accept Nguanamthom as another king of Sukhothai. The genealogy of the Pra Ruang dynasty should therefore be revised as follows :-

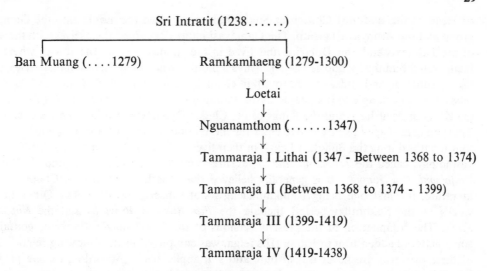

Sri Intratit (1238 . . . . . .)

Ban Muang (. . . . 1279)        Ramkamhaeng (1279-1300)
↓
Loetai
↓
Nguanamthom (. . . . . . 1347)
↓
Tammaraja I Lithai (1347 - Between 1368 to 1374)
↓
Tammaraja II (Between 1368 to 1374 - 1399)
↓
Tammaraja III (1399-1419)
↓
Tammaraja IV (1419-1438)

LOETAI AND LITHAI.    If Ramkamhaeng's successors had been warriors like him, the Kingdom of Sukhothai might have lasted longer than it actually did. His son, Loetai, succeeded him but he was nowhere near his calibre.    During Loetai's reign most of the vassal states such as Nan, Luang Prabang and Nakhon Si Thammarat took the opportunity to get rid of the Thai yoke and declare themselves independent. The King of Pegu, Saen Muang Ming, went beyond those vassal states.   Not only did he throw off his allegiance to Sukhothai but he also attacked and captured Tavoy and Tenesserim.   A Thai army marched against him, but was not successful in recovering the two cities.

In the lower part of the Menam valley, a Thai prince who ruled the Principality of Supannaphum or Utong proved himself to be a powerful rival of Loetai.   With an army which he had raised from the men of Utong, Ratchaburi and Phetchaburi, he won back Tavoy and Tenesserim for himself.   King Loetai was unable to bring him to submission, since he was deeply involved in the affairs of his dynasty. Meanwhile trouble had arisen in Sukhothai over the seizure of the throne because Loetai had appointed his eldest son, Lithai, as Maha Uparat (Deputy King) of Si Satchanalai and another as governor of Jakungrao later known as Kamphaeng Phet.   He built Jakungrao and endowed it with the same status as Si Satchanalai.   The two princes failed to maintain brotherly relations, because they were rivals and were planning to seize the throne.   So long as Loetai was alive, they remained quiet, showing no signs of insubordination.   Hearing that his father was seriously ill, the governor of Jakungrao, hurried with his army to Sukhothai, where he was confronted by Lithai's troops and in the ensuing battle, he was decisively beaten.   Lithai then succeeded to the throne in 1347.   A question might be asked as to how long Nguanamthom who succeeded Loetai ruled Sukhothai.   No stone inscription mentions anything about his reign. He might have occupied the throne for a few days or a few months and then he merely passed out from history, while the two princes were fighting for the Kingdom.

LITHAI was a great scholar and patron of Lanka Buddhism so much so that he bore the title of Maha Tammaraja or Dhammaraja.   Throughout his reign, he devoted himself to the advancement of this religion. He made a Ceylonese high monk the Sangharaja or Head of the Buddhist Church at Sukhothai and divided the monks into the Gamavasi group and the Arunyavasi group. The Gamavasi monks occupied themselves with the study of the Pali texts and the Doctrine and lived in the monasteries of the towns where they inaugurated Buddhist schools. The Arunyavasi monks, who lived in forest monasteries, practised meditation and endeavoured to attain emancipation from suffering and rebirth. Lithai himself set an example to his people by becoming a monk for a time; this was followed by the Kings of Ayutthaya and the Kings of the Chakri Dynasty and it became the custom for Thai young men aged twenty-one to enter the monkhood for at least a short period—usually four months during the Buddhist Lent—in their lives. He also wrote a treatise on Buddhist cosmology, called the *Tribhumikatha* (The Three Worlds—Heaven, Earth and Hell) or the *Traibhumi Pra Ruang*. It is generally believed that it is the second oldest book of Thai literature, the first one being Ramkamhaeng's stone inscription of 1292. Other literary works of the Sukhothai period include the *Pra Ruang's Proverbs* and the *Nophamas Story*. The compilation of the present versions of the *Pra Ruang's Proverbs*, containing some material added to it in Rama III's reign, was completed in the following reign. Some of these proverbs are never out of date and still applicable. According to one proverb, "Seek knowledge when young; seek wealth when grown up," while another one says "Do not put a boat against a strong current." Some additions were made at the beginning of the Bangkok period to the present version of the *Nophamas Story*, explaining many royal customs and ceremonies in the days of Sukhothai.

He spent both time and money in building monasteries, Buddha images and roads, the ruins of which still remain to-day. The art of making Buddha images, both large and small, may be said to have reached perfection in his reign. The famous image of the Buddha, Pra Buddha Jinaraj or Lord of Victory which now occupies one chapel of the Sriratana Mahathat monastery at Phitsanulok is generally recognized as a masterpiece of the Sukhothai plastic art. He made a road from Si Satchanalai to Sukhothai and Kamphaeng Phet, only the traces of which can now be seen. It is called the Pra Ruang road. He raised Song Kwae (Phitsanulok) to be a royal city and rebuilt Nakhon Jum.

He was fully aware of the strength of his Kingdom and so he made no attempts to subdue his former vassals, particularly Ramatibodi I of Ayutthaya. Recent research appearing in *A Declaration of Independence and its consequences*, an article by A.B. Griswold and Prasert na Nagara in the Journal of the Siam Society, has brought out the fact that "Lithai was an able statesman and a competent soldier. By attracting a number of the vassals who had broken away, and by subduing others, he recovered a territory stretching from above Uttaradit in the north to Nakhon Sawan in the south, from the valley of the Ping in the west to that of the Sak in the east. If his gains were modest compared with those of Ramkamhaeng, they were nevertheless impressive, for he was faced with a limiting factor which did not exist in Ramkamhaeng's time: the territory south of Nakhon Sawan now belonged to so powerful a ruler that Lithai had to dismiss all hope of recovering it. Instead he cultivated friendly relations with him." Owing to his wise policy, he was therefore able to preserve the independence of the Kingdom of Sukhothai.

TAMMARAJA II, TAMMARAJA III AND TAMMARAJA IV. Sukhothai became a vassal state of Ayutthaya in the reign of Maha Tammaraja II (Between 1368 to 1374 to 1399). In pursuance of his expansionist policy, King Boromaraja I (P'angoa) of Ayutthaya attacked it in 1371, but meeting with a strong resistance of the people lasting about six years, he could advance only as far as Chai Nat and then he made one more attempt to conquer Sukhothai in 1378 when he sent an army to seize the town of Jakungrao. Watching the Ayutthaya troops in action, Tammaraja II came to the conclusion that it would be helpless to fight the enemy. So he surrendered the town and made submission to Boromaraja I in that year. Thus Sukhothai lost its 140 year old independence. The King of Ayutthaya split up his new vassal state into the northern territory and the southern territory with a view to reducing Tammaraja II's power. However, Tammaraja II was not deposed, but was assigned by Boromaraja I to rule the northern territory which included the Meyom and the Nan valleys with Sawankhalok, Phitsanulok and Phichit as principal towns. For the sake of administrative convenience of this territory, he moved his capital from Sukhothai to Phitsanulok and consequently the city of Sukhothai itself was neglected. The southern territory in the Meping valley was ruled by Boromaraja I's step son, Phya Yarnnadis, who made Kamphaeng Phet his government headquarters.

Tammaraja II was succeeded in turn by Maha Tammaraja III (1399-1419) and Maha Tammaraja IV (1419-1438) who continued to show subservience to Ayutthaya. Maha Tammaraja III's death without a legal heir brought about confrontation between his two half brothers, Phya Ban Muang and Phya Ram, who fought for the throne. Through the mediation of King Intaraja of Ayutthaya who was their overlord, Phya Ban Muang won the crown of Sukhothai, while Phya Ram received the governorship of Kamphaeng Phet. After Maha Tammaraja IV's death, King Boromaraja II installed his son and heir, Ramesuan, as ruler of the northern provinces with his seat of office at Phitsanulok. This event marked the extinction of the Pra Ruang Dynasty. Sukhothai became completely part and parcel of the Kingdom of Ayutthaya.

# CHAPTER V

# AYUTTHAYA FROM ITS FOUNDATION
# AS THE CAPITAL TO ITS FIRST FALL

RAMATIBODI I (1350-1369). Ayutthaya was a thriving town before it was founded as the capital of Siam by King Ramatibodi I in 1350, and was already a trading centre where people congregated and worshipped the famous Buddha statue, Panuncherng, which had been erected at the monastery or wat of the same name in 1324. Before it fell into the Thai hands, it used to serve as an outpost of the Khmers or Cambodians who ruled Lavo or Lop Buri. Situated on an island, the confluence of three rivers, the Chao Phya, the Lopburi and the Pasak, it became an important centre of trade and communications, being at a distance of approximately 70 miles or 110 kilometres from the sea.

Before his accession to the throne, King Ramatibodi I had distinguished himself as the Prince of Supannaphum or Utong. Utong is now an Amphur or district in the province of Suphan Buri. The Principality had been extending its boundaries since the beginning of the fourteenth century, as it had annexed a large part of the kingdom of Sukhothai as well as the western portion of the Cambodian Empire including Ayutthaya and Lop Buri, thus helping to increase its strength both in men and natural resources. Nothing definite is known about Ramatibodi I's ancestry or even his personal name. It is believed that he married a daughter of the preceding Prince of Utong and became himself the ruler of Utong on the death of his father-in-law. The people of Utong had depended on the supply of water from a small river (now known as the Chorakhesampun tributary) nearby, but it had become silted up. Despite the fact that wells had been dug, a scarcity of water occurred and this caused an outbreak of an epidemic, believed to be cholera, which decimated the people. If he lived on there, he saw no possibility of the city becoming a progressive one. He had also been seeking a town which was centrally located, so that he could control his expanding principality more effectively. For these reasons, he abandoned Utong and moved his capital to Ayutthaya, which was a growing town. In 1963, excavations, undertaken by the Thai Department of Fine Arts in co-operation with Professor Jean Boisselier, a French expert on South-East Art and Archaeology, have revealed that Utong was an important city in the Kingdom of Dvaravati and lasted until about the eleventh century. It then became a deserted city presumably due to some natural disaster, for approximately 100-200 years before the founding of Ayutthaya as the capital. Opinion therefore differs as to the location of his original city prior to his accession to the throne, and may be summarised in this way. Ramatibodi I might have resided on the southern bank of the Chao Phya river opposite the City of Ayutthaya somewhere near the Panuncherng monastery. Due to an outbreak of cholera, he evacuated his people across the river to the northern bank where he built his capital. Or he might have evacuated from Suphan Buri, another name for Supannaphum or Utong, to Ayutthaya. His original city might have been located in the district of Ban Rairoth or Nonglang, now in the district of Donchedi in the province of Suphan Buri. Having thoroughly scrutinized the map of Suphan Buri showing Ban Rairoth being at a distance of about 40 kilometres from Utong as the crow flies, the author of this book subscribes to the latter view.

After his coronation, Ramatibodi I appointed his son, Ramesuan, as Governor of Lop Buri which was the largest northern outpost bordering on the Kingdom of Sukhothai, and he assigned his brother-in-law, Prince Pa'ngoa, to the governorship of Suphan Buri on the west of Ayutthaya, with the exalted title of Boromaraja. Pa'ngoa was the elder brother of his Queen. These appointments were in harmony with Ramatibodi's policy of consolidating the Kingdom of Ayutthaya, in which only the princes whom he trusted fully ruled the important regions.

During Ramatibodi's reign, the government assumed the form of an absolute monarchy, the main structure of which was similar to that of Sukhothai, but it was inextricably tinged with strong Cambodian influences. The Thais had been living for some hundred years side by side with the Cambodians and inevitably they had adopted many features of their civilization which was in turn based on that of India. According to Thompson's *Thailand: The New Siam*, "It was the most sophisticated Khmers who supplied the Thais with a theory of divine kingship. Khmer words, ideas, and royal ceremonial were absorbed slowly through proximity." The Thai King became an autocrat, no longer in paternal relationship with his people in the same way as in the Sukhothai period. He was the "Lord of Life." The land in the whole country belonged to him and a court language grew up to designate anything concerning himself or his possessions. Besides the court language, there are now four kinds of Thai language-the religious, the polite, the common language and the slang. But his autocracy was tempered by the observance of ten Buddhist kingly duties: liberality, piety, charity, freedom from wrath, mercy, patience, rectitude, mildness, devotion, and freedom from enmity.

For the administration of the Kingdom, he created the offices of the four Great Officers of State as follows:-

1. Khun Muang corresponded to the Minister of Local Government whose duties included the maintenance of peace and order and the punishment of criminals.

2. Khun Wang corresponded to the Minister of the Royal Household. In addition to his regular duties, he acted as a judge who decided cases among the people.

3. Khun Klang corresponded to the Minister of Finance. Not only was he a collector of taxes, but he was also a custodian of state properties.

4. Khun Na corresponded to the Minister of Agriculture whose extra duty it was to store up food for the capital.

These Great Officers would require proper laws in the execution of their duties and so Ramatibodi I promulgated the following laws:

The Law of Evidence (A.D. 1350), classifying people as witnesses. In a quarrel between the principal wife and a minor wife, for instance, only local people, friends and neighbours were permitted to act as witnesses, the husband being barred from this owing to his inability to maintain impartiality. In a quarrel between sailors on the high seas, fellow sailors could serve as witnesses.

The Law on Offences against the Government (A.D.1351)

The Law of Husband and Wife (A.D.1351)

The Law on Receiving Plaints (A.D.1355)

The Law on Abduction (A.D.1356)

The Law on Offences against the People (A.D.1357)

The Law concerning Robbers (A.D.1350 and 1366)

The Law on Miscellaneous Matters (A.D.1359)

There is one point in the Law on Abduction, to which special attention should be drawn, concerning slaves. The question as to whether slavery was in existence under the Pra Ruang Dynasty has been widely discussed and it is generally agreed that it was unknown as an institution in the independent Kingdom of Sukhothai; otherwise the people there would not have called themselves "Thai" which, as has been explained, means free. Nevertheless ex-prisoners of war who mingled with the free citizens of Sukhothai might serve as slaves. Ramatibodi I adopted the slavery system from the Cambodians and Thai slaves in the Kingdom of Ayutthaya knew that according to the law, if they could escape to the dominions of Sukhothai, freedom would be their prize. As time wore on, slavery permeated the Thai social system until the end of the nineteenth century.

Ramatibodi I followed the example, set by Ramkamhaeng the Great and his successors, in the support of Lanka Buddhism, and this constituted a normal practice for the later kings of Ayutthaya to follow. With regard to Cambodia, after he had been on the throne for more than one year, he was convinced that the Cambodians had become increasingly inimical to Ayutthaya. In order to forestall any possible Cambodian attack, he placed his son, Prince Ramesuan, at the head of an army for the invasion of his eastern neighbour in 1352. Owing to faulty tactics, the Thai army was defeated and the King had to despatch Prince Boromaraja (Pa'ngoa) with another army to save his nephew. Boromaraja (Pa'ngoa) made a forced march to Cambodia, where he inflicted a severe defeat on the enemy and captured its capital, Angkor Thom. So he returned to Ayutthaya with an enhanced reputation and the Thai eastern frontier was extended to the area which now spreads from Nakhon Ratchasima to Chanthaburi and the neighbouring provinces.

In short, Ramatibodi I laid the firm foundation of Ayutthaya for his successors to build on, and so Ayutthaya continued to be the capital of Siam for 417 years, almost three times longer than Sukhothai.

THE EXPANSION OF AYUTTHAYA. King Ramatibodi I died in 1369 at the age of fifty seven, and in accordance with his wishes, his son Ramesuan ascended the throne. Being unable to cope with his distinguished uncle, Boromaraja(Pa'ngoa), Ramesuan meekly surrendered the throne to him and went back to Lop Buri as its governor for the second time.

The new King (Pa'ngoa) took upon himself the title of Boromaraja I whose rule covered a period of eighteen years (1370-1388). Having shown himself to be an extremely competent and skilful general, he pursued Ramatibodi I's policy of expansion. In 1372, he invaded the Kingdom of Sukhothai and advanced as far as Jakungrao, but was unsuccessful in taking it. Subsequently he made two more attempts to conquer the same Kingdom which proved to be equally fruitless, since the troops of Lannatai or Chiang Mai had moved down to help in its defence. Nevertheless his attack of Jakungrao was crowned with complete success in 1378, resulting in the submission of Sukhothai as a vassal state to Ayutthaya. Consequently for the safe rule of the new vassal state, Pa'ngoa adopted the "divide and the rule" policy by dividing Sukhothai into the northern territory which continued to be under its king, and the southern territory under Phya Yarnnadis, Boromaraja I's stepson.

The Kingdom of Lannatai had, through its assistance to Sukhothai, incurred Boromaraja I's wrath. As soon as he settled the government of his newly won vassal state, he marched with an army against Chiang Mai, the capital of Lannatai, in 1370. Lampang barred his way and after trying in vain to take it, he made his retreat. His plan to subdue Chiang Mai was by no means abandoned, and in 1388, he led another army against this City, but illness overtook him and he died during the expedition. The Thai army therefore had to return to Ayutthaya.

With the consent of the high officials the throne devolved on Boromaraja's son, Tonglun, who was a mere boy of fifteen. He was the King of Ayutthaya for only seven days. The ex-King Ramesuan, who was the Governor of Lop Buri, still nurtured his rightful ambition to the throne, and immediately proceeded to Ayutthaya, where he seized the young King and had him done to death in the royal manner — clubbing him to death in a velvet sack with a sandalwood stick. This was indeed a shameful crime. Probably Ramesuan had forgotten his own fate at the time of his abdication. He should have shown mercy to Tonglun by letting him retire to a monastery or exiling him to a distant town. Such an idea would most likely have never occured to him as an autocrat who was flushed with unlimited power.

King Ramesuan (1388-1395) thus became King for the second time. He followed up Boromaraja I's policy with regard to Chiang Mai. Good fortune favoured him and the city fell to him after an attack, supposedly by cannon. His use of cannon might have been possible, since it had appeared for the first time about 1335 during the Hundred Year's War in Europe, but no picture or description of the cannon has, so far, been found. He transplanted to Ayutthaya a large number of Chiang Mai people who were then assigned to settle down in Chanthaburi, Nakhon Si Thammarat and Songkhla. They were Thai, but they had their own dialect, and with the passing of time, they were eventually assimilated with the local people. A son of the former King of Chiang Mai was installed in his place.

Cambodia continued to be a thorn in the side of Ayutthaya. The Cambodians raided Chon Buri and Chanthaburi and carried off some people with them to their country. In 1393, King Ramesuan therefore retaliated by putting himself in charge of an army which advanced against them. After dealing a crushing defeat to them, he entered their capital, Angkor Thom, from which he removed 90,000 Cambodian prisoners to Siam and this virtually terminated the Cambodian threat to the Thai power.

King Ramesuan died in 1395 at the age of sixty-two. Ramaraja, his son, occupied the throne from 1395 to 1409, but nothing is recorded of his reign. Presumably the people enjoyed peace and tranquillity for a change, if one recalls that no news is good news. He lost his throne, because his principal Minister, Chao Phya Mahasena, turned against him and invited Prince Nakorn In, Governor of Suphan Buri, to Ayutthaya. When the Prince arrived there with his forces, King Ramaraja abdicated in his favour and retired to a private life, making no move whatsoever to regain his power. Perhaps he was a prince of no ambition, a rare example of self-satisfaction.

The new King bore the title of Nakarin or Intaraja (1409-1424). He was the son of one of the younger brothers of King Boromaraja I. At the time of his accession, he was more than fifty years old and possessed considerable experience in government, as he had been governing Suphan Buri for some time and had in 1377 visited Nanking which was then the capital of the Chinese Emperor of the Ming dynasty. During his reign, he maintained friendly intercourse with the Emperor Yung Lo through the exchange of diplomatic missions.

The succession dispute between the two brothers of Sukhothai, Phya Ban Muang and Phya Rama, claimed Intaraja I's attention. When his army advanced to Nakhon Sawan, they came down to pay him their respects, and with his persuasion, they reached a compromise, whereby one of them was made King Tammaraja IV and the other received the governorship of Kamphaeng Phet.

King Intaraja had three grownup sons who had each a number of adherents. The first one was Prince Ai' phya (Prince One), who governed Suphan Buri, and the second was Prince Yee'phya (Prince Two), governor of Prack or San, while the third was Prince Samphya (Prince Three), who held the governorship of Chai Nat. Hearing of their father's death, the two elder brothers struggled for the throne. They hurried with their troops and retainers to Ayutthaya, where they met at a spot called Sapan Than (Charcoal Bridge) and fought a duel from their elephants. Neither of them was the winner, as both of them were thrown from the elephants and were killed immediately. The youngest brother, Prince Samphya, who won the throne without any exertion, was then proclaimed king as Boromaraja II.

KING BOROMARAJA II (1424-1448) took measures to strengthen the Kingdom along the same lines as his father, Intaraja. In 1431, King Tammasoke raided the outlying districts of Siam and removed a number of Thai people to Cambodia. In pursuit of his enemy, King Boromaraja II put himself in command of an army which penetrated to Angkor Thom. Having invested the Cambodian capital, he managed to capture it after a siege of seven months in 1431. With an intention to turn Cambodia into a vassal state of Ayutthaya, Boromaraja II set up his own son, Pra Intaraja, as King of Cambodia, before the army started its return journey, bringing back to Siam a vast number of prisoners and a large quantity of valuable objects of art including bronze images of animals. But Pra Intaraja occupied the Cambodian throne only for a short time. The hot climate affected his health very badly, as the result of which he was taken ill and died. Thus the first Thai attempt to hold Cambodia in subjugation ended in a failure. The country slipped back into its former status and apparently Boromaraja II made no further efforts to retake it. Meanwhile the new King of Cambodia considered that the reconstruction of Angkor Thom would not be worth a large amount of expenses that were needed, as the city was dangerously near the Thai frontier. He therefore abandoned Angkor Thom with Angkor Wat nearby in 1432, and transferred his Court first to Basan on the eastern side of the Mekong river, and in 1434 to Phnom Penh which was situated further down the Tonlesap or Great Lake. Angkor Thom and Angkor Wat crumbled into ruins with the passage of time, and the interest in these colossal structures was not revived until the end of the nineteenth century by the French who undertook to clear up the jungles and restored them. However, Phnom Penh was the capital of Cambodia for only a short time, and the Cambodian king substituted for it Lowek or Lawak, about 30 kilometres north of it. Finally the capital was moved back to Phnom Penh in the nineteenth century.

The eastern region of Siam was thus secure for some time. The death of Tammaraja IV of Phitsanulok afforded Boromaraja II an opportunity to take another important step in the consolidation of the Kingdom of Siam. He incorporated the two territories of Sukhothai in it and appointed his eldest son, Prince Ramesuan, as Viceroy of the northern region or old dominions of Sukhothai with his seat of government at Phitsanulok in 1438. The reason was that King Tilokerat of Chiang Mai, who was reputed as a warrior, might be tempted by the heirs of the Pra Ruang line to make an inroad on the northern border of Siam.Taking advantage of another succession struggle in Chiang Mai, Boromaraja II intervened in it with his army in 1442, but his attempt to bring Chiang Mai under the Thai rule proved in vain. Six years later, when his army advanced as far as the southern frontier of Chiang Mai, death overtook him. The army, however, transplanted some Chiang Mai people to Ayutthaya.

BOROMTRAILOKANAT AND RAMATIBODI II. Prince Ramesuan, who succeeded his father, Boromaraja II, was seventeen years of age, and he assumed the title of Boromtrailokanat (1448-1488), usually shortened to Trailok. He achieved wide fame for his scholarship; he was well versed in arts, jurisprudence and statecraft. He was the first prince of Ayutthaya to rule the old dominions of Sukhothai. While holding the viceroyalty at Phitsanulok, he made a profound study of the royal history and customs of Sukhothai, from which he selected only the good and appropriate features as a basis to work on. For instance, he dedicated a piece of land within the precincts of the royal place at Ayutthaya as the site of a Buddhist chapel which was erected under his patronage. The chapel was originally known as Wat Buddhawas and later had its name changed to Wat Pra Srisanpet, which was a replica of Wat Mahathat in Sukhothai.

His monumental work was the reorganization of the government with a view to achieving centralization of the affairs of the State and in doing so, he established the military administration and the civil administration. The military administration which was under the Samuhakalahom or co-prime minister for military affairs was divided into departments, whose heads had high rank. In the performance of his routine duties such as the supply of troops, weapons, draught animals and provisions, he was assisted by a hierarchy of officials, beginning with the Under-Secretary of State. For the conduct of warfare, two armies were kept in readiness—one under Phya Siharajdejojai and the other under Phya Tainam, both under the Samuhakalahom. Should the King lead his soldiers in a battle, all the armies were at his command. The civil administration, headed by the Samuhanayok or co-prime minister for civil affairs, had four great offices, each under a Minister or Senabodi, namely: (1) the Krom Muang or Ministry of Local Government which was in charge of the affairs of the capital; (2) the Krom Wang or Ministry of the Royal Household which dealt with the Palace affairs and the administration of Justice; (3) the Krom Klang or Ministry of Finance which also served as the Royal Treasury and dealt with the foreign affairs and foreign trade; (4) the Krom Na or Ministry of Agriculture which was in charge of the cultivation of rice and other crops, food supply and land tenure. Certainly each Minister or Senabodi controlled a hierachy of officials.

For the provincial administration, King Trailok divided the towns into four classes, first, second, third and fourth. At the head of each town was the governor who performed his duties with the assistance of officials of the military and the civil sections corresponding to those in the capital, but lower in rank. Subsequently the Samuhakalahom took charge of the north, while Samuhanayok was in charge of the south of the kingdom. Needless to say, both of them were directly responsible to the King.

It is interesting to note that all these offices were not hereditary as was the practice in Europe, since they were held at the King's pleasure. Nor did the titles of nobility, as created by King Trailok, pass down from father to son, and they were divided into seven grades as follows: 1. Phya; 2. Pra; 3. Luang; 4. Khun; 5. Muen; 6. Pun; and 7. Tanai. The Chao Phya grade was created afterwards. The titles varied in grades according to the importance of the offices. A Chao Phya and a Phya might be equivalent to an English Marquess and a Lord respectively, since they were not numerous in number. Normally the highest title, Chao Phya, was for the Minister of State or the Governor of a first class town; the second title, Phya, was for the Under-Secretary of State, the Head of a Department of Bureau, or the Governor of a second class town; and so on. Often the titles also went with certain posts. Chao Phya Mahasena for instance, was the Samuhakalahom, while Chao Phya Chakri was the Samuhanayok; Chao Phya Praklang or Kosatibodi was the Minister of Finance; Chao Phya Yomarat was the Minister of Local Government; Phya Sripipat was the Under-Secretary of State for Finance. Phya Rajwangsan was the commander of the navy.

The officials, both civil and military, received no salaries. Partly to help them to find an income and partly to regulate the system of land tenure, King Trailok issued, in 1454, a law governing the Sakdi Na grades. It specified the different classes of people and amounts of land to be assigned to each. For example, a prince of high rank could have 20,000 rais or 8,000 acres ($2\frac{1}{2}$ rais being equal to 1 acre). A Chao Phya was entitled to 4,000 acres, while a commoner held only 10 acres. For the sake of clarification, one would say that the Sakdi Na system placed a value on every man in the Kingdom. If he did something wrong and was fined, the amount of the fine was determined by his Sakdi Na grade; so too was the compensation to be paid for any injury done to him or for his death. Every government official received the amount of land prescribed by the Sakdi Na system and had to live on the revenue from the produce of his land. But his land tenure was not hereditary, and on the degradation of his title of nobility or his death, it reverted to the King. His children were commoners and could have land in accordance with their status, unless they were made noblemen by the King and in such a case, the amount of land they could hold was increased. However the conferment of the Sakdi Na grades did not include land at the beginning of the Bangkok period. One of the reforms, effected by King Chulalongkorn at the end of the nineteenth century, was the payment of salaries in cash to government officials instead of land. The bestowal of titles on them still carried with it an assumed grant of land in the days of the absolute monarchy. In other words, the Sakdi Na system prevailed until the revolution of 1932 in Siam. At one time confusion existed in the mind of some people who thought that Trailok's system of government might be a feudal one. In fact this was not the case. Titles of Thai nobility, for instance, were not hereditary as in Europe, and land tenure was at the King's pleasure.

In 1450, King Trailok promulgated the Palace Law or Kot Montien Ban which formulated the customs, ceremonies, rules and regulations, connected with the Court and the Royal Family. This was in conformity with his policy of systematizing all branches of government. The Palace Law, for instance, specified the neighbouring States which sent gold and silver trees as tribute to Ayutthaya; it defined the relative rank of different classes of queens and princes, and it laid down the procedure, whereby a prince who committed an offence or a crime was to be punished. He was bound with gold or silver fetters before he was put in a velvet sack and was beaten to death with a sandalwood club. A person who committed certain offences against the Palace Law was also severely punished, two examples of which are quoted here. If he introduced amatory poems into the palace, he would be put to death. If he kicked the door of the palace, his foot would be cut off. The idea behind such punishment was to exalt divine kingship, which would overawe the people and deter them from hatching a plot to cause harm to the King.

Malacca claimed King Trailok's attention after he had occupied the throne for seven years. In fact, the land where Malacca was located had belonged to Siam since the reign of Ramkamhaeng the Great of Sukhothai, but his rule there was not effective. No mention of Malacca, however, is found in the stone inscription concerning the boundaries of the Kingdom of Sukhothai under Ramkamhaeng. King Ramatibodi I asserted his power over Malacca at the beginning of the Ayutthaya period. According to the Malay and Portuguese sources Malacca was a fishing village before it was, in 1399, founded as a town by Prince Parameswara who had descended from the Sailendra dynasty and had married a Majpahit princess in Java. The outbreak of a war of succession forced him to seek refuge at Tumasik (an old name of Singapore) and begin an adventurous career until he became the governor of Malacca. He changed his religion from Buddhism to Islam, very probably assuming the name of Megat Iskander Shah and recognizing the King of Siam as his suzerain. In his effort to throw off the allegiance of Ayutthaya, he travelled to China where he was accorded an audience with the Emperor, seeking his assistance, but the request fell on deaf ears. At the instigation of the Arab merchants, one of his successors rebelled against Siam. In 1455, at King Trailok's command, a Thai army moved to the south in order to crush the rebellion. It was successful in carrying out its mission with the capture of the town of Malacca. But Malacca submitted to Siam for a short time only and then it slipped out of the Thai hands again.

In 1456, King Trailok became involved in a war with Chiang Mai. Phya Yutistira, the Governor of Phitsanulok had secretly transferred his allegiance from Ayutthaya to Chiang Mai. Seeing that this was a chance to strike a blow at Siam, King Tilokerat led his army down to Kamphaeng Phet and took it. His vanguard moved further down to take away a number of people from Chai Nat. King Trailok chased the Chiang Mai troops out of his dominions and followed them to Toen, where they engaged in a battle. The result was that the Thai army was victorious and King Trailok ordered the arrest of the Governor of Sawankhalok who had by then fled to Chiang Mai. Not only did he stir up King Tilokerat to invade Siam, but he also volunteered to lead the Chiang Mai soldiers to Sukhothai. In 1461, Sukhothai was lost to them, and their next objective was Kamphaeng Phet, but as soon as they heard about an invasion of the Yunnanese from the north, they beat a hasty retreat, thus leaving the way open for Ayutthaya to regain its northern territory. Sukhothai was taken and controlled by Siam once more.

In 1463, King Trailok's invasion of Chiang Mai ended in a failure. In view of the fact that the north might be subject to a Chiang Mai attack again in the event of his complete withdrawal to the south, he made up his mind to live at Phitsanulok. His purpose in doing so was to put up a strong and effective defence of the north against any incursion. After the appointment of his elder son, Prince Boromaraja as Governor or Regent of Ayutthaya, he transferred his headquarters to that city which became for practical purposes his capital for twenty five years until the end of his reign.

The incessant war between Ayutthaya and Chiang Mai benefited neither side and actually it bore down on both King Trailok and King Tilokerat. Once in 1473, the latter went out of his mind and had his son and heir executed. Seizing this opportunity, the former invaded the Chiang Mai territory in the following year, but did not achieve the result for which he had set out. He merely brought back the people who had been removed by the treacherous Governor of Sawankhalok. Realizing the uselessness of the struggle, King Tilokerat made overtures for peace, which was agreed to by King Trailok. The normal relations were thus restored by Ayutthaya and Chiang Mai.

Special mention must be made of the cultural aspect of King Trailok's reign. He gave a strong impetus to the arts and literature. At his command, the *Mahajati* volume was written, while the *Pra Law* was composed at about the same time. The former was a religious poem of some length, dealing with the Buddha's last incarnation before being born as Prince Siddhatta, and the latter relates a love story which is brought to a tragic ending by the feud between the two lover's families. The King was particularly interested in the improvement of the Buddhist Church, and with this object in view, he invited a high monk from Ceylon to undertake its reorganization. A Buddha relic having been discovered, he had it enshrined in a stupa at Ayutthaya. Like King Tammaraja I (Lithai) of Sukhothai, he took the vow of a Buddhist monk temporarily in 1465 and resided at Wat Chulamani in the southern part of Phitsanulok. The first white elephant caught in the Ayutthaya period was presented to him, which was considered a good omen for his prosperous reign, being so far the longest in Ayutthaya.

The succession question had been settled before King Trailok died. His elder son, Prince Boromaraja, who was the Regent of Ayutthaya, mounted the throne as a matter of course, while his younger son, Prince Jetta, continued to rule the north as the Maha Uparat or Deputy King, with his headquarters at Phitsanulok. The reversion of the capital to Ayutthaya was thus confirmed. The new King assumed the title of Boromaraja III (1488-1491). The only event worth mentioning was the loss and recapture of Tavoy. His reign was a short one, as he died in 1491, at the age of about 45. He was peacefully succeeded by his brother, Prince Jetta, known as Ramatibodi II.

At his accession to the throne, King Ramatibodi II (1491-1529) was nineteen years of age. He had in him the royal blood of the Pra Ruang dynasty, since his mother was a princess of Sukhothai, thus helping to get rid of any ill-will towards Ayutthaya, which might have remained on the part of the offsprings of that royal House. In compliance with a precedent, he appointed his son, Prince Atityawong, as Governor of Phitsanulok bearing the title of Boromaraja towards the end of his reign.

King Ramatibodi II took the following measures in improving the military system, basing it on universal compulsory service. A registration of able bodied men for the military and civil services was organized and placed under the Conscription Department or Krom Surasvadi. These services were obligatory to all men whose ages were between eighteen and sixty, and for exemption they must have each at least three sons serving in their place. They were divided into two classes, namely, probationary retainers (Prai Som) and permanent retainers (Prai Luang). Enrolled in the national register at the age of eighteen, the probationary retainers were required to undergo the training appropriate to their particular service for a period of two years, after which they became permanent retainers. The latter were split up into two categories, namely, those who devoted their time to the service took turn in doing it, and those who lived at a great distance from their towns paid for it in kind and were consequently known as retainers-in-kind. All these retainers were virtually soldiers in reserve and were called up to serve the country at an outbreak of war. Every town was commanded by the King to arrange a ceremony for a trial mobilization. As the retainers answered a call-up, they were assigned to the army for the maneuvres. To serve as a manual for those responsible for the conduct of war, a treatise of military strategy was issued in 1518.

The King also focussed his interest on a building programme which was implemented for the glory of the Buddhist Church as well as for the benefit of the people. After the cremation of the remains of his father and elder brother, he caused their ashes to be placed inside two stupas built for this purpose in Wat Pra Srisanpet at Ayutthaya. The two stupas together with the one erected for Ramatibodi II were renovated under the auspices of Field Marshal P. Pibulsonggram during his second premiership (1948-1957). Within the compound of Wat Pra Srisanpet, Ramatibodi II ordered the construction of a royal chapel and a huge image of the Buddha in a standing posture. The Buddha image was 48 feet high with a 25 feet pedestal and was covered with about 800 lbs of gold. Actually the wat or monastery was named after this image. With the fall of Ayutthaya in 1767, the image was stripped of its gold plates and destroyed beyond repair by the enemy. The inland communication by klongs or canals was greatly facilitated through the digging of new canals and the improvement of the existing ones. The Samrong canal and the Tubnang canal which linked the Chao Phya river with the Bangpakong river, for instance, were considerably deepened so as to enable large boats to pass through.

Chiang Mai again disturbed the peace of Siam, starting with an attempted invasion of Sukhothai in 1507 to be followed by another unsuccessful attempt to capture that city and a useless attack on Kamphaeng Phet in 1513. The ire of King Ramatibodi II was thus aroused and undoubtedly he would not let Chiang Mai remain unpunished. In 1508, a Thai army captured and held Prae for a short time, and in 1515, the King advanced with his army as far as Lampang where he utterly defeated the northern invaders, and he returned to the south with considerable booty. The reason why he did not bring the conquered territory under the direct rule of Ayutthaya was probably the inadequacy of troops to undertake this task in a mountainous terrain.

King Ramatibodi II's reign is most memorable for the opening of intercourse between Siam and Europe, for which credit went to the Portuguese. They were the first Europeans who arrived at Ayutthaya.

Towards the end of the fifteenth century, Portugal and Spain encouraged the exploration of sea-routes through the offer of financial assistance, men and ships for the following reasons: firstly to find a passage toAsia in order to purchase spices, silk, porcelain, ivory and other luxury goods for the European market, since the trade route to Asia which passed through the Levant was blocked by the Ottoman Turks who had already taken possession of Constantinople in 1453; secondly, to discover new lands for settlement and colonization; thirdly, to spread Christiantity through missionaries. The Portuguese and the Spaniards soon became keen rivals in search of new lands and trading interests and might come to blows. Being well aware of the fact that both of them were Catholic countries and ardently assisted in the propagation of the religion, Pope Alexander VI intervened as a mediator and persuaded them to come to an agreement. Portugal and Spain held the Pope in high esteem, and therefore signed the Treaty of Tordesillas in 1494, by which the world was divided into the eastern hemisphere and the western hemisphere, with the imaginary line of demarcation drawn from the north to the south of the Atlantic Ocean at a distance of 370 leagues to the west of the Azores. The eastern hemisphere was to be the Portuguese field of action, while the western hemisphere was reserved for Spanish expansion.

The Portuguese continued to carry on their exploration work. In 1498, Vasco da Gama sailed round the Cape of Good Hope, crossed the Indian Ocean and finally reached Calicut, a town on the Malabar coast of India where he traded and made an unexpectedly large profit. This induced his fellow countrymen to venture out to that country, where they soon obtained some territory on which to build their settlements. Goa, which was a town on the Malabar coast, became their headquarters with the Viceroy in charge.

On assuming his office as the second Portuguese Viceroy, Alfonso d'Albuquerque laid down a plan to extend the Portuguese power in the east and the west of Bengal. In the east, he desired to take possession of the Malay archipelago where he would be able to control the trade in spices. Malacca on the west coast of Malaya was an extensive market for oriental goods and therefore the Portuguese wanted to trade with it. Four ships under the command of Diego Lopes de Sequeira arrived at Malacca in 1509.

Malacca was at that time governed by a Malay Sultan, who proved himself to be a difficult vassal of Siam. In 1489, he rebelled against Siam. The Thai troops were sent to Malacca and a fierce battle ensued. They captured the town and secured the Sultan's submission.

With the Sultan's permission, Lopes de Sequeira and his men set up a trading station at Malacca. The Arab merchants who had been trading there before the Portuguese strongly resented the intrusion of the latter into their business. At their instigation, the Sultan determined to get rid of the Portuguese and therefore ordered his men to attack the Portuguese station. Twenty Portuguese were taken prisoner, but Lopes de Sequeira escaped, sailed in his ship to Galle in Ceylon, another Portuguese settlement, and sent a secret message to Alfonso d'Albuquerque, imploring him to rescue his fellow countrymen from Malacca. In 1511, d'Albuquerque brought a fleet of eighteen ships from Goa into the Straits of Malacca, and ordered the Sultan, who had defied a previous demand, to surrender the town. At the refusal of the order, Malacca was stormed and occupied by the Portuguese. The town thus became a Portuguese possession.

Having learnt that the Thai King claimed some suzerain rights over Malacca, d'Albuquerque decided to enter into relations with him in order to avoid trouble with the Thais. In that year, he despatched Duarte Fernandez, who was one of de Sequeira's officers and knew a little Thai, to Ayutthaya with a report which had led to the capture of Malacca by the Portuguese. He travelled by a Chinese junk to the Thai capital, where soon after his arrival, he was granted an audience by Ramatibodi II, informed him of his mission and presented to him a sword with a golden scabbard encrusted with diamonds. The King seemed to raise no objection to the Portuguese occupation of Malacca. The first Portuguese envoy was thus well received at the Thai Court, the reason being that he showed no superiority towards the Thais.

Fernandez returned to Malacca by way of Tenesserim and was accompanied by a Thai envoy bearing a gift for d'Albuquerque and also having the duty to report upon the strength and nature of the Portuguese establishment. In reply to the King's congratulatory message, d'Albuquerque sent by the overland route a second envoy, Antonio Miranda de Azevedo, who was the first of the European explorers of southern Siam. However, beyond the fact that the journey was taken in 1512, there is no record of it. A Portuguese by name of Fragoso accompanied him to Ayutthaya, where he spent two years writing a report on the customs and manners of the Thais. He then left for Goa, bringing a Thai envoy with him. The Thai envoy met d'Albuquerque and handed him a letter from King Ramatibodi II with a request that it be transmitted to the King of Portugal.

In 1516, the Portuguese governor of Malacca appointed Duarte de Coelho as the third envoy to Ayutthaya, who concluded a treaty of friendship and commerce between Siam and Portugal in due time. The envoy was well acquainted with the conditions of the country having visited Ayutthaya twice, the first time with de Azevedo and the second time with de Andrade who had to seek shelter in the Thai territory, due to a violent storm, while his ship was on the way to China. According to the terms of the treaty, which was the first one between Siam and a western State, the Portuguese agreed to supply her with guns, and ammunition and gained the right to reside and trade at Ayutthaya, Ligor, Pattani, Tenesserim and Mergui. Moreover, they were granted permission to practise their religion. Apart from the treaty, the Portuguese expressed their admiration for Ayutthaya as being the most powerful and progressive country in the Indo-Chinese peninsula and also their readiness to welcome the Thais who wished to settle down in Malacca, because the Arabs had made their exodus soon after its conquest. It is interesting to point out that the Portuguese met with no difficulty in opening relations with Ayutthaya and also enjoyed religious freedom, a rare concession to them, simply because suffering from no prejudices the Thais adopted a liberal attitude towards foreigners. To celebrate the signing of the treaty, de Coelho was permitted to place in Ayutthaya a "Padrao," that is, a stone pillar with the coat-of-arms and surmounted with a wooden cross. After one year's stay, he returned to Malacca. During the five years between the first visit of Fernandez to Ayutthaya and the signature of the treaty in 1516, the Thais had time to observe that the Portuguese policy in the East aimed at the development of trade rather than the acquisition of territory. Indeed foreign trade was needed by an agricultural country like Siam, as it would contribute to the progress of the country. Firearms and ammunition, bought from the Portuguese, could be used in the defence of the realm. For these reasons, the Portuguese were accorded a warm welcome. They began their trade at the southern towns such as Pattani, Ligor or Nakhon Si Thammarat, Mergui and Tavoy. Their connection with Pattani deserves mention here. In 1516, the year of the treaty, Manoel Folcao established a trading station at Pattani which flourished so quickly that by 1538 there were three hundred Portuguese living there and doing business with merchants from Arabia, Persia and other lands, according to Fernando Mendez Pinto. Pinto spent his youth in the East in the sixteenth century, and in his old age composed a story of his adventures entitled **Perigrinacam** or Peregrinations. He appears to have drawn upon his imagination more often than on his memory in composing this work. Many of his statements are clearly unreliable. He claims to have visited Chiang Mai in company with the Siamese expeditionary force. The inaccuracies of his geography throw suspicion upon the authenticity of his own fantastic adventures.

In 1529, Ramatibodi II died at the age of fifty seven, after a reign of thirty eight years. His son, Prince Atityawong, who was the Governor of Phitsanulok, succeeded him as King Boromaraja IV (1529-1533). During his short reign, Boromaraja IV appointed his half brother, Prince Prajairaja, as Governor of Phitsanulok. So the north of Siam with its centre at this city became the training ground for a future king, but nothing occurred to disturb the peace of the north, since Ayutthaya maintained friendly relations with Chiang Mai. In the

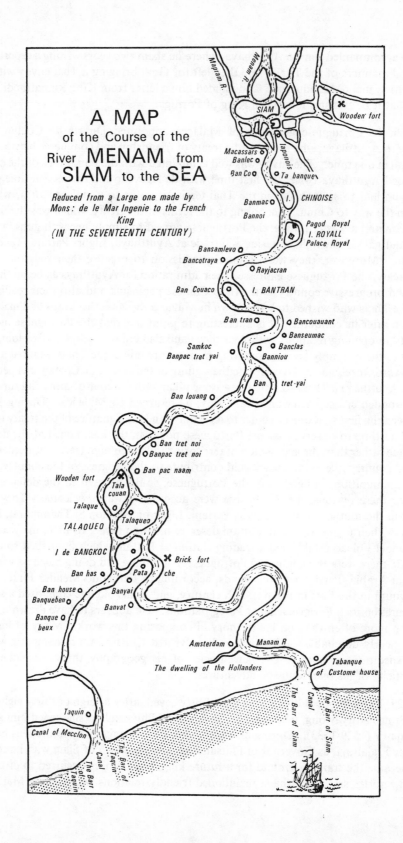

A MAP
of the Course of the
River MENAM from
SIAM to the SEA

*Reduced from a Large one made by*
*Mons: de le Mar Ingenie to the French*
*King*
*(IN THE SEVENTEENTH CENTURY)*

Mapiam R.

Menam R.

SIAM

Wooden fort

Macassars Banlec
Ban Co
Ta banque
Iaponois

Banmac
Bannoi
I. CHINOISE

Pagod Royal
I. ROYALL
Palace Royal

Bansamlevo
Bancotraya
Rayjacran
Ban Couaco
I. BANTRAN

Ban tran
Bancouauant
Banseumac
Banclas
Banniou

Samkoc
Banpac tret yai
Ban tret-yai

Ban louang

Ban tret noi
Banpac tret noi
Ban pac naam

Wooden fort
Tala couan
Talaque
Talaqueo
TALAQUEO

I de BANGKOC

Brick fort

Ban has
Pata che
Ban house
Banqueben
Banyai
Banvat
Banque beux

Amsterdam
Manam R
The dwelling of the Hollanders

Tabanque of Custome house

Taquin

Canal of Mecclon

The Barr of Taquin
Canal of Taquin
The Barr of Taquin

The Barr of Siam
Canal
The Barr of Siam Canal

capital, the King built another stupa at Wat Pra Srisanpet as a repository for Ramatibodi II's ashes.

Boromaraja IV was stricken with smallpox and passed away in 1533, leaving the throne to his son, Prince Ratsadatiratkumar, a child of four. After occupying the throne for five months, the boy King was got rid of by Prajairaja, who had brought down his army from Phitsanulok to Ayutthaya with a firm intention to seize the power. Thus history repeated itself in the case of Prajairaja's usurpation of the throne which was similar to that of King Ramesuan, who had King Tonglun done to death.

THE WAR WITH BURMA. The twelve years' reign of Prajairaja (1534-1546) was concerned with the improvement of the river navigation, the promulgation of the Law for Trial by Ordeal, the war with Burma and the intervention in the affairs of Chiang Mai. Before his time, the River Menam or Chao Phya was meandering at Bangkok, as it followed the course through the present Bangluang and the Bangkok Noi canals. Knowing about a short cut on the dry land between the canals, the King ordered a channel to be dug through it in 1534. The new channel soon became the main waterway, thus shortening the distance from the sea to Ayutthaya. Now it is the River Chao Phya in front of the Grand Palace at Bangkok.

In 1536, he put on the statute book the Law for Trial by Ordeal, the introduction of which in Siam postdated that of Europe by about four hundred years. The Law describes many kinds of ordeal such as diving under the water. The winner of the case was the one who stayed under the longer.

Burma achieved unification under King Tabengshweti or Tabinshwehti (1531-1550) of the Taungu dynasty, and thus became a threat to Siam. The King was a great warrior, imbued with insatiable ambition, and sought to become a Chakravatin. In 1539, he subdued the Mon country or Pegu. During the war with Burma, the Mons who did not desire to be ruled by Tabengshweti fled to Chiengkran or Chiengran (Gyaing), a town on the western border of Siam. It had, in fact, belonged to Siam since the Sukhothai days. In the course of rounding them up, the Burmese King occupied the town in 1538, which brought Prajairaja into action at once. With a strong army, the Thai King defeated the Burmese and drove them out of his dominions. Chiengkran was again under the Thai rule. But this short war produced later repercussions to Siam, as it assumed the nature of a curtain raiser to long and sanguinary wars with Burma.

According to Fernando Mendez Pinto, 120 Portuguese mercenaries rendered a signal service to Prajairaja in the first war with Burma, as a reward for which he gave them land at Ayutthaya to build their church and houses. The Portuguese also taught the Thais the arts of cannon foundry and musketry and assisted in the reform of the army, thus making it a formidable force. It should, however, be noted that as soldiers of fortune, the Portuguese served the Burmese king in that war and continued to fight on the Burmese side in other wars against Siam.

The rivalry for the throne of Chiang Mai claimed Prajairaja's attention in 1538, but by the time he had arrived there with his army, Princess Jiraprabha was the Mahadevi or Regent. The Princess Regent received him in a friendly manner, thus putting at rest temporarily any doubt about her loyalty to Ayutthaya. Seven years later, Chiang Mai made a volteface, showing signs of yielding to Burma, whose king, Tabengshweti, was very powerful having converted Pegu or Hanthawadi into his capital. Prajairaja therefore made up his mind to prevent the union of Chiang Mai with Burma, which, if finalized, would in all probability pave the way for an attack or incursion on the Thai frontier towns. In 1545, he commanded an expedition to the north, took Lampang and Lamphun, and laid siege to Chiang Mai. Finding herself at wit's end to fight the Thai troops, the Mahadevi surrendered Chiang Mai as a vassal state of Ayutthaya. Soon after a return from the north, Prajairaja died in 1546.

TAO SRISUDACHAN. Prajairaja had two sons by Tao Srisudachan who was his Chao Chom or Royal Lady Companion, namely, Prince Keofa or Yodfa, aged eleven, and Prince Srisin aged five. Prince Keofa mounted the throne as a minor with Prince Tienraja, who was his father's half brother, acting as Regent, while Tao Srisudachan was now Queen Mother in complete control of the palace affairs. She showed herself to be an exceedingly ambitious lady who wished to concentrate all the power in her hands, thus coming into conflict with the Regent. There is a story that Prince Tienraja was not favourable to her amorous advances, since he had no desire to hurt the feelings of his wife, Suriyotai, who was by birth a princess. Whether the story is true or not, it does not make any difference. The fact is that he chose the line of least resistance, resigned the Regency, and donned the yellow robe as a Buddhist monk for his safety.

Thus Tao Srisudachan got the absolute power in the affairs of the country. In the meantime, she had fallen passionately in love with her relative, Pun Butsritep, who was a minor official in charge of a Buddha images pavilion of the outer palace. She transferred him to the same post in the inner palace with the title of Khun Jinaratraksa so as to be near and dear to her, and in due course she became pregnant. She tolerated no criticism of her way of life. On hearing that Chao Phya Mahasena had expressed his disapproval of the relations with her lover, she had him stabbed to death while he was leaving the palace, and others who held the same opinion about her shared a similar fate. She promoted Khun Jinaratraksa to be the commander of the palace guards with the title of Khun Worawongsatirat and at about the same time she gave birth to a daughter. Deeply ashamed of his mother's flagrantly immoral conduct, King Keofa (1546-1548) entered into an intrigue with his close officers with a view to doing away with Khun Worawongsatirat, but his Mother's lover got wind of it and took a decisive action in this matter. The King was murdered; according to Pinto, he was poisoned by him. This point is really immaterial. The result was that Prince Srisin, who was a mere boy of seven, became King with Khun Worawongsatirat acting as Regent.

Doubtless a strong reaction arose against the new Regent among two groups of officials who conspired to destroy him. One group secretly contacted the northern towns with a request to render assistance to them, while the other had as the ringleader Khun Pirentoratep who was working hand in glove with Khun Intoratep, Luang Srisongyot and Muen Rajsaneha. Queen Srisudachan happened to have some inkling about the rebellious attitude of the northern towns, and she therefore believed that in order to deal with them effectively, it was absolutely necessary to have a strong man on the throne. She deposed her own son, Srisin, publicly proclaimed Khun Worawongsatirat as King in November 1548, and appointed his brother, Nai Chan, the Maha Uparat, thus quieting those who hoped for assistance from the north. On the contrary, Khun Pirentoratep and his three friends settled a plan to kill the usurper and to invite Prince Tienraja to assume the crown. Although they were assured of the Prince's co-operation, a hitch occurred, due to their hesitation, and they proceeded to Wat Pakeo in Ayutthaya, where they cast their lot by means of two lighted candles, one representing Prince Tienraja and the other Khun Worawongsatirat. If Prince Tienraja's candle went out first, they would give up their conspiracy. What happened was that Khun Worawongsatirat's candle was extinguished, probably due to Khun Pirentoratep dropping the remnants of his chewed betel leaf and areca nut on it unintentionally. It was also said that a Buddhist monk bestowed his blessings on them and then disappeared mysteriously. Encouraged by this good omen, they spread a rumour about a white elephant roaming near the capital. Khun Worawongsatirat and Queen Srisudachan went in search of the animal at once, which, if caught would augur well for his reign. While they were travelling by boat to the hunting ground, they were attacked in an ambush by Khun Pirentoratep and his fellow conspirators at a bend in the river. They were dragged ashore and hastily beheaded together with their infant daughter. The ex-King, Srisin, who witnessed the execution, was put under the care of his uncle, Prince Tienraja. Almost at the same moment, the Maha Uparat was shot to death by Muen Rajsaneha. Khun Worawongsatirat occupied the throne for forty two days, and being a usurper, he has not been counted as one of the Kings of Ayutthaya.

MAHACHAKRAPAT (1549-1569). At the invitation of Khun Pirentoratep and his party, Prince Tienraja left the monkhood and ascended the throne as Mahachakrapat in 1549 at the age of thirty six. He had two sons, Prince Ramesuan and Prince Mahin, and two daughters, Princess Wisutkasatri and Princess Tepkasatri, by Queen Suriyotai. Being the elder son, Prince Ramesuan was the heir to the throne. The King bestowed a special reward on Khun Pirentoratep; he made him a prince with the old Sukhothai title of Maha Tammaraja, appointed him Governor of Phitsanulok, and gave his elder daughter, Princess Wisutkasatri as a bride to him. In fact, Prince Maha Tammaraja had already royal blood in his veins, his father being descended from the Kings of Sukhothai and his mother being related to King Prajairaja. The other members of his party also received high honours and titles of nobility from King Mahachakrapat.

Mahachakrapat occupied the throne for only six months when he was confronted with the first Burmese war in his reign. Hearing of the violent changes that had led to his accession to the Thai throne, King Tabengshweti thought that Ayutthaya would be in great difficulties and so in order to fulfill his revenge, he invaded Siam in 1549. His powerful army advanced by way of Martaban, the Three Pagoda's Pass, Kanchanaburi and Suphan Buri, and laid siege to Ayutthaya. During that time, Mahachakrapat made a sortie against the enemy and was accompanied by his two sons as well as Queen Suriyotai and Princess Tepkasatri dressed in warrior's grab, all riding on elephants. In his single combat with the Prince of Prae or Prome, one of the Burmese leading generals, he was put at a dangerous disadvantage, being chased by the enemy. In trying to rescue him Queen Suriyotai drove her elephant in between and was herself cut down. Her sons then forced the Burmese troops to retire and escorted her body back into the city. She has since been regarded as one of the greatest heroines of Thai history, due to her unique bravery, love, devotion and faithfulness to her husband. This was the first time that a Queen appeared on the battlefield in Siam.

PRA CHEDI SRI SURIYOTAI,
ENSHRINING THE ASHES OF QUEEN
SURIYOTAI AT SUAN LUANG
SOBSAWAN MONASTERY, AYUTTHAYA

Faced with the rapidly diminishing food supply coupled with the prospect of being attacked in rear by Maha Tammaraja's army, Tabengshweti withdrew to his country by way of Tak. But in the pursuit of the enemy, Maha Tammaraja and Ramesuan were ambushed and captured near Kamphaeng Phet by Burengnong, an extremely competent Burmese general. Mahachakrapat had to redeem them by making peace and offering two strong elephants to the Burmese.

Before the second war with Burma in 1563, Mahachakrapat undertook the task of strengthening the defences of the Kingdom in general and of the capital in particular. He dismantled the fortifications of Suphan Buri, Lop Buri and Nakhon Nayok, because it was difficult to hold these towns and the enemy might use them as bases for an attack on Ayutthaya. Only Phra Pradaeng with its forts was kept in good shape, since it commanded the communication from the sea. The mud walls of the capital which were nearly two hundred years old were replaced by brick walls and forts built in the European design.

An outer moat was dug in the north of the city, in addition to the already existing inner one, so that the city itself was not within the guns' range and soon it became generally known as the Mahanak canal. The towns of Saraburi, Chachoengsao, Nonthaburi, Sakornburi or Samut Sakhon, and Nakhon Chaisi were then founded to serve as an outer ring of defences. The list of inhabitants was ascertained with a view to calling up able bodied men for military service. Moreover, a stockpile of military supplies, guns and ammunition was laid. Many river warships of a new type were added to the fleet and nearly three hundred elephants were caught and trained for warfare. Out of this number, seven were white elephants which were considered a good augury for Mahachakrapat's reign. The Thai people humbly called him the "Lord of the White Elephants."

In the intervening years between the first and the second war with Burma, Cambodia caused some trouble to Siam. A Cambodian raid on Prachin Buri was followed by a Thai punitive expedition in 1551, and the Thai forces suffered defeat in a short war with the Cambodians in 1556. The ex-King Srisin, who had been brought up by Mahachakrapat, rebelled against him in 1561 and was killed in an action against the forces of Prince Ramesuan and Prince Mahin.

Soon after his return from the expedition against Siam, Tabengshweti went out of his mind, due to excessive drinking, and could not govern the country. He was assassinated in 1550, thus plunging Burma into utter confusion, and the vassal princes took the opportunity to declare themselves independent. However, such chaotic conditions did not last long, thanks to Burengnong or Bayinnaung, who was the brother-in-law of Tabengshweti. He assembled his forces quickly and proceeded to quell the recalcitrant vassal states one by one, namely, Taungu, Prome and Pegu, and crowned himself King at Hanthawadi in 1553. He then conquered the Shan States and Chiang Mai. Mekuti was permitted to rule Chiang Mai as a vassal of Burma in 1556. Siam was the next target of his ambition to realize the expansionist policy. Certainly his vast dominions would stand him in good stead in this undertaking. Pegu and Chiang Mai, which were already under his control, would serve as bases for a converging attack on Ayutthaya.

Burengnong then made a request for two white elephants presumably on the ground of strengthening the cordial relations between the two countries. It was submitted for consideration to the grand council of princes and high officials which soon split up into two parties—one in favour of complying with it for the sake of peace and the other, which was opposed to it on the ground that the transfer of two white elephants would not satisfy the Burmese King. The latter included the King's elder son, Ramesuan, Phya Chakri, and Phya Sunthornsonggram. Mahachakrapat gave his decision to the opposing party.

Basing as his pretext Mahachakrapat's refusal to give him the two white elephants, Burengnong declared war on Siam in November 1563. The Thais committed a great blunder in miscalculating his strategy, since preparations had been made in anticipation of a Burmese invasion by way of the Three Pagodas' Pass. The people in the surrounding towns had been assembled and all the available food supply stored up in the capital. No measures had been taken to improve the defences of the north. Burengnong chose to lead his large army through the Melamao Pass. According to the *Royal History of Siam*, the army numbered 200,000, but based on the estimated population and conditions of Burma, this figure should be reduced to less than 100,000. His troops spread out to capture the towns in the north. Phitsanulok was beleaguered by the Burmese. However

THREE PAGODAS' PASS IN THE PROVINCE OF KANCHANABURI

hard he tried to defend the city, Maha Tammaraja could not hold it, because famine and smallpox had played havoc with the inhabitants. So he surrendered to the Burmese King and, to add an injury to the insult, he was ordered to accompany him in his advance to Ayutthaya. The Burmese besieged the city in February 1564, and subject it to a continual connonade, destroying buildings and houses and causing unspeakable hardship to the helpless inhabitants.

Being convinced that any further resistance against the enemy would be useless as the result of the pressure that the people had brought on him, King Mahachakrapat communicated with Burengnong and made peace with him according to his terms. Four white elephants were given to the Burmese, and Prince Ramesuan, Phya Chakri and Phya Suntornsonggram, who had led the war party against Burma were delivered up as their hostages—a bitter pill for Mahachakrapat to swallow. Prince Ramesuan did not live long, as he died during an expedition to Chiang Mai with the Burmese King.

An immediate result arose from the Thai defeat. The Governor of Pattani, who had under his command an army and a fleet of two hundred boats, had arrived at Ayutthaya too late to help in fighting the Burmese. Hoping to carry off a large booty, he turned a traitor and plundered the palace. The rebellion, however, was quickly suppressed.

There was a gap of nearly six years between the second and the third war with Burma. Burengnong still nursed his ambition to conquer Siam and so he sowed the seeds of disunity in the Thai Royal Family so as to undermine the defence of the country. At the request of King Jaijetta of Luang Prabang (Laotian-kingdom), Mahachakrapat agreed to send Princess Tepkasatri to be his Queen with a view to securing his alliance. Maha Tammaraja and his consort, Wisutkasatri, disapproved of this impending marriage. Unable to prevent it himself Maha Tammaraja sought the Burmese help, which was willingly given. At Burengnong's command, a Burmese force intercepted the Princess near Phetchabun while she was on her way to Wiengchan, Jaijetta's new capital, and she was carried off to Hanthawadi. Filled with sorrow and shame at Maha Tammaraja's chief role in the abduction of his daughter, Mahachakrapat retired to a monastery once more and before doing so, he appointed Prince Mahin to be Regent. This event proved to be a great disaster for the Kingdom of Siam, as it caused a complete rift between the Regent and Maha Tammaraja. The one tried by every possible means to destroy the other. Prince Mahin relied on King Jaijetta, while Maha Tammaraja had recourse to Burengnong's assistance, which fitted in exactly with his dearest ambition to force the most powerful of all the Thai states to submit to his authority. Filled with great anxiety for the safety of the realm, Mahachakrapat abandoned the yellow robe and took over the helm of the government again.

In October 1568, Burengnong departed from Pegu (Hanthawadi), with a much larger army than the previous one, for Ayutthaya by way of the Melamao Pass, and two months later, he began to invest the city with his forces who were joined by Maha Tammaraja's Thai troops from Phitsanulok. It is unquestionalbly sad to record that the Thais fought the Thais themselves, being the result of Maha Tammaraja's excessive selfishness which caused him to forget the national interest. In January 1569, Mahachakrapat died at the age of fiftysix and Prince Mahin ascended the throne. During that time, the Thai soldiers were showing extraordinary bravery in defending Ayutthaya hoping to hold the enemy until the flood moved down from the north towards latter part of the rainy season. The Burmese encampment, which was put up on a low ground, would then be inundated. For the successful prosecution of the war, Burengnong called for consultation Maha Tammaraja, who willingly offered his service to find a way to reduce Ayutthaya to submission. Through a letter to Pra Wisutkasatri, Mahin learnt that if Phya Ramronarong, who was the mainstay for the defence of the capital, was handed to Burengnong, the Burmese would make their withdrawal. Realising that any further resistance to the enemy would be of no avail, he sacrificed Phya Ramronarong to the Burmese King who then made a very strong demand for Siam to surrender to him unconditionally. In the meantime, King Jaijetta sent a force to the assistance of Ayutthaya, but the Burmese ambushed it and drove it off at Saraburi. In the seventh month of his siege, Burengnong made no further progress in his war and resorted to a stratagem, whereby Phya Chakri who had been removed as a hostage to Burma after the 1563 war was sent into the city as a fifth columnist. One day this general appeared in chains before the city ramparts, saying that he had fled from the Burmese in order to serve the Thai King. Without a long and thorough test of his loyalty, Mahin put him in charge of the defence of the capital, thus opening the way for him to proceed with his treacherous design. Acting on Phya Chakri's report about his half-brother, Pra Srisaowarat, who though he fought the enemy very well was accused of treason, he ordered him to be executed for this crime. Phya Chakri transferred able men from the points which would facilitate entry, thereby weakening them considerably. At Phya Chakri's signal, the Burmese attacked Ayutthaya in full force and on all sides and captured it on August 30, 1569. Had the Thais summoned up all their available resources and continued to hold the city for about one more month, the Burmese would most probably have struck camp, in anticipation of the flood which would engulf them. To summarise, the fall of Ayutthaya could be ascribed to the treachery of Phya Chakri, the incompetence of King Mahin and the disloyalty of Maha Tammaraja. This constitutes an object lesson to the Thais, which is often referred to or emphasized to-day.

In order to make up for the heavy losses in the war, Burengnong gave orders for the removal to Burma of the unfortunate King Mahin, most of the members of the Royal family and government officials in capitivity as well as a vast number of prisoners and a tremendous amount of booty, leaving only 10,000 inhabitants in the city with its dismantled fortifications. Mahin died of fever on the way to the enemy country, having occupied the throne of Ayutthaya for nearly one year and thus ended the life of the King who bore the brunt for the loss of Thai independence to the Burmese for the first time. Burengnong prolonged his stay in the shattered city until the rainy season was over. Death was the reward for Phya Chakri, a notorious traitor to his fatherland. Burengnong found a pretext for his execution. Before his departure for Hanthawadi, he crowned Maha Tammaraja as King of Siam under the vassalage of Burma. Thus the Suphannaphum dynasty which had ruled Ayutthaya after the Utong dynasty came to an end.

The genealogy of the two Royal Houses which ruled Ayutthaya from 1350 to 1569 is as follows:-

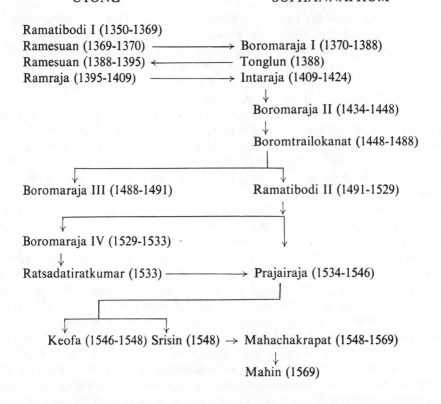

UTONG          SUPHANNAPHUM

Ramatibodi I (1350-1369)
Ramesuan (1369-1370) ⟶ Boromaraja I (1370-1388)
Ramesuan (1388-1395) ⟵ Tonglun (1388)
Ramraja (1395-1409) ⟶ Intaraja (1409-1424)
Boromaraja II (1434-1448)
Boromtrailokanat (1448-1488)
Boromaraja III (1488-1491)     Ramatibodi II (1491-1529)
Boromaraja IV (1529-1533)
Ratsadatiratkumar (1533) ⟶ Prajairaja (1534-1546)
Keofa (1546-1548) Srisin (1548) ⟶ Mahachakrapat (1548-1569)
Mahin (1569)

# CHAPTER VI

## RESTORATION OF THAI INDEPENDENCE
## BY NARESUAN THE GREAT

In 1569, Maha Tammaraja assumed the official title of Pra Srisanpet, but he is generally known in history as King Maha Tammarajatirat. Queen Wisutkasatri bore him three children, namely, Princess Suwandevi, Prince Naresuan and Prince Ekatotsarot. In order to cement his ties with Burma, Maha Tammaraja handed the Princess as a bride to Burengnong on his accession to the throne of Ayutthaya, probably in exchange for Prince Naresuan or Naret, who, born in 1555, had, at the age of nine, been taken as a virtual hostage to Hanthawadi after the second war in 1564, but Burengnong had not succeeded in brainwashing him by making him a Burmese tool. He returned to Ayutthaya, full of good intention for the country. The Burmese official explanation was that he had been adopted and brought up by Burengnong. At that time he was fifteen years old and became heir to the throne. His father appointed him in this capacity as Viceroy of Phitsanulok. Naresuan was given the nickname of "The Black Prince," because his complexion was darker than that of his younger brother, Ekatotsarot, who was generally known as "The White Prince."

Burmese laws and institutions were introduced into Siam, two of which were adopted by the Thais and continued in use down to the Bangkok period, namely, the Burmese Dhammasat and the Burmese era. The Dhammasat or jurisprudence, which was based on the Indian Laws of Manu, was grafted on the laws of Siam. The Burmese era which began in A.D. 638 became known in Siam as the Chulasakarat or Little Era which displaced the Mahasakarat or Great Era starting in A.D. 78. It was due to the Indian King Kanishka of the Gupta dynasty that the Mahasakarat Era was invented. It would be beyond anybody's guess as to how and when it spread to the Indo-Chinese Peninsula. Anyhow it appeared on the stone inscriptions of Sukhothai. King Chulalongkorn substituted the European calendar for the Chulasakarat era in 1889, but he called it the Ratanakosin or Bangkok Era and fixed April 1st as the first day of the new year. This era started in 1782. King Rama VI or Vajiravudh introduced the Buddhist Era on April 1, 1911 (B.E. 2454), preferring it to the Ratanakosin era. Finally the Western calendar was enforced in to by the Pibulsonggram Government which announced the commencement of the Thai new year on January 1, 1941, (B.E. 2484) for the first time.

Profiting from the weakness of Siam, King Boromaraja of Cambodia led a large raiding party of 20,000 soldiers against her and ventured to advance as far as the outskirts of Ayutthaya in 1570, but when the commander of his forward troops was killed by a gun shot, he retired and carried a large number of Thai people back with him. Five years later, when Prince Naresuan was compelled by the Burmese King to accompany him on his expedition against Wiengchan, he was taken ill with smallpox and had to return to Ayutthaya just in the nick of time to repel another Cambodian raid. The Cambodians never learnt their lesson and conducted a few more raiding parties, all of which ended in failure.

Maha Tammaraja, however, was not the type of the king who was contented with the status of a Burmese vassal. The Cambodian raids provided him with a good excuse to restore the fortifications of the capital and strengthen its defences without stirring up the suspicion of the Burmese King. The city walls, for instance, were extended, additional forts were constructed, and cannon and other military supplies were purchased. The population was swollen by those who had sought shelter from the Cambodians. At the same time, Prince Naresuan was implementing the same policy as his father in improving the defences of the north, as his real and ultimate objective was to liberate the country from the Burmese. Nobody else would be more suitable than he was in tackling the most perilous, but unquestionably patriotic task of restoring national independence. Naresuan was born and grew up in the north, where he became well acquainted with the mentality and conditions of the people who in turn held him in high regard, thus obviating any difficulty in governing them. His six years' residence in Burma proved to be a blessing in disguise. Not only did it afford him undreamt-of opportunities to examine quietly the strengths and weaknesses of the Burmese in general, but it also led to his study of their language, character and art of war amid sons of princes and nobles in particular. He had the fortune of being the first foreign educated Thai prince. Certainly he could speak Burmese. The knowledge thus acquired, he utilitized for the good of his country afterwards. Besides being a born soldier, he was endowed with an extraordinary degree of intelligence, re-sourcefulness and courage. He collected young men into a small and compact army and he himself trained them in the new methods of warfare which he had devised. He would fearlessly lead his soldiers into a battle, and in skirmishes, he would resort to surprise tactics such as an ambush and a sudden swoop by local guerrillas, who became known as Wild Tigers and Peeping Cats.

Naresuan's army proved its worth in regaining and preserving the independence of Siam afterwards. Meanwhile he was showing himself to be a great warrior in dealing with the Cambodians who made a series of raids. On one occasion, being unmindful of any danger which might happen to him, he had pursued Phya Chin Chantu to the sea. The latter was a Cambodian nobleman of Chinese ancestry who had sought asylum as a political refugee at Ayutthaya, but as soon as he gathered enough information about it, he made good his escape by ship. When Naresuan was approaching the ship, he fired at the Cambo-dians who returned the fire, smashing his gun barrel. Admiring Naresuan's intrepid leadership, the Thais centred their hopes of "risorgimento" on him.

In Burma, Burengnong never deviated from his policy of extending his dominions. In 1578, Princess Jiraprabha, who had once more taken the reins of government as Regent of Chiang Mai after Mekuti, died. Burengnong appointed one of his sons, Tharawadi Min, as Prince of Chiang Mai, with the title of Nohrata Zaw in order to secure a firm control of the principality. In 1581, Burengnong was peacefully succeeded by his son, Nandabureng or Nanda Bayin, on his death, but the new King was not by any means of the same calibre as his father who later won fame as "The Victor in Ten Directions," and consequently the fissiparous tendencies of the Burmese princes began to assert themselves. In conformity

STATUE OF KING NARESUAN
THE GREAT (1590-1605)

with a Burmese custom, the vassal princes were required to renew their homage to the
new king on his accession. Prince Naresuan volunteered to represent his aging father,
Maha Tammaraja, with an intention to investigate how Nandabureng's reign was affecting
the conditions of Burma in general and of Pegu in particular. By the way, Pegu soon came
to be regarded as the main base by Siam and Burma for an invasion of the other country.
While he was staying in Hanthawadi, the Prince of Kung, one of the Shan States, revolted
against Nandabureng who thereupon directed three separate forces to subdue him. The
Hanthawadi contingent was commanded by the Burmese Crown Prince, while the Taungu
and the Ayutthaya ones were under Prince Sangatat and Prince Naresuan respectively.
The two Burmese Princes failed ignominiously to capture the town of Kung, but the Thai
Prince discovered a secret passage at its back before his turn came to attack it. While
pretending to throw all his available troops into a frontal encounter with the rebels, he

stormed it by that passage and succeeded in taking the Prince of Kung as a prisoner to the Burmese capital, where he was rewarded in the usual manner. The campaign of Kung provided him and his men with practical and valuable experience of real warlike operations as well as the much needed intelligence about the attitude of the vassal princes towards Nandabureng, but it brought about the displeasure of the Burmese King and the Crown Prince towards him. Naresuan came to the conclusion that the vassal princes were making sub-rosa preparations to overthrow Nandabureng's yoke, since they did not respect or fear him like his father. In such an eventuality, he would certainly strike the blow for the recovery of national independence.

Naresuan did not have to wait long for serious trouble to break out in Burma. In coping with the rebellion of the Prince of Ava who was his brother-in-law, Nandabureng summoned to his support his vassals, namely, the Prince of Prome, the Prince of Taungu, the Prince of Chiang Mai, the King of Luang Prabang or Srisatanacanahut, and the King of Siam. The first four Princes joined forces with the Burmese King according to the prescribed schedule, but Siam reported to him that Prince Naresuan would command a Thai contingent on behalf of King Maha Tammaraja. However, Naresuan's wilful delay in keeping the schedule aroused the suspicion of the Burmese King, who, before his departure with an expedition against Ava, left his Crown Prince in complete charge of the capital with secret instructions to do away with the Thai Prince as soon as he reached Burma.

Naresuan left Phitsanulok with an army for the Burmese frontier in February 1584 and in accordance with his dilatory tactics, he arrived at the Mon town of Krang on the Thai border in May of the same year. Should Nandabureng suffer defeat at the hands of the rebellious Prince of Ava, Naresuan would attack Hanthawadi at once, and in the event of the contrary, he would move back the Thai inhabitants, who had been transplanted to Burma, so as to augment the population of his land. The Burmese Crown Prince had, in the meantime, entrused two Mon chiefs, Phya Kiart and Phya Ram, with a secret mission to murder Naresuan, but they balked at the act and disclosed the whole plan to him, due to the fact that the Mons entertained strong hatred against the Burmese. Prince Naresuan therefore called a meeting of all his generals and the Mon officials who had very recently transferred their allegiance to him and, with his father's full consent, he proclaimed the independence of Siam at the town of Krang on May 3, 1584, thus terminating the Burmese vassalage of fifteen years. Most of the Mons at Krang sided with the Prince and helped him in his advance to Hanthawadi.

By the time he was approaching the Burmese capital, Naresuan learnt that Nandabureng had won a victory against the Prince of Ava and was returning. Realizing the hopelessness of an attack against Hanthawadi, he turned back to his country, bringing with him approximately ten thousand Thai prisoners who had been deported to Pegu during Burengnong's wars. The Burmese Crown Prince hastened to send a general by name of Surakamma in hot pursuit of Naresuan's army. He followed him up with his army. The Thai Prince faced the enemy on the opposite bank of the Sittaung River. There was an exchange of heavy fusillade and Surakamma was shot dead on the neck of his elephant by Naresuan, thus forcing the Burmese to turn back. As a result of the declaration of independence at Krang, King Maha Tammaraja handed to Prince Naresuan the absolute power in making preparations against a new Burmese invasion. The Prince sent out

PAINTING OF KING NARESUAN THE GREAT, PROCLAIMING
INDEPENDENCE OF SIAM AT KRANG, MAY 3, 1584

troops to destroy all the Burmese pockets of resistance in the north, but the Governors of Sawankalok and Pijai, fearing Burmese vengeance, rebelled against him. He stormed their stronghold and executed both of them. A country which declares its independence must be ready to encounter the full reaction of its former ruler who will unhesitatingly attempt to re-subjugate it. In throwing off the English yoke, the Americans had to fight the American War of Independence, while the Greeks who declared their independence against the Sultan were involved in war with Turkey for some time. Similarly, in the case of Siam, Naresuan certainly anticipated a new Burmese invasion, and made thorough preparations to meet it. According to his firm belief, therefore it was absolutely essential to concentrate men and their families, weapons and ammunition and food supplies in the capital in order to fight the Burmese effectively with fewer number, and for this reason he decided on the so-called scorched earth policy. The northern towns were evacuated of the population; everything which might be utilized by the enemy was removed and their forts and ramparts were completely dismantled.

As was expected, the Burmese made several attempts to re-subjugate Siam, but all in vain. In December 1584, a Burmese army under the Prince of Bassein was driven back from Suphan Buri. In April 1585, the Prince of Chiang Mai who was commanded by the Burmese King to attack Siam was routed at some distance from the village of Sraket near Ang Thong. Subsequently Nandabureng invaded Siam with a large army by the Melamao-Kamphaeng Phet route in November 1586. Meeting opposition, he advanced down to

Ayutthaya and in January 1587, he laid siege to it. Naresuan relied on his tactics, soldiers and fortifications of Ayutthaya in putting up an impregnable defence against the Burmese holding them back for five months. During the siege, he achieved an amazingly daring feat when he led the assault of a Burmese camp by climbing the wooden stockade with the blunt side of a sabre in his mouth. He was stabbed and fell down. The Burmese tried their best to capture him but he successfully drove them back and cut his way out. In the end, famine and disease forced the Burmese to retire to their own country. Thus Ayutthaya was once more saved from external aggression. Naresuan made preparations for a punitive expedition against Cambodia, being exceedingly incensed at the treacherous attitude of King Satta who had conducted a large scale raid on Prachin Buri while the Burmese siege of the Thai capital was in progress. Towards the end of 1587, he invaded Cambodia, and having captured Battambong and Pursat, he withdrew owing to lack of supplies.

In July 1590, King Maha Tammaraja died at the age of seventy five. He is still an enigma in Thai history. Why did he join the Burmese in the invasion of his fatherland? Was he really a traitor to Siam? In any case, Naresuan made good his father's reputation. He became king in his own right when he was thirty-five years old. He took the unprecedented step of bestowing the highest honours in the realm upon his brother, Ekatotsarot, who had been through thick and thin with him. He appointed him as Maha Uparat or Second King with all the kingly distinctions.

Undeterred by his past failures, Nandabureng commanded his Crown Prince to lead two more invasions of Siam. In November 1590, the Burmese invaders marched through the Three Pagodas' Pass and were utterly defeated by the Thais in a hand to hand encounter near Kanchanaburi. The climax of the subsequent invasion came in a duel on elephants, in which King Naresuan slew the Burmese Crown Prince at Nong Sa Rai near Suphan Buri in January 25, 1593. In commemoration of this event, he caused a chedi (pagoda) to be built on the spot where he won his resounding victory. The chedi was a prey to the rapidly spreading jungle for more than three hundred years until it was found in an almost unrecognizable state in 1913. A monument which was erected on the spot of the original chedi was unveiled by His Majesty, King Bhumibol on January 25, 1959. It is now known as Don Chedi. Naresuan also caused another chedi to be enlarged at Wat Pakeo at his metropolis, later known as Jaimongkol Chedi.

Naresuan thus raised Siam to be a mighty Kingdom and it was now the turn of the Thais to take the offensive against Burma. In the battle against the Burmese Crown Prince, some high Thai officers in his army had failed in their duties. Phya Srisainarong had disobeyed the royal command by deciding to attack the enemy with a result that he had suffered defeat and withdrawn to the main Thai army. Chao Phya Chakri, Phya Praklang, Phya Teb-orajun, Phya Pijaisonggram and Phya Ramkamhaeng had not followed the King with their men promptly. Otherwise Naresuan would probably have turned the Burmese defeat into a complete rout. Being angry with them, he intended to mete out the most severe punishment to them, that is, they were to be beheaded after the Buddhist sabbath day. Fortunately for them, he granted a request to pardon them, made by a group of the 25 high monks under the leadership of Somdech Pra Wannarat on the condition that they were to win back Tavoy and Tenesserim which had belonged to Siam. So in 1593, two armies—one under Chao Phya Chakri and the other under Phya Praklang, marched against the Burmese and, in due course, recovered the two towns and their adjoining

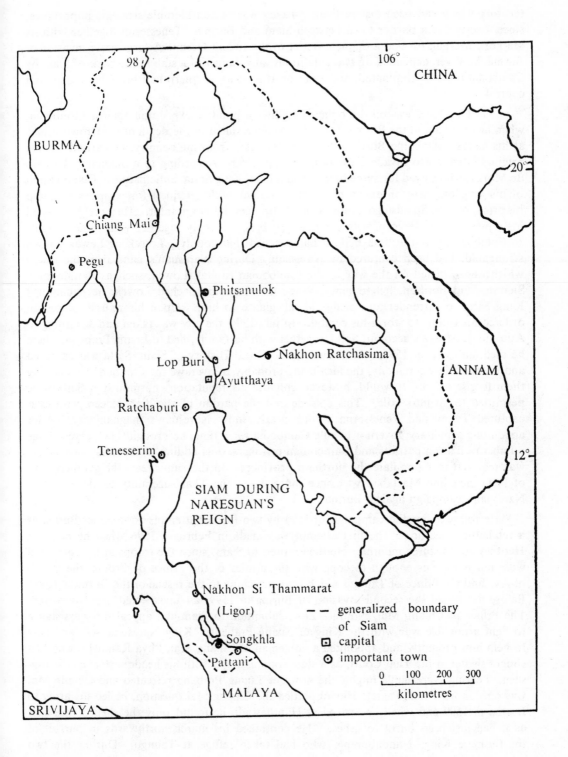

98

106°

CHINA

BURMA

20°

Chiang Mai

Pegu

Phitsanulok

Nakhon Ratchasima

Lop Buri

ANNAM

Ayutthaya

Ratchaburi

Tenesserim

12°

SIAM DURING
NARESUAN'S
REIGN

Nakhon Si Thammarat

(Ligor)

— — — generalized boundary
of Siam

Songkhla

capital

Pattani

important town

MALAYA

0    100    200    300

kilometres

SRIVIJAYA

territory which had been lost to them. Tavoy was of considerable strategic importance, since it served as a barrier town between Siam and Burma. Tenesserim together with its sea-port, Mergui, formed a Siamese outlet to the Indian Ocean. A large scale invasion of Burma, however, depended on two conditions; any danger of a stab in the back of Siam by Cambodia must be eliminated, and Pegu or at least its southern half must be under Thai control.

The Thai King was on the point of leading a punitive expedition against Cambodia, when he heard about the Burmese invasion which resulted in the death of the Crown Prince at his hands. After the Burmese had been expelled from the country, he carried out his original intention to invade Cambodia in May 1593. According to a Spaniard, Antonio de Morga, who stayed for some time in Cambodia, King Satta, anticipating a Thai invasion of his kingdom, sent an envoy to Manila in 1590, with a request for weapons to equip his army, but the Spanish governor of the Philippines did not grant it. He merely entrusted his representative, Belloso, with a mission to bring his reply together with some presents to Cambodia. By the time Belloso had reached that country, Lowek or Lawak Satta's stronghold, had been captured by Naresuan. During Naresuan's campaign, the towns which were situated on the way to the Cambodian capital, Lowek, such as Battambong, Siemrap and Boribun, fell to him. When his army approached Lowek, he summoned King Satta to surrender and pledge his allegiance to him. Upon his refusal, Naresuan ordered his troops to storm his capital. In july 1594, the city was taken and according to Antonio de Morga's account, Satta, together with his family, fled to Luang Prabang, where he died, an exile, in 1596. According to the Royal History of Siam, Satta was captured and executed in a ceremony, the idea being probably to overawe the Cambodians, detering them to rise again. It would, however, enhance his reputation enormously if Satta were permitted to go into exile. This episode and the pardon of the high officers who later captured Tavoy and Tenesserim would clearly show Naresuan's magnanimity. After appointing a military governor to rule Cambodia for a time, he brought back a very large number of his compatriots and Cambodian prisoners, thus adding to the manpower which was required to repopulate the northern provinces. In the same year, the southern half of Pegu including Martaban was once more under the Thai suzerainty as the result of Naresuan's campaign against Burma.

He followed up the campaign of 1594 by two further attempts to conquer Burma as a retaliatory measure. The first attempt was made in February 1596 when he besieged Hanthawadi for three months. He then retired to Siam, since the troops at his command were not numerous enough to cope with the armies of the Prince of Prome, the Prince of Ava and the Prince of Taungu which were marching to the rescue of the Burmese King. Before he started the second invasion of Burma in 1599, an unexpected event occurred. The Prince of Chiang Mai, Nohrata Zaw, submitted to Siam and appealed for assistance to fight a possible war with the King of Luang Prabang. King Naresuan sent an army to help him promptly and appointed a nobleman of Chiang Mai, Phya Ramdejo, who had sought shelter at the Thai Court, as a state commissioner with his headquarters at Chiang-saen. Fearing Naresuan's might, the army of Luang Prabang retreated and Chiang Mai was once more a Thai vassal. Having settled the Chiang Mai question, he led his army to Burma in 1599 and when he arrived at Hanthawadi, he found only the shell of the city, as it had just been burnt to ashes. He continued his march northwards in pursuit of the Burmese King, Nandabureng, who had taken refuge at Taungu. During the two months' siege of the town, he tried again and again to break through its defences, but he faced a stubborn resistance and had to fall back to his camp. Lack of food supplies, diseases and excessive rainfall were the factors that contributed to his withdrawal from Burma in May 1600.

However, Naresuan's invasion of Burma was not entirely in vain. It led indirectly to the death of Nandabureng and the disintegration of Burma once more. After he was poisoned to death at Taungu in December 1600, his kingdom was broken into Taungu, Prome, and Ava, while Pegu and three Shan States, namely, Muang Hang, Muang Nai and Muang Hsenwi came under Thai control and the other sixteen Shan States were independent. The Prince of Ava, Nyaung Yan Min, determined to unify Burma and soon won a large following under the halo of his father, Burengnong. In 1603, he crowned himself as King Sihasha Tammaraja of Burma. In pursuance of his policy, he subdued the Shan States one by one until he approached Muang Hsenwi which was under Thai vassalage. On hearing about the Burmese advance, Naresuan became enraged and so marched northwards with his army to aid his vassals. At Muang Hang or Hin Myo to the west of the River Salween, where he set up his camp for a hat, he fell seriously ill with a carbuncle on his face. Prince Ekatotsarot, who was at Muang Fang, hastened to be at his sick bed. On May 16, 1605, King Naresuan passed away at the age of fifty. In spite of the wars with Burma and Cambodia, Naresuan found time to cultivate friendly relations with the Europeans. Besides the Portuguese, he extended a cordial welcome to the Spaniards who had established their headquarters in the Philippines. For this reason, when Don Tello de Aguirre went on a diplomatic mission from Manila to Ayutthaya in 1598, he met with a good reception and concluded a treaty of friendship and commerce with Siam. This was the second treaty which Siam made with a European Power. The terms of the treaty were similar to those in the Portuguese treaty, that is to say, the Spaniards had the right to reside, to trade and to practise their religion in Siam. But the signing of the treaty with Spain did not bring about any noticeable increase in trade between Ayutthaya and Manila, which concentrated its trading interest in other countries. The Spaniards were followed by the Dutch who went to Siam in 1604.

Truly indeed Naresuan deserved the honour of being the Great among the kings of Siam. Not only did he restore the national independence, but he also made Siam such a powerful country that no enemy saw the walls of Ayutthaya again for a period of one hundred seventy three years, no matter from what direction he came. The musket with which he shot Surakamma, the sabre which he carried in his mouth during his assault on the Burmese camp at Ayutthaya, and the leather hat which he was wearing and which had its brim cut off in the shape of a crescent moon when he engaged in a duel on elephants with the Crown Prince of Burma, have constituted the royal regalia down to the present time.

# CHAPTER VII

# THAI INTERCOURSE WITH OTHER COUNTRIES

EKATOTSAROT (1605-1610). Having succeeded Naresuan on his death, Ekatotsarot called off the expedition into the Shan States and brought back his remains to Ayutthaya for cremation. Naresuan the Great had no queen or children. Muang Hang, Muang Nai and Muang Hsenwi then reverted to Burmese vassalage. In connection with the years of Ekatotsarot's reign, the evidence has been conflicting. According to Prince Damrong Rajanubhab's *The Thais Fight the Burmese*, he ruled Siam from 1605 to 1620, dovetailing with the *Records of the Relations between Siam and Foreign Countries in the 17th Century* which says that "The King of Siam, Raja Api (or the Fire King) (King Naresuan) died in 1605, whom his brother (called the White King) did succeed. He died also 1620, and his son inherits," being an extract of an anonymous report submitted to the English East India Company. Ekatotsarot's reign, as mentioned here, is corroborated by a book written in Portuguese by Major Jacinto Jose Do Naccimento Mouar on the Relations of the Portuguese with Siam. According to the *Royal History of Siam* (Royal Autograph Edition), however, Ekatotsarot occupied the Siamese throne for eight years, while the *Royal History of Siam* which has been found at the British Museum and Bradley's *Royal History of Siam* mention periods of seven and seven and a half years respectively. In his *Sanggitivangsa* written in 1789, Somdech Pra Wannarat, Lord Abbot of Wat Pra Jetubon stated that King Songtam succeeded to the throne of Ayutthaya at the age of 19, thus fitting in with Van Vliet's Historical Account of Siam mentioning Songtam's death at the age of 38 and his reign of 19 years. An English merchant, Peter W. Floris, who arrived at Ayutthaya in 1612 recorded that "....anno 1605, when as the Black King deceased without any issue. He was a man of great understanding, and left his kingdom to his brother who was called the White King, who was a very covetous man but enjoyed his kingdom in peace, doing no other thing worth of remembrance. He died anno 1610, leaving divers children behind him." According to Wood's "A History of Siam," "During his short reign of five years, the White King, as he was called by European writers, devoted his time more to the reorganisation of the finances of Siam than to warlike pursuits. He thus gained among foreigners the reputation of being a covetous man," while in Prince Chula Chakrabongse's *Lords of Life*, "......the White Prince's reign was but a short one of five years with the King becoming insane before he died in 1610." Having carefully considered the evidence from these sources, particularly those submitted by Mr. Kachorn Sukhabanij, a member of the Committee for the Revision of Thai National History, one is inclined to accept Ekatotsarot's reign as having been five years (1605-1610).

Ekatotsarot concentrated mainly on the development of his kingdom. In order to increase the national revenue, he levied a tax on shops and markets and a ten percent tax on goods, and permitted the payment of dues in cash instead of manual labour. In addition, as foreign trade would greatly benefit the country, he showed his friendship to the Dutch and the Japanese who entered into relations with the Thais. The Portuguese also enjoyed his favour.

In 1601, the Dutch reached Pattani, a small Thai vassal state in the south, where they received permission to build a trading station. One year later, the United East India Company (V.O.C.) was founded by the Dutch who proceeded to establish their headquarters for East Asia at Batavia (now known as Jakarta) in Java. They set out to study possibilities of trade in the neighbouring countries. Their arrival at Ayutthaya in 1604 was marked by an audience which Naresuan the Great gave to their chief, Cornelius Specx. They came to an agreement with Siam, whereby they obtained permission to trade and to build a trading station at the Thai capital. In 1608, the first Dutch trading station was established with Specx as its director. The Thais were eager to transact business with the Dutch, as they took their cotton goods in exchange for hides and pepper. In the same year, by command of King Ekatotsarot, a Thai embassy travelled by a Dutch ship which took seven months to reach the Netherlands where it was accorded a cordial reception at the Hague and was received by the Stadholder, Prince Maurice of Orange Nassau on September 10, 1608. A printed record of the Thai embassy says that "The two envoys from the King of Siam were introduced to make their reverence to His Excellency (the Stadholder) and, having arrived at the door of his chamber, they both knelt, straightened their hands, and holding them before their forehead, bowed their hands several times to the ground, and though having been given signs to stand up, they went nevertheless three or four paces over the ground on their knees, until His Excellency extended his hand which after having been touched, made the envoys stand up."

This embassy is the first appearance on record of the Thai in Europe. It brought back cannons and small arms as well as other valuable gifts from the Stadholder and the Dutch East India Company to the Thai King. The primary intention of the Dutch was to use Ayutthaya as a depot for China trade; that is to say, the produce of Europe could be exchanged in Siam for hides which could be shipped to China and disposed of there for goods acceptable to the home market, but their trade with the Thais proved to be so profitable that they became inextricably involved in it for its own sake. On June 12, 1617, the Dutch signed their first treaty with Siam, obtaining definite terms for the purchase of hides.

The actual text of the treaty reads as follows:-

"The skins purchased shall be stored by us until the arrival here of the Javanese (should be Japanese) junks, when the total amount, in accordance with the price obtained from the Japanese shall be divided equally between us, on the understanding that we shall pay in addition only the costs of first purchase and the commission for the opra.

"We also understand that we shall be permitted to decide whether or not to accept the skins at the selling price stated and that the opra named shall be given a free hand in respect of sale and supply, unless, as stated in the foregoing, we are not satisfied with our half of the skins at the combined selling price. In that case the merchandise shall be at his entire proposal, provided he refunds to us the money that he received from us for the first purchase."

The Japanese came on the Thai scene for the first time in the reign of Naresuan the Great. When he fought a duel on elephants with the Burmese Crown Prince in January 1593, he had 500 Japanese soldiers in his army and many of them had probably lived in the country for some time. They had reached the shores of Siam as soldiers of fortune, adventurers, sailors and traders, and as they had not brought out their wives, they had married Thai girls. They had formed a sizable community by the beginning of King Ekatotsarot's reign, living in their own settlement at Ayutthaya. The majority of the Japanese continued to engage in trade, while others entered the King's service as Japanese guards. It was probably through these expatriates that the Shogun Iyeyasu Tokugawa learnt of Siam's wealth and power. It was again through them that friendly relations were opened between King Ekatotsarot and the Shogun of Japan and were followed by the usual exchange of letters and presents on many occasions. According to some of these Japanese letters, the Shogun expressed his desire to procure firearms and ammunition from Siam.

Simultaneously King Ekatotsarot maintained cordial relations with the Portuguese whose community was increased by their missionaries.

The first group of missionaries sponsored by the Portuguese, the Dominicans, Jerome de la Croix and Sebastien de Cantu, had arrived at Ayutthaya in 1555. They were followed by a Portuguese Jesuit missionary, Balthazar de Sequeira, who reached Ayutthaya in 1606 by an overland route from Tenesserim. In 1617, however, the Portuguese quarrelled with the Thais, because they had seized a Dutch ship in the Thai waters. They rejected the Thai request to return the ship to its owner. Both sides then had recourse to force and fought one another for a while. Eventually this matter was amicably settled.

King Ekatotsarot had two sons by his Queen, namely, Prince Sutat and Prince Srisaowapak, and his Royal Lady Companions bore him three other sons whose names were Prince Intaraja, Prince Srisin, and Prince Tong. Prince Sutat who was the Maha Uparat died before his father and so the throne devolved on Prince Srisaowapak who proved himself to be a weak and incompetent king. After a reign of less than one year (1620), he was forced to abdicate by a party of prominent officials who proceeded to invite Prince Intaraja to mount the throne.

SONGTAM (1610-1628). This Prince had been a Buddhist monk with the title of Pra Wimontam and left his monastery on the acceptance of the throne. He is generally known as King Songtam or the Just King. He was a great scholar, learned in liberal arts, profoundly devoted to Buddhism and firmly impregnated with the kingly virtues. For the government policy, he preferred peace to war. This accounts for the recovery of Cambodian independence by King Jaijetta in 1618, since all the attempts which were made to bring him under Thai suzerainty in Songtam's reign ended in failure. However, he succeeded in keeping the Burmese at bay at the beginning of his reign. The Burmese attempt to capture Tavoy and Tenesserim was beaten back in 1613, and the efforts made by the Burmese King to invade Chiang Mai and Lampang in order to regain his prestige proved to be equally useless in the following year, but in 1622, Tavoy was lost to Burma, and in the opinion of the Thai King, it was not worth while to recapture it. Chiang Mai slipped out of Thai control and became again independent.

King Songtam welcomed the English and showered favours on the Dutch and the Japanese. At the beginning of his reign came the English, who began to take interest in Ayutthaya after the founding of the English East India Company on December 31, 1600.

Captain William Keeling went with three company ships to Bantam in West Java in 1608 where he became acquainted with one of the Thai envoys who were on the way to the Netherlands. According to E.W. Hutchinson's *Adventurers in Siam in the Seventeenth Century*, he learnt from him that "a thousand Clothes red could vend in his country in two days, and great quantities yearly, they clothing their Elephants and Horses therewith," and then he passed on the information thus acquired to the Company. Impressed with this report, the East India Company ordered Captain Anthony Hippon to take one ship, the "Globe," for a visit to Siam.

Hippon sailed from England on February 5, 1611, and called at Ceylon, Masulipatam, and Bantam on the way to Ayutthaya. On June 23, 1612, the "Globe" cast anchor off Pattani with Peter Williamson Floris and other English merchants on board. At factory was opened there, but Hippon was taken ill and died. He was not really the first Englishman to stop at Pattani. In 1605, an English navigator, John Davis, was killed in a fight with Japanese pirates off the town. Thomas Essington continued the voyage in command of the ship, leaving Floris in charge of the factory there.

On August 15, 1612, the "Globe" arrived at Ayutthaya, and the English were well received. After disembarking a cargo of goods and four merchants to dispose of them, the "Globe" made its departure from the city. One of these English merchants, Lucas Antheuniss, had an audience with the King on September 17, 1612, when he presented to him a letter from King James I (1603-1625) of the Stuart dynasty. The King evinced much pleasure at the receipt of this missive and gave a small golden cup and a piece of clothing to each member of the English party. Not only did he allow them to trade at Ayutthaya, but he also allotted them a plot of land to build their factory on the east side of the Chao Phya River between the Dutch and the Japanese settlements.

The English factories at Ayutthaya and Pattani did not make any profit. On the contrary, they suffered considerable losses for the following reasons. One of the most serious difficulties which faced the English was that English ships did not visit Siam frequently; another difficulty arose from the fact that goods could not be disposed of on a cash basis; goods had to be sold against the promise of other goods, such as copper, which were to be delivered at a later date, when they arrived from abroad. Promises of this nature often developed into bad debts. Meanwhile the Agent of the Company had to borrow money from the Thai Treasury at interest in order to help along with the daily business. The Agent himself did not seem to carry on his work in a proper manner. In 1621, the Agent at Ayutthaya was reported to be drunk every night. Some of the factors or officers of the Company were not honest in doing their duties, as they gambled away 1,000 rials in a single night. Moreover, the Portuguese and the Dutch did all they could to hamper the English trade. There is a story of one Benjamin Fairlie being poisoned to death, presumably by the Portuguese. In Pattani, trade came to a standstill owing to civil troubles.

In view of the unfavourable trading conditions, the East India Company ships, the "Fortune," the "Bee" and the "Roebuck" visited the Thai capital before the trade between Siam and the English East India ceased in 1625. Stress should be put on the fact that the East India Company withdrew of its own accord from Siam the first time and no pressure was brought to bear upon it.

Hearing about the good treatment accorded to its people, the Dutch government sent Songtam a letter, thanking him for the assistance that had been rendered for their benefits. The English and the Portuguese were afraid that their trade might suffer as a result of the treaty between Siam and the Netherlands. The English therefore decided to chase off Dutch ships from the seas, while the Portuguese seized a Dutch vessel but were compelled to release it. They also sank a Thai boat with the result that a state of war arose between Portugal and Siam and lasted until after the end of King Songtam's reign. The Dutch, however, could hold their position against the English and the Portuguese.

Both Ekatotsarot and Songtam rewarded the Dutch for the services that had been rendered to the Thai government, especially in connection with the foreign trade. The former parcelled out to them land at Ayutthaya on which to set up their quarters, while the latter permitted them to build another trading station on the right bank of the Chao Phya River near the sea (at Paknam). The Dutch turned this place into a small town of their own and named it New Amsterdam, no traces of which remain to-day, as they crumbled into the river a long time age, due to rapid erosion.

After the death of King Ekatotsarot, some Japanese had tried to seize the palace at Ayutthaya and had been forgiven. But the Japanese guards who served Siam in Songtam's reign were loyal to him. They were organized as a regiment under a Japanese commander named Yamada Nagamasa who was created Okya Senabhimuk. He was born in the province of Suraga, Japan, and it is said that as a young man, he served Okubo Jiemon as a palanquin bearer. He was about thirty years of age when he set foot on the Thai soil in 1610, and he soon entered the Kings' service where he rose to be a Thai nobleman — an appreciation of his good deeds shown by Songtam.

King Songtam undertook to promote friendly intercourse with the Shogun of the Tokugawa family by sending the following envoys to Japan, namely, Khun Pijitsombat and Khun Prasert in 1621, Luang Thongsamut and Khun Sawat in 1623, and Khun Raksasitti-phorn in 1629. The Shogun reciprocated Songtam's goodwill with letters. In reply to a Thai letter asking the Japanese not to join the Cambodians in resisting Siam, the Shogun stated that as the Japanese were merchants, they should keep away from politics, and if they were found taking part in it, they should be punished according to the law of the land. According to another letter, which Songtam addressed to the Shogun. "The fact that the sea is between Siam and Japan has made intercourse difficult. But now our merchant ships ply between the two countries, thus strengthening the friendly relations. Obviously you show sincere love to us and, in fact, love us more than your close relatives." The Shogun's reply was that "the friendly relations between our two countries will be unbreak-able, and since we have mutual trust, the fact that there is the sea between our countries is by no means of any importance." Such relations were backed up by an exchange of presents. The Japanese appreciated the good quality of Thai guns and ammunition which had been delivered to them, while the Thais admired horses from Japan. Connected with diplomacy was the trade which proved to be beneficial to both of them. Japan paid silver bullion and copper for her imports of deerskin, tin, teak, sandalwood, sugar, coconut oil, lead and other commodities from Siam.

Like the English, the Danes made themselves known to the Thais in King Songtam's reign. In 1621, a ship belonging to the Danish East India Company visited Mergui and Tenesserim. It was under the command of the Dutch captain, Cruppe. The Governor of Tenesserim informed him that as Siam would like to be an ally of Denmark, she would be prepared to reduce the customs and dues for the Danes as a special favour. But the Danish East India Company did not engage in trade to the same extent as the English or the Dutch East India Company. It purchased elephants which found a ready market in India and a few other goods in exchange for firearms which Siam always needed.

Nowadays the Thais recall with deep veneration King Songtam's name owing to the discovery of a huge footprint of the Buddha by a hunter named Boon in 1623 at the foot of a hill in the province of Saraburi, now about 150 kilometres from Bangkok. It was beautifully carved on a rock with all the superhuman characteristics of the great Teacher, and the King caused a Mondhob or tapering structure to be erected over it. Large scale celebrations were held to mark the inauguration of the annual pilgrimage to the Buddha Footprint which has continued down to the present day. Every year, during the full moon of February and March, people travel from Bangkok and other neighbouring towns to worship the Buddha Footprint at Saraburi. Another feature of King Songtam's active patronage of Buddhism was the revision of the Mahajati, a long religious poem written in the reign of King Boromtrailokanat. For the convenience of the reader, the Pali text was entirely separated from the Thai text in this poem.

King Songtam must have been familiar with the stories of the boy kings on the throne of Ayutthaya. When he fell seriously ill, he worried a good deal about the succession to the throne of his eldest son, Prince Jetta, who was a boy of fourteen. In an assembly of the high officials which was called to discuss this question, one party headed by Phya Sriworawong, was strongly in favour of Prince Jetta as the next king, while Chao Phya Mahasena and his supporters were of the opinion that the King's brother, Prince Srisin, should have priority in succeeding him on account of his maturity. It is not certain whether the Prince Srisin, who was living under the protection of the yellow robe, was informed of the whole affair. Nevertheless King Songtam persisted in his plan to install Prince Jetta as his successor and gave confidential instructions to his Lord Chamberlain, Phya Sriworawong, to assist him. In his endeavour to win support for the Prince, Phya Sriworawong managed to persuade a large number of people to join him. Yamada Nagamasa, who was Okya Senabhimuk, and 600 Japanese guards also espoused his cause.

JETTATIRAT (1628-1629). In 1628, King Songtam died at the age of thirty eight, having occupied the throne for eighteen years. Prince Jetta was proclaimed King by Phya Sriworawong who then required all the leading officials to drink the holy water as a sign of swearing allegiance to him. Chao Phya Mahasena and the other prominent members of his party who had opposed the new King were arrested and beheaded at once with their properties being confiscated and distributed to those who had rendered valuable services to him. King Jettatirat promoted Phya Sriworawong to be the Co-Prime Minister for military affairs with the title of Chao Phya Kalahom Suriyawong.

Since the King could not very well govern the country, being a boy, Chao Phya Kalahom was in actual practice the power behind the throne and soon entered into an intrigue with his adherents to seize the throne. He was born in 1600, being a son of Phya Sritammatirat, a Royal Chamberlain, whose younger sister was the mother of King Songtam. He was thus intimately connected with the royal family, being a cousin of King Songtam and a distant uncle of King Jettatirat. He served King Ekatotsarot as a page and rose to be a senior Chamberlain when he was seventeen years of age. Endowed with extraordinary cleverness and bravery, he tended to assert himself in a bad way. He aroused Songtam's ire for attacking the Mock King of the Ploughing Ceremony and was sentenced to a prison term. On the intercession of Lady Manichan, Naresuan's consort, with the King, he was pardoned after a period of five months in prison, and rejoined the royal service. The King conferred upon him the title of Phya Sriworawong and he subsequently became the King's trusted favourite.

At the beginning of King Jettatirat's reign, Chao Phya Kalahom worked step by step with a view to winning the crown. Believing that Prince Srisin might be a serious obstacle to his grand design, he entrusted Yamada with the task of luring him from his sanctuary. Trusting Yamada's promise that the Japanese troops would help him to seize the throne, the Prince discarded the yellow robe. He was at once taken prisoner and condemned to death. Having pity on his uncle, the King commuted the death sentence to exile at Petchaburi. The Prince revolted again, but he was defeated and was clubbed to death.

King Jettatirat had been on the throne for about one year and seven months when he had no highest officer of the State to consult, because Chao Phya Kalahom was turning against him. At one of the royal audiences when he transacted the State affairs, only a few high officials were present and the rest attended the cremation of the mother of Chao Phya Kalahom at Wat Jaiwattanaram. The King thus became suspicious of his treacherous intention and threatened to destroy him. Learning about the threat before the King took any action about him, he decided to save himself, and with his supporters, he stormed the palace. The King was captured and executed in 1629.

ATITYAWONG (1629). On his refusal to accept the throne, offered by an assembly of the prominent officials, Chao Phya Kalahom set up as King the little Prince Atityawong, Jettatirat's brother, aged only ten, and he himself acted as Regent of the realm. In other words, he possessed the kingly power, but Phya Kampangram and Yamada who were his leading accomplices might oppose his eventual accession to the throne. Finding a pretext to accuse Phya Kampangram of plotting to seize the throne, he caused him to be arrested and liquidated. However, he did not dare to harm Yamada, since he commanded the Japanese guards, and in order to get him out of the way, he appointed Yamada as Chao Phya Nakhon Si Thammarat to rule the city of that name instead of the former governor who had been deprived of his position, due to a rebellion. In doing so, he used as an excuse a rumour of the sinister Dutch design on it. The whole regiment of the Japanese guards accompanied Yamada to Nakhon Si Thammarat.

The leading officials then made an appeal to Chao Phya Kalahom to assume the throne on the ground that King Atityawong did not keep his royal dignity and indulged in childish amusements.

PRASATTONG (1630-1655). Chao Phya Kalahom accepted this offer and became King Prasattong—the King of the Golden Mansion. Atityawong was deposed after a reign of more than one month and lived until 1637 when he was executed, due to his involvement in a rebellion. Prasattong was really a usurper, as he had no hereditary claim to the throne. Opinions differ as to his place in the history of Thailand. Joost Schouten who was the Dutch Agent at Ayutthaya in 1630 praised him as ruling with great reputation, but his successor, Jeremias van Vliet who held the same office from 1636 to 1641 used unkind words about him in his book — A Historical Account of Siam. Nevertheless an objective discussion of his reign would show that he had what is now called nationalistic tendencies. He was firm in dealing with foreigners and upheld national dignity and interests, despite the fact that he was beset with difficulties almost throughout his reign.

Chiang Mai, which had declared itself independent, was completely conquered by the Burmese in 1632, and Phya Luang Tipanet was set up as Burmese Viceroy there. However, the King was successful in bringing Cambodia under Thai overlordship once more, and he fell under the cultural influence of the beautiful ancient Khmer architecture of Angkor Thom and Angkor Wat to such an extent that he set up in his capital of Ayutthaya a big model of Angkor Wat. It was perhaps about this time that Khmer influences in various fields of culture became strongly manifest and an outward form of the ancient Khmer cult, the Devaraj, was adopted at the Court especially in matters of obsequial ceremonies and the coronation.

Peace reigned in Nakhon Si Thammarat which was in the firm hands of Yamada, but he held the governorship of the city for only a short time. After he was poisoned to death, his son, Oin Yamada, succeeded him as governor and soon became involved in constant hostilities with the adherents of the ex-governor. Unable to hold his position any longer, he evacuated his family and compatriots to Cambodia for a brief stay. Thence they returned to Ayutthaya, where some of them aroused the King's suspicion. Van Vliet related that they were not afraid to declare that they would seize the King on his throne. Nor did the King look kindly upon them. He also resented the refusal of the Shogun of Japan to recognize him as King and to extend a welcome to his envoys. With these considerations in mind, he decided to extirpate the Japanese, whom he had found difficult to cope with. Suddenly his men made a night attack on the Japanese settlement during the flood season of 1632 and killed many of the Japanese, while the rest escaped by boat to Cambodia. Such was the end of the relations between Siam and Japan and was, in due time, confirmed by the general exclusion laws which the Shogun issued in 1636, initiating the period of Japanese isolation which lasted until 1854. Still a few Japanese hid themselves in Siam, and again made known their presence in King Narai's reign.

At the beginning of Prasattong's reign, the Princess of Pattani proved to be recalcitrant. She refused to send the usual tribute and declared herself independent of Siam. The royal army failed to subdue Pattani in 1632 and 1634. The Dutch offered to help Prasattong to crush that city, as they were maintaining good relations with him. In 1632, Prince Frederick Henry of the Netherlands sent two ships and a letter of congratulations to him on his accession. By the advice of the Dutch, however, the Princess of Pattani surrendered to Prasattong in 1636 and sent her envoys to beg his forgiveness and to present him with the customary miniature trees made of gold and silver.

It should be borne in mind that the Dutch were then in a strong position owing to their thriving trade. They paid a royalty equivalent to 5,000 florins for the right to carry on their business. Within the compound of their settlement at Ayutthaya, they built a solid brick headquarters for their Agent, van Vliet, who gave good protection to his men. In December 1636, two Dutchmen were involved in a brawl with the Thais. The next day they were charged with attacking the house of the King's brother and were sentenced to be trampled to death by elephants. Van Vliet managed to obtain their release by giving presents to the King and principal officials and signing a pledge of unquestioning obedience to the Praklang's orders. Three years later, van Vliet saved his assistants from the King's anger. They were ordered to leave Siam within a day under pain of death. But nothing happened, as the Dutch Agent threatened to use force against the King and the episode ended.

In spite of Prasattong's threatening attitude towards the Dutch, the Prince of Orange and the Governor-General of Batavia deemed it necessary to curry his favour for them, and so in 1641 they sent to him two letters which pleased him immensely. When Songkhla (Singgora) rose against him in 1648, the Dutch promised to send him twenty ships to assist in attacking that town, but they did not show up. On hearing this news, he flew into rage against the Dutch and ill treated their representative, Westerwolt, who was van Vliet's successor as Agent. The Thai Government forbade the Thais and the Mons to work in the Dutch station at Ayutthaya. If this order was carried out to the letter, their business would suffer in consequence. They therefore determined to teach Prasattong a lesson and proceeded to make a naval demonstration of force in the Gulf of Siam. This caused the King to change his policy by conciliating them. Subsequently the rebellion of Songkhla was subdued. As soon as the Dutch showed themselves to be friends with the Thais, he let them carry on their trade as before and bestowed favours on them. For instance, he gave Westerwolt a silver box and conferred upon him a title of nobility as Luang Ritsakorn. Thus the Dutch got back their influence at the Court of Ayutthaya towards the end of Prasattong's reign.

To the Portuguese, he meted a harsh treatment. Siam was at war with Portugal, a legacy from King Songtam's reign. He arrested all the Portuguese in the Kingdom and put them in gaol for three years. Portugal was united with Spain for sixty years (1580-1640), and so the Spanish Governor of the Philippines took charge of the Portuguese in the East. King Prasattong sent him a letter, expressing willingness to resume friendly relations with the Portuguese. In fact, the Portuguese themselves were desirous of taking such steps and a Portuguese envoy arrived at Ayutthaya in 1633, thus terminating the war between the two countries. Three years later, a Thai envoy returned the Portuguese visit when he went to Manila instead of Goa. A remark should be inserted that although Portugal regained her independence in 1640, her decline in the East had set in. Malacca was taken from her by a Dutch conquest in 1641 and the Portuguese coastal towns in Ceylon fell to the Dutch in 1660. Probably recognizing their diminishing power, the Portuguese held aloof from political matters in Siam and so they pursued their trade quietly until the end of the Ayutthaya period.

The reign of King Prasattong was noted for a certain amount of legislation. Among the laws which he put on the statute book were the Law of Appeal 1633, the Law of Inheritance 1635, the Law on Slavery 1637 and the Law of Debts 1648. Only a few words will be said about some of these laws. The Law of Appeal allowed an appeal against the judge for injustice, favouritism or slackness, while the Law of Inheritance rested on the principle of witnessing.

King Prasattong believed in magic and superstition. In 1635, one of his daughters died and was cremated, but a part of her flesh remained unconsumed. In his opinion, this must have been due to magic, caused by his enemy. Using the incident as a pretext, he ordered the arrest and execution of a few thousand persons. According to the Chulasakarat Era, there was a cycle of twelve years, and each year bore the name of an animal, beginning with the rat followed by the ox, the tiger, the rabbit, the dragon, the serpent, the horse, the goat, the monkey, the cock, the dog, and the pig. The 1000th year of the Chulasakarat

Era, which coincided with the year of the tiger, corresponded to 1638-1639. He feared that the year of the tiger might bring terrible disaster to the country. In order to avert such a calamity, he organized a so-called Brahmanic ceremony in which he performed the changing of the year of the tiger to that of the pig. The result was that he felt greatly relieved and that the people would continue to enjoy peace and happiness. But the change was not popular and caused some confusion in the Thai calendar.

CHAO FA JAI (1655-1656). Having occupied the throne for twenty five years, King Prasattong died in 1655, at the age of fifty five, and was succeeded by his eldest son, Prince Jai or Chao Fa Jai. After a reign of about one year, King Chao Fa Jai fell victim to a conspiracy, engineered by his uncle, Prince Srisutammaraja, and his younger brother, Prince Narai. He was captured and was put to death in the royal manner. Indeed this crime constituted a shame on the royal family of Prasattong, and strange to say, it was repeated three months later.

SRISUTAMMARAJA (1656). Not long after his accession, King Srisutammaraja alienated the feelings of his own nephew, Prince Narai, whom he had created the Maha Uparat. Being an amorous man, he showed improper attention to his own niece, Princess Kalyani, who was Narai's younger sister. She strongly resented the King's conduct and, after an escape from the palace by hiding herself in a Buddhist book case, she made a complaint to her brother about the whole incident. Filled with exalted ambition, he used it as an excuse to attack the King's palace with his followers, thus causing an outbreak of a civil war which lasted for a few days. Finally, King Srisutammaraja was defeated and done away with.

NARAI THE GREAT (1656-1688). After winning the throne in 1656, Narai crowned himself as King of Siam. Born in 1632, as a son of King Prasattong, he acquired a legend about his godlike appearance and his invulnerability. At his birth, his relatives thought that he had four arms, and so the name of Narai after the God Narayana (Vishnu) in Brahmanism was conferred upon him. Later, while he was standing near a long pole in the palace, lightning struck it, causing his governess to faint, but he was not hurt at all.

Chiang Mai and Burma claimed Narai's attention four years after his accession. The Prince of Chiang Mai sent him a letter requesting the protection of Siam, since he was afraid that the Chinese might attack his principality after Ava in Burma. The request of Chiang Mai being a good opportunity to reunite it with Siam, he led an army to the north. But on hearing that the Chinese had retired from Ava, due to shortage of supplies, the Prince of Chiang Mai changed his mind and renewed his allegiance to the Burmese King. Thus he escaped from any vengeance that Burma might wreak on him, but he stirred up Narai's wrath to such an extent that the Thai troops were detailed to deal with a hostile Chiang Mai. As they were not numerous enough to crush the Prince, they withdrew to Ayutthaya in 1661. Chiang Mai was under Burmese suzerainty as before.

In the same year, a rebellion at Ava enabled the Prince of Prome to seize the Burmese throne with the title of King Mahasihasurasutammaraja. Profiting by this event, King Narai made a second attempt to subdue Chiang Mai. The first army of 40,000 under Chao Phya Kosatibodi (Khun Lhek), and the second under of 60,000, under the King, moved towards the north once more. By throwing all the available forces into an all out attack on city of Chiang Mai, the King was successful in taking it in March 1663, Chiang Mai, however, proved to be elusive to Siam, and after less than one year under Thai control it reverted to Burma.

Soon after the invasion of Chiang Mai, Siam had to deal with Burma again. Strongly resenting the terrible treatment meted out to them, the Peguans or Mons revolted against the King of Burma and plundered Martaban. As they could not hold the town against superior forces from the Burmese capital, they and their families, numbering about ten thousand, emigrated to Siam where they settled down with the King's permission. In order to follow up their demand for the return of the Peguans, the Burmese troops marched through the Three Pagodas' Pass for an invasion of Siam in 1663, but they were heavily defeated by the Thais at Saiyoke near Kanchanaburi and hastily retreated, leaving large military supplies in the hands of the Thais.

King Narai took the same retaliatory measures as King Naresuan the Great in ordering an army of 60,000 under Chao Phya Kosatibodi (Khun Lhek) to invade Burma in 1664. The Thais advanced by Pegu and Prome, and besieged Pagan or Pukam. The Burmese never flinched in putting up a stubborn resistance to the Thai army which was compelled to strike camp, due to lack of provisions. Although the wars with Chiang Mai and Burma did not benefit Siam, they helped to show that she was still a Power to reckon with.

In his foreign relations, Narai became the most talked of Thai monarch, since he adopted a friendly policy towards foreigners, especially the Europeans, and Ayutthaya was a metropolis where peoples from many lands congregated. Among the Europeans with whom he came into contact, the Dutch and the English caused him a great disappointment.

The Dutch assumed a friendly attitude towards the Thais for a few years only and then reverted to their high handed policy. In 1661, they captured a ship, flying the Portuguese flag, in the gulf of Tongkin, but the goods it was carrying belonged to the Thai King. In 1661, the English reopened their factory or trading station at Ayutthaya, thus causing displeasure to the Dutch, since they were afraid that the English might take away part of their trade. The Dutch were also dissatisfied with the Thai government. In 1664, they were threatened by the Chinese and they blamed the Thai authorities for this lack of proper protection. The system of Royal Monopolies which had been initiated by King Songtam and revised by King Prasattong was not to their liking.

Siam had levied a tax on foreign trade on the basis of the size of the ship's beam before Songtam's reign. This tax was paid to the Praklang or Minister of Finance (well-known to foreigners as Barcalong or Barcalon) who was responsible for foreign trade, and thus had the duty of conducting the foreign affairs of the Kingdom as well. The main purpose of the system of Royal Monopolies was to conserve the natural resources of the country and to control foreign trade at a close range, and its principal features were as follows: 1. The Thai people were forbidden to deal with foreign merchants in such rare commodities as ivory, hides, and sandalwood. If they had them in possession, they must sell them to the Royal Warehouse Department which fixed the prices. If a foreign merchant wanted these goods for exports, he bought them from the Royal Warehouse. 2. Permission must be obtained for the export of paddy rice and polished rice. 3. For other commodities which were not specified in the regulations of the Royal Warehouse, a foreign merchant could purchase them directly from the local people for exports.

The Dutch accused Siam of failing to observe the treaty of 1617 which had been made with them. In order to safeguard their trade interests, they demanded various commercial privileges from the country, which naturally refused to give them at first. In 1664, therefore, a Dutch fleet blockaded the mouth of the River Chao Phya. Having no fleet which could fight the Dutch ships, King Narai had eventually to grant the Dutch demands, and on August 22nd of the same year, Siam signed a treaty with them. The treaty comprised one short document and one long document which could be summarised as follows: 1. The King of Ayutthaya and the Dutch East India Company agreed to promote friendly relations. 2. The Dutch were free to trade in Siam without restrictions, but they must pay taxes and dues in accordance with the current practice. 3. Siam undertook not to employ any Chinese on her ships. If a Chinese was found on any Thai ship, the Dutch could confiscate it. 4. The export of deer hide and cow hide was a Dutch monopoly. 5. "In case (which God forbid) any of the Company's residents should commit a serious crime in Siam, the King and the Judges shall not have the right to judge him, but he must be handed over to the Company's Chief, to be punished according to the Netherlands laws."

The treaty was extremely disadvantageous to Siam. It was almost impossible for her to compete with the Dutch in the China trade, because the term "Chinese" in clause 3 of the treaty included the Japanese and the Cochin-Chinese, some of whom sailed in Thai ships. Clause 5 constituted the beginning of the extraterritoriality system, although it applied only to the Dutch at their trading station. Apparently King Narai had no intention of abiding by the terms of the treaty. According to *Thailand the New Siam* by Virginia Thompson, "At first the treaty worked to Dutch satisfaction; but soon the wily king, by controlling prices, managed to rob the Dutch of almost all their newly won advantages."

The English resumed their relations with Ayutthaya in King Narai's reign. In 1654, the English East India Company opened a branch or factory in Cambodia, with John Rollins as its agent, but its trade was not satisfactory. John Rollins preferred Siam to Cambodia, as is seen from his report to his Company that "Siam goes much beyond this place both for largeness and cheapness......and none of those northern places gives such justice as they, only this inconvenience, no coming to sight the King." In 1659, the invasion of Cambodia by Annam forced the English traders to leave the country. They took a ship to Ayutthaya, where King Narai accorded them a friendly reception. Through them, he sent a message to their chiefs which induced the Company to reopen its factories in Siam. By that time the Company was prosperous. It paid an annual toll of £400,000 to the English Government and the profit to England of its trade with India was estimated at a million pounds per annum. In 1661, a factory was re-established at Ayutthaya. Although the Thais were willing to do business with them, the English were not greatly interested in the trade. Pattani and Songkhla were in a state of rebellion. In 1678, King Narai made an offer to cede Pattani to the Company which declined to accept it. On the contrary, one of the Company's factors proceeded to Songkhla, where he helped the rebellious Governor to fortify the town against the Thai troops. Needless to say, this brought the Company into disfavour with the Thai authorities.

Siam hoped to benefit from the trade with the English and to play them off against the Dutch whose considerable influence was felt at Ayutthaya, because at the beginning of Charles II's reign (1660-1685), England went to war once with the Netherlands. The

English, however, alleged that the Thai foreign trade was a state monopoly. Certain specified exports, as already mentioned, could be bought and sold only through the Royal Warehouse Department. Although a free deal was allowed for other goods, the Thai Government reserved the right of pre-emption and juggled with prices as it thought fit. The Company asked the Royal Warehouse Department to announce the exact amount of goods it would deal with and the prices it was prepared to fix. Naturally the Thai authorities could not comply with this request, because it conflicted with their foreign trade policy. It might be said without exaggeration that the Company also adopted the trade policy for its selfish interests. By its foundation Charter, the Company enjoyed trade monopoly in Siam in so far as it concerned Englishmen. Those who were not members of the Company were deprived of the right to trade at Ayutthaya. There were still so ne Englishmen who defied the Company's order and carried on trading transactions, and they were known officially as "interlopers." Such men were the White brothers, George and Samuel. It was George White who introduced Constantine Phaulkon to Siam in 1675.

Phaulkon was a Greek, born in the island of Cephalonia not far from Athens, about 1650. His father was a small inn-keeper named Gerakis or Yerakis (meaning Falcon in modern Greek). When he was about ten years old, he joined the crew of an English ship, apparently with his mother's consent. He lived in London until about 1669, when he went to sea again as Captain White's cabin-boy. He had in the meantime anglicised his name to Falcon, and his shipmates re-hellenised it again to Phaulkon. However, he was generally known by his Christian name Constantine, or by a diminutive of it, Constant, Constans, Conse or Kance, if written in French. At first he worked under George White and his party, Richard Burnaby, at Ayutthaya. In the course of sundry trading ventures. he once suffered shipwreck on the same spot as the Thai ambassador to Iran. Possessing a flair for languages, he mastered the Thai language in about two years. In fact, he was a linguist, as he knew English, Portuguese, Malay and Thai, besides Greek which was his native tongue. With such rare and appropriate qualifications, Phaulkon joined the office of the Praklang as an interpreter in 1679. He was very clever and energetic in the performance of his duties. The Thais, for instance, were amazed at his method of weighing a heavy siege gun. He had the gun placed on a boat, the water-mark of which was then noted down. The gun was removed from the boat and pieces of stone were in turn dumped into it until it reached the same water-mark. The stone was taken out from it and was weighed. Thus the weight of the stone corresponded to that of the gun. Being conversant with the merchants' trickery, he filled up the loopholes in the collection of customs and duties. Consequently he won rapid promotion as a Thai nobleman; he was Luang Wijayen and rose to be Pra, Phya and Chao Phya by the same name in succession.

Some officers of the English East India Company did not like him, because he had been encouraging many of the English interlopers to transact business at Ayutthaya, apart from being at one time an interloper himself. They were searching for a pretext to smear his good name in the eyes of the Thai authorities. On December 6, 1682, the house and the factory of the Company were burned down. Samuel Potts, one of the joint chiefs of the factory, accused Phaulkon of having caused the fire in order to destroy the evidence of his debt. Phaulkon alleged that Potts himself had set fire to the factory so as to conceal his embezzlements. He was originally a member of the Greek Orthodox Church and became a Protestant while serving in English ships. As a typical adventurer of his days, he was a bachelor, and while he was working at Ayutthaya, he married a Catholic girl of

Japanese ancestry. Through the influence of the French priests, he embraced Roman Catholicism and his conversion to the new faith exacerbated the relationship he had with the Company, which then regarded him as being pro-French. Actually he endeavoured to cultivate friendship with the English, and so he sent expensive gifts to his former patron, George White in London, for distribution to those which could influence the English policy towards Siam. Some of the gifts were presented to Charles II (1660-1685) and acknowledged by James II (1685-1688) who wrote to thank Phaulkon, addressing him as "Our well beloved friend." In 1684, the second Thai embassy to France stopped at Margate, a town on the south-eastern coast of England. All these efforts, however, failed to bring about the improvement in the relations between Phaulkon and the East India Company.

As a high government official with the title of Chao Phya Wijayen, Phaulkon was entrusted with the duties of managing the foreign trade and conducting the foreign affairs in the name of the Praklang, who normally bore the title of Chao Phya Kosatibodi. He was enjoying Narai's favour and confidence, but he refused to accept the office of the Praklang for fear of arousing jealousy among the Thai officials. He launched out into trade on his own too for the sake of raising an income to defray his current expenses.

On Phaulkon's recommendations, King Narai appointed Richard Burnaby and Samuel White as Governor and Port Officer (Shahbander) of Mergui respectively. Burnaby, who was the former Chief of the Company's factory at Ayutthaya, had joined the Thai service. He held the title of Pra Marit and with the co-operation of the Thai Governor of Tenesserim, he controlled Mergui. Samuel White was the brother of George White who had been Phaulkon's benefactor and he carried on private trading abroad, especially in India. His ships sailed under the Thai flag, and if they had any dispute, Siam would surely become involved in it. Samuel White had a quarrel with the merchants of Golconda on the Coromandel coast of India, since his ship had been sunk there. In 1686, Captain John Coates was sent in command to arrange the dispute. As a retaliatory measure, he seized several ships belonging to Golconda. A strong complaint against this hostile act was made by Golconda to the East India Company on the ground that it might have connived at it. In fact, the Company was already extremely dissatisfied with White, who was looked upon as an interloper. To settle the whole question of interlopers in Siam once for all, it ordered two frigates to sail to Mergui, where they were to take the town, seize the Thai ships pending settlement of a claim for £65,000 by Siam and arrest the Englishmen in the Thai service such as White. Believing that the English were about to violate the sovereignty of his country, the Thai Governor of Tenesserim which took charge of Mergui resisted them and sank one ship, while the other ship escaped. King Narai backed up his Governor, and on August 11, 1687, he declared war against the East India Company. It should be noted that he did not consider himself to be at war with the English Government. The Thai authorities did not interfere with the daily life of the Englishmen who were outside the Company.

The war fizzled out on Narai's death in 1688. In his farewell message to the last batch of the Englishmen who left Ayutthaya, the Praklang emphasized Siam's willingness to render facilities to English merchants. The English ships which continued to call at Ayutthaya were few and far between, for the simple reason that the trade with Siam was not profitable to the Company. To summarise, the Thai relationship with England in the Ayutthaya period produced no durable results. Perhaps the English, a good many of whom entered the Thai service as captains of the King's ships, taught navigation to the Thais.

Meanwhile King Narai had turned to the French in the hope of using them to counteract the Dutch influence in Siam. It was a wise step in the beginning, since the Dutch and the French were enemies in Europe and fought the Franco-Dutch war of 1672-1678, the war of the League of Augsburg (1689-1697) and the war of Spanish Succession (1701-1713). Doubtless the credit for opening the relations between Siam and France went to the French Catholic missionaries who belonged to the French Foreign Mission with its headquarters at the Rue du Bac in Paris. The main aim of the Mission was to propagate Roman Catholicism in Annam, Tongkin and China. The Pope recognized the Mission in 1659 and consecrated three members of the Mission, Pallu, de la Motte Lambert, and Cotollendi as bishops. Thus Pallu became Bishop of Heliopolis; Monsignor de la Motte Lambert's title was Bishop of Berytus, while that of Monsignor Cotollendi and later of Monsignor Laneau was Bishop of Metellopolis.

Bishop Lambert intended to go to China first for his missionary work, but forseeing the difficulties in travel, he decided to set up his mission in Annam. He reached Mergui in April 1662 and continued his journey to Ayutthaya, where he hoped to find a boat which would take him to his new destination. He set out for Annam in 1663, and, due to a shipwreck, he had to return to Ayutthaya, where he lived in the Annamite district.

Bishop Pallu arrived at Ayutthaya in 1664 almost two years after Bishop Lambert, being accompanied by four priests and a secretary. Having studied the conditions of the country, he established the headquarters of the Mission in the East at Ayutthaya, because it was centrally located and within easy reach of the neighbouring countries, the climate was not hot, the cost of living was low, the general atmosphere was agreeable to religious propaganda, and what was of supreme importance was that religious toleration prevailed among the people, no matter whether they were Thai or foreigners. In fact, there were many foreign communities living in the metropolis and thus constituting good material for the evangelical work.

King Narai became interested in the French Mission when he learned about the reputation of Father Thomas Valguarnera as a skilful architect and engineer. The King ordered new forts to be built at Bangkok, Nonthaburi, Ayutthaya and other towns for the defence of the Kingdom. Fr. Thomas, who was Italian by birth and a member of the Mission, designed and superintended the construction of these forts. In view of the proximity of Ayutthaya to the sea, the King was afraid that it might be attacked easily. For this reason, he moved his residence to Lop Buri, where Fr. Thomas and the French architects and craftsmen helped to put up a new palace, forts and other buildings, the ruins of which stand to-day as undisputed evidence of their handiwork. As a reward, King Narai gave the French missionaries land and houses as well as facilities to build churches. During the twenty four years which followed, the Mission expanded considerably, with a large church, a few elementary schools, and a boarding school for boys who intended to enter the seminary for the Holy Order. The French missionaries made an attempt to romanize the Thai script, as they set up a printing press which used the Roman letters for publishing religious books in Thai, but it was closed down at the end of King Narai's reign, due to the expulsion of the French priests by Petraja. The Mission staff consisted of more than twenty priests from Paris, and a few of them spread out to Bangkok and Phitsanulok, where they built chapels. In Ayutthaya, they divided their time between teaching and administering to the sick. A medical attendant, M. René Charbonneau, came out from

France to help the priests at the dispensary and hospital. Having been the governor of Phuket for a short time, he returned to his medical work at Ayutthaya, where he lived until the end of his life.

According to the French missionaries, it was very unusual for the King who professed a different religion to favour them with the gift of land and houses, and consequently they believed that he was attracted to their religion. When Bishop Lambert and his followers had an audience with the King in 1665, they took the opportunity to expound to him the principles of Christianity. But their hope to win him over to Christianity did not materialise. The King still remained a good Buddhist. A remark should be made here that he did not show particular devotion or make any special contribution to Buddhism, but he never swerved from it. Nor was he inclined to any other religion. In 1668, a group of Mohammedan missionaries arrived from Atcheh or Acheen in North Sumatra and tried to persuade him to accept Islam, but he turned a deaf ear to them. Later he entered into friendly relations with them, but nothing came out of this contact. Narai also welcomed in an audience the Persian Ambassador who arrived at the Thai capital about 1685, thus bringing Siam and Persia into official relationship for the first time. In fact, some descendants of the Persians who lived in Siam had already entered the King's service and made a name for themselves.

Meanwhile the French missionaries submitted reports of their activities to the Pope and Louis XIV, requesting further assistance for their work. This was granted, as the Pope and the French King were pleased with King Narai who continued to lavish goodwill on the missionaries, since Louis XIV considered himself as the Defender of the Catholic faith. The French evinced interest in the Thai trade. Jean Colbert, Louis XIV's chief Minister, was the prime mover in founding the French East India Company (Compagnie Royale des Indes Orientales) in 1664. After the establishment of its headquarters at Pondicherry in 1672, the Company examined the trading possibilities of the Indo-Chinese peninsula. In 1680, the Company's ship, the "Vautour," commanded by Boureau Deslandes, sailed to Ayutthaya, where he met with a good reception, and thus the trade between Siam and France began. King Narai then decided to send an embassy to France with a view to securing a true understanding with that country and a friendship that would withstand the passage of time. Phya Pipatkosa was the first Thai ambassador to France, accompanied by an interpreter, Fr. Gayme, and two secretaries, Luang Sriwisan and Khun Nakornwichai. He was more than sixty years of age and possessed considerable experience in diplomacy, having conducted three embassies to China. The embassy left Siam by the "Vautour," and at Bantam, changed to another French ship, the "Soleil d' Orient." After a stop for water at Mauritius in 1681, the ship was never heard of again. Probably it was wrecked by violent storms near the Cape of Good Hope.

Constantine Phaulkon, who wielded considerable influence with King Narai, aimed at promoting friendly relations and fostering trade with France. He was by then a Catholic and was intimate with the Jesuits who were the French missionaries. The general opinion was that he was more powerful than the Praklang. Probably at his suggestion, the King appointed the second embassy to France. It was headed by Khun Pijaiwanit and Khun Pijitmaitri and accompanied by a French priest, Fr. Vachet, as guide and interpreter. This embassy was entrusted with the duty of inviting France to send an embassy to Siam with a view to concluding a treaty of friendship. The members of the embassy sailed from

BRONZE ENGRAVING OF
THE THAI DIPLOMATIC MISSION, GRANTED AN AUDIENCE
BY LOUIS XIV AT VERSAILLES

Ayutthaya in January 1684, taking with them the first group of Thai students ever to go to Europe, and called at Margate in England on the way to France.

The second Thai embassy achieved the desired result. In 1685, Louis XIV despatched his first embassy to Siam, thus bestowing a great honour on King Narai, and the Chevalier de Chaumont was the French ambassador. He was a French nobleman, a recent convert from the Huguenots as well as a religious zealot. He brought with him a large suite including the Abbé de Choisy as well as six Jesuits whose mission was to verify the maps and correct the soundings in the course of the voyage. These Jesuits were ultimately bound for China. However, five of them prolonged their stay in Siam for some years, while the sixth Jesuit, Fr. Tachard, returned to France on a secret mission which brought him back again as a member of the second French embassy.

The Chevalier de Chaumont and his party travelled to Siam by two ships which had Khun Pijaiwanit and Khun Pijitmaitri as passengers. The voyage from France to Siam occupied 204 days including two stops of eight and ten days at the Cape of Good Hope and at Batavia respectively. On October 18, 1685, the French ambassador proceeded to the palace in a procession with Louis XIV's letter being laid upon a golden salver and borne along on a palanquin. King Narai received him in state, with Phaulkon acting as an interpreter during the audience. De Chaumont tried his best to convert Narai to Christianity, but he met with no success. King Narai remained a firm believer in Buddhism, a shining example to the Thai people. The role of the Abbé de Choisy as religious instructor to the

Thai King thus became superfluous. Nevertheless, the King agreed to sign with France a convention containing the following terms: 1. Facilities were given to the French to trade with the Royal Warehouse Department, provided that they paid dues and customs to Siam. 2. The French obtained a monopoly of tin in the island of Phuket. 3. Songkhla was ceded to them, with full power to fortify it. (The Governor of this town rebelled against Narai a few years before). 4. The manager of the Company's branch at Ayutthaya received extra-territorial jurisdiction over his men.

The convention was meant to be a provisional document which must be confirmed by a treaty. King Narai therefore despatched Pra Wisutsuntorn as ambassador to France with a mission to express, on his behalf, a sincere appreciation of Louis XIV's friendliness and to complete the negotiations with the French Government for the treaty. Pra Wisutsuntorn is generally known in Thai history as Kosa Parn. Subsequently he was made the Praklang with the title of Chao Phya Kosatibodi, his elder brother, Khun Lhek, having previously occupied this post.

PAINTING OF PRA WISUTSUNTORN
(KOSA PARN), THAI AMBASSADOR
TO FRANCE IN 1686

Leaving Ayutthaya in company with M. de Chaumont on his return to France in December 1685, the third Thai embassy arrived at Brest in June 1686 and was granted an audience by Louis XIV in the Gallery or Hall of Mirrors of the Palace at Versailles on September 1, 1686. During his stay in France, Kosa Parn proved himself to be an astute diplomat who took the interests of his country to heart. The French wanted Mergui instead of Songkhla, but the Thai ambassador pointed out that Mergui was very far from the Thai capital. A sea voyage from that town to Ayutthaya would necessarily include a detour round the Malay Peninsula, while a land journey would take many days. When the French looked at the map, his explanation was borne out by facts and they dropped their request accordingly. So he saved Mergui for Siam, and it was a sea port of considerable importance, serving as the Thai outlet to the Indian Ocean. It has been asserted that the Thai embassy asked for French troops to garrison some of the forts in Siam, but any evidence in support of this statement is lacking. The Thai request was for French experts in various fields including those in the military service. It is most likely that Siam did not desire the despatch of French soldiers to her shores. The Royal History of Siam records an amazing feat of invulnerability, demonstrated by 17 Thais who accompanied Pra Wisutsunthorn. Having donned a coat of the arabesque design and muttered some cryptic incantations, each of them took his seat in a small pavilion specially erected in front of a grandstand occupied by the French King. 500 French sharpshooters were ordered to shoot at them, but the shots fell short of the target.

Pra Wisutsuntorn and his assistants returned to Siam with the second French embassy, which arrived at Ayutthaya on September 27, 1687. The French party consisted of two envoys, Father Tachard, 636 soldiers under the command of General Desfarges. Only 492 soldiers arrived in Siam. The first envoy was Claude Cébéret du Boullay, a Director of the French Company—a calm and honest man. The second envoy was Simon de la Loubère, a barrister who had gained some experience in diplomacy under St. Romain in Switzerland. The French envoys presented Phaulkon with the patent of knighthood in the Order of St. Michael and carried out successful negotiations with the Thai authorities with a result that a commercial treaty was signed on December 1, 1687. According to the treaty, the French East India Company obtained the right to trade at Ayutthaya without payment of duties. Exception was, however, made in the purchase and sale of prohibited goods, namely, white saltpetre, black saltpetre, sulphur, firearms and weapons, for which permission must be secured from the Thai Government. The Company monopolised the tin business at the town of Thalang Bangclee in the island of Phuket, and was permitted to set up stations in the islands near Mergui. The Agent of the Company in any town had the right to decide a case involving his employees on the basis of equity. In a case between a Company employee and any person outside the Company, a Thai judge conducted the trial and gave out his decision, having a Frenchman sitting with him. Immediately after the signing of the treaty, Cébéret left Siam, and about one month later, de la Loubère followed him. During their stay at Ayutthaya, the former occupied himself with the negotiations, while the latter spared some time to collect material for his book on the *Description of the Kingdom of Siam*, which was published in 1691. The fourth Thai embassy headed by Khun Chamnan to the Court of Louis XIV travelled in company with de la Loubère and returned home quietly at the beginning of King Petraja's reign.

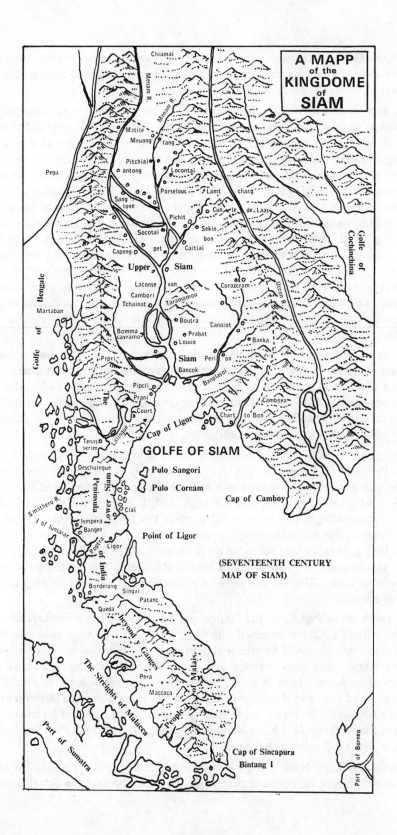

A MAPP
of the
KINGDOME
of
SIAM

Chiamai

Menam R.

Mztile
Meuang fang
Pitchiai antong
Locontai
Porselouc Lamt charg
Sang love
Pichit Cun le de Laas
Socotai Sekin bon
pet Caitiai
Capeng

**Upper Siam**

Laconse van
Cambori Taramamou
Tchainat Corazcram
Boutra
Bomma cavramo Prabat
Louuo Canaiot

**Siam**
Bancok Peri on Banka
Banplasol

Prpri

Pipcli Camboya
Prani Chart to Bon
Court

Tenas serim
Latingue Cap of Ligor

Pegu

Golfe of Bengale

Martaban

Golfe of Martaban

Golfe of Cochinchina

Ucon R.

**GOLFE OF SIAM**

Pulo Sangori

Pulo Cornam

Cap of Camboy

Deschuingue

Smathero R.
I of Iunsalar
Isespera
Banger

Peninsula of Siam

Popra of India

Ligor
Bordelong
Singvi
Patanc
Queda

beyond y Ganges

Pera
Maccaca

The Streights of Malacca

People of Malais

Part of Sumatra

Joi

Lower Siam

Clai

**Point of Ligor**

(SEVENTEENTH CENTURY
MAP OF SIAM)

Cap of Sincapura
Bintang I

Part of Borneo

The Thai Government was perhaps not quite sure how the French troops might react to any event concerning the throne, and so they were dispersed into groups to man various forts at Bangkok, Mergui and other towns.

Many factors contributed to the formation of an anti-French or nationalist party which aimed at saving Siam from the clutches of the French. Not only did the leading Thai officials envy Phaulkon for being the King's favourite, they were also much afraid that he might achieve the King's conversion in order to serve the French purpose and that the country might be brought under French domination, as a large French garrison was already stationed in the Kingdom. The Thai party was led by Pra Petraja, who was the Commander of the Royal Regiment of Elephants. He had distinguished himself in the Chiang Mai campaigns and the expedition against Burma and had up till then been very close to King Narai, being one of his foster-brothers. He had as his right hand man his son, Dua, who was a remarkable young man, being extremely ambitious and aggressive. As Luang Sorasak, he was an officer of the Guards. A rumour circulated that Luang Sorasak was a son of the King, conceived with a northern woman during a campaign to Chiang Mai. The King was apparently ashamed of the fact, and Pra Petraja obliged his master by accepting her as his wife. Anyhow Luang Sorasak served Pra Petraja dutifully and loyally.

King Narai had no son who would be his direct heir. The royal family comprised his daughter, Princess Yotatep, his sister, Princess Yotatip, and two brothers, Chao Fa Apaitot and Chao Fa Noi. The King had brought up a distant relative as his adopted son, whom he appointed as Pra Piya meaning the beloved lord. In the hope of seeing Pra Piya as Narai's successor, Phaulkon had successfully persuaded him to join his party and to embrace Roman Catholism—so it was alleged.

Learning that King Narai had become seriously ill with dropsy at Lop Buri in March 1688, Pra Petraja and Luang Sorasak acted immediately according to the plan. They ordered the guards to mount a strict watch of the King's palace; they lured Pra Piya from the King's apartment and had him done to death, and they arrested Phaulkon on a charge of treason. It was alleged that he intended to place Pra Piya on the throne, with himself acting as Regent. He was condemned to death with all his property being confiscated, and about June 5, 1688, he was beheaded on the edge of Tale Chupsorn, a lake just outside Lop Buri. It is common knowledge that a meteorite flashes in the sky at a great speed and disappears in no time. The rise and fall of Constantine Phaulkon could appropriately be described as meteoric.

After the death of Phaulkon, Pra Petraja sent for the King's two brothers who lived at Ayutthaya. Chao Fa Apaitot hastened with Chao Fa Noi to Lop Buri, as he was under the false impression that he would be offered the throne. The two princes were well received, but two days later, they were arrested and done away with at Luang Sorasak's order. He thus forced his father's hand in seizing the throne. The next task was to rid the country of the French, and acting in the name of the King Pra Petraja ordered Desfarges to move his troops to Lop Buri. On his refusal to comply with his wishes, he sent his trusted soldiers to attack the fort at Bangkok. King Narai died on July 11, 1688, and Pra Petraja mounted the throne without difficulty, at the age of fifty six.

Not only was King Narai's reign well known in Europe, but it also saw a revival of Thai literature. Under his constant patronage, his Court became the centre where poets congregated to compose verses and poems. King Narai and Pra Rajdevi certainly made their poetical mark in the history of Thai literature and enjoyed the literary works which were admirably produced by such outstanding poets as Pra Maharajkru, Pra Horatibodi, and Sriprachya. At the command of King Narai, Pra Horatibodi wrote a book for the study of Thai language entitled *Chindamani* in order to counterbalance the French cultural influence. The King worried about Thai children who attended the Catholic schools in increasing numbers, as they might adopt the European culture and be converted. Summing up the elements, the grammar, the prosody, the versification of Thai language as well as official forms of correspondence, the *Chindamani* became a popular textbook in due time and continued to be in use until the commencement of King Chulalongkorn's reign (1868-1910). It is generally accepted as the first textbook of Thai language.

Thus ended the reign of Narai. In view of his record of achievements already mentioned, it is generally agreed that the last king of Prasattong's dynasty certainly deserved the title of the Great like Ramkamhaeng and Naresuan.

The genealogy of the Royal Houses which ruled Ayutthaya from 1569 to 1688 is as follows:-

## DYNASTY OF MAHA TAMMARAJA

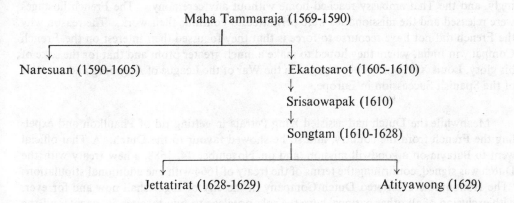

Maha Tammaraja (1569-1590)

Naresuan (1590-1605)   Ekatotsarot (1605-1610)

Srisaowapak (1610)

Songtam (1610-1628)

Jettatirat (1628-1629)   Atityawong (1629)

## DYNASTY OF PRASATTONG

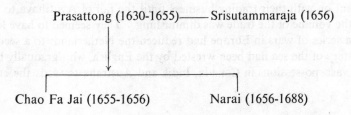

Prasattong (1630-1655)——Srisutammaraja (1656)

Chao Fa Jai (1655-1656)   Narai (1656-1688)

# CHAPTER VIII

# END OF AYUTTHAYA

PETRAJA (1688-1703). Petraja was faced with the difficult task of expelling the French from the country, on his accession. The Thai troops besieged the fort at Bangkok, where the French garrison held out for two months. In the end, due to their desire for repatriation coupled with lack of provisions, the French appealed to the King for the cessation of hostilities, and this was agreed to. So all the French soldiers as well as General Desfarges left Siam, leaving Bishop Metellopolis and a few French merchants as hostages for the safe return of the fourth Thai embassy from France. This condition was carried out accordingly, and the Thai embassy reached home without any ceremony. The French hostages were released and the missionaries were permitted to continue their work. The reason why the French did not have recourse to force is that they focussed their interest on the French Company in India, where they hoped to make a much greater profit and that for the sake of his glory, Louis XIV was deeply engaged in the War of the League of Augsburg and the War of the Spanish Succession in Europe.

Meanwhile the Dutch had assisted King Petraja in getting rid of Phaulkon and expelling the French from the country, and so he showed favour to the Dutch. A Thai official went to Batavia on a goodwill mission, and on November 14, 1688, a new treaty with the Dutch was signed, confirming the terms of the treaty of 1664 with one additional stipulation: "The Honourable Chartered Dutch Company in the city of Ligor shall now and for ever, with exclusion of all other nations, have the sole privilege to buy through its agents, all the tin, with the exception only of such quantity as His Majesty may, according to usage, require for its proper use."

The Dutch went on with their trading business until the fall of Ayutthaya to the Burmese in 1767, but the volume of the trade was diminishing. They seemed to have lost interest in Siam, since a series of wars in Europe had reduced the Netherlands to a second class power. Their mastery of the sea had been wrested by the English, who gradually became a Great Power with vast possessions in Canada, India and Australia towards the end of the eighteenth century.

Petraja hailed from the district of Ban Plu Luang in the town of Suphan Buri. So his Royal House is known as the Ban Plu Luang dynasty, the genealogy of which is as follows:-

# BAN PLU LUANG DYNASTY

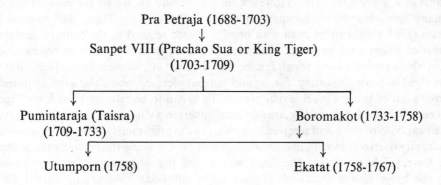

Pra Petraja (1688-1703)

↓

Sanpet VIII (Prachao Sua or King Tiger)
(1703-1709)

Pumintaraja (Taisra)
(1709-1733)

Boromakot (1733-1758)
↓

Utumporn (1758)

Ekatat (1758-1767)

Petraja's reign of fifteen years (1688-1703) was by no means a peaceful one. As a commoner who usurped the throne, he was naturally confronted with a violent reaction from a section of the people, and four rebellions broke out. In 1690, a Mon impostor named Tammathien, who claimed to be Chao Fa Apaitot, led a rebellion at Nakhon Nayok, to the east of Ayutthaya, and advanced as far as the outskirts of the capital, but he was defeated and beheaded, and his followers fled from their home towns for fear of punishment. About the same time, the King became strongly suspicious of the Prince of the Rear Palace, Nai Chobkotprasit, who had been his chief collaborator in the usurpation of the throne. By using the theft of his golden salver as a pretext, he ordered his arrest. The Prince was accused of treason and was duly executed. Another collaborator, Chao Phya Surasong-gram, who dared to make a protest against the King, suffered the same fate. Towards the end of 1691, the Governor of Nakhon Ratchasima (Khorat), Phya Yomarat, rebelled, and the Governor of Nakhon Si Thammarat followed suit. Eventually they were vanquished after putting up a daring resistance for two years. The last rebellion of Petraja's reign was caused by a visionary or fanatic named Boonkwang, with only twenty eight followers, at Khorat, and was suppressed in 1700.

The King had two young sons, Chao Pra Kwan aged fourteen, and Tras Noi aged ten in 1703. The first prince was the child of Queen Yotatip, King Narai's sister, while the second prince had as his mother Queen Yotatep, that monarch's daughter. Chao Pra Kwan was very popular, greatly respected and generally regarded as the heir to the throne, as he was a descendant of King Narai. Fearing his rivalry for the throne, Luang. Sorasak, who was the Maha Uparat, enticed him to his villa, where he was clubbed to death. Learning about the murder of his beloved son, the King who was seriously ill, flew into uncontrollable rage against Luang Sorasak and proclaimed his nephew, Chao Pra Pijaisu-rindr as his heir. Foreseeing that the acceptance of the throne would be his own tragedy, Chao Pra Pijaisurindr, who never expected the highest nomination in the realm, handed the reins of government to the Maha Uparat as soon as King Petraja had breathed his last breath. In saving Siam from foreign domination, Petraja performed one of the truly patriotic deeds for his country, which to-day remains implanted in the mind of the Thai people. His other young son, Tras Noi, successfully sought his salvation as a Buddhist monk and passed out of history.

SANPET VIII (1703-1709). On his accession, the Maha Uparat assumed the official name of King Sanpet VIII. However, he is generally known by the popular name of King Luang Sorasak or by the nickname of Prachao Sua or King Tiger. His reign of about six years (1703-1709) can be dealt with briefly. Peace reigned in the country, and the people, most of whom were peasants, continued to pursue their livelihood as before, except for a very short period during which famine and drought stared them in the face. But the King indulged in boxing, hunting, fishing and sensual pleasure, and as he soon acquired the bad reputation of being a cruel sexual pervert, he began to be referred to as King Tiger. Being a keen boxer, he fought in disguise two local boxers in a village match not far from Ayutthaya. He beat both of them and received two bahts as the prize money from the ringmaster. However, pity overtook him on one occasion, when he was being rowed along the Mahajai canal in his royal barge during the flood season and the coxswain, Norasingh, unavoidably let the barge hit the bank with its prow being smashed. According to the Palace Law of 1450, this was an offence punishable by death, and Norasingh unflinchingly insisted on the law taking its course, in spite of the King's immediate pardon. His lugubrious wishes being honoured, he was beheaded, and a small shrine was erected to his memory on the bank of the canal. Recently a play and a film have been built on this famous story of self-sacrifice for the firm upholding of the dignity of his profession as well as the sanctity of the Law.

Of his two sons, the elder, Prince Pejr, was the Maha Uparat, while the younger, Prince Porn, became Pra Bantun Noi or the Prince of the Rear Palace. The King's excessive self-indulgence shortened his own life. He was only forty five years of age, when he died in 1709. He was succeeded by the Maha Uparat, Prince Pejr, who adopted the official name of King Pumintaraja, but was generally known as King Taisra (meaning "by the side of a pond"). His favourite residence was a hall, situated by the side of a pond in the palace of Ayutthaya. The vacancy of the Maha Uparat was filled by his younger brother, Prince Porn.

PUMINTARAJA OR TAISRA (1709-1733). The peaceful twenty four years reign of King Taisra (1709-1733) was interrupted in 1717 by an intervention in the internal affairs of Cambodia in order to maintain his overlordship. Otherwise the King spent his time in improving the internal water communication and the foreign trade. Thirty thousand workers were conscripted to complete the Mahajai canal, the redigging of which had been started by King Luang Sorasak, and a few ships were built to transport elephants to foreign markets, for instance, to India. Besides his activities in the field of economic development, he built or repaired a number of Buddhist monasteries. A vihara was erected to house the huge lying Buddha image at Wat Pamoke in the province of Ang Thong. For relaxation, he enjoyed hunting and fishing.

King Taisra's reign ended in the same terrible manner as that of King Prasattong, being a struggle between an uncle and two nephews. He had three sons, the eldest of whom was Prince Naren, and the second and the third were Prince Apai and Prince Parames respectively. Before his death, the King began to entertain suspicion against the Maha Uparat, Prince Porn, who was his own brother, and so he contemplated raising Prince Naren to be his successor. This Prince, however, expressed his reluctance to accept the appointment for the simple reason that the Maha Uparat should succeed to the throne, and not long after he entered the monkhood. Taisra therefore handed the throne to Prince Apai before he passed away at the age of fifty-four. A struggle for the throne now broke out and developed into a civil war between the Maha Uparat having his palace as his stronghold, and Princes Apai and Parames, making the Grand Palace as their base. It lasted several days, as both sides had erected the fortifications in the heart of Ayutthaya separating the palaces. Eventually the two Princes were defeated, and after being fugitives for a week, they were captured. They were put to death in the royal manner, and a large number of their followers who failed to escape into the countryside shared their fate.

Taisra's reign is noteworthy for the renewal of Spanish intercourse with Siam. In 1717, Spain resumed diplomatic relations with Siam. At the command of Philip V, the governor of the Philippines appointed Don Gregorio de Bustamente Bastillo as the King's envoy to the Court of Ayutthaya. He arrived there with two ships, and Taisra granted him an audience. As a result of their negotiations, Spain gained the following privileges:-

1. To establish a trading post on the Chao Phya river. The Spaniards set up a flag pole on the site of the proposed station in order to show that they had been given permission by the Thai King for this purpose.

2. To build ships in Siam. The Thai agreed to supply the Spaniards with teak at a reasonable price.

But the trade between Ayutthaya and Spain did not develop in the way it had been expected. The unsatisfactory treatment which the Spaniards meted out to the Thai trading ships which had been calling at Manila since Narai's reign, became a source of discontent to Thai merchants who then decided to stop their business with the Philippines. Still a few Spaniards were found living in Siam. In 1725, they built a trading ship on the banks of the Chao Phya river with the assistance of the Thai king. The Spaniards passed out of Thai history at the fall of Ayutthaya in 1767.

BOROMAKOT (1733-1758). The Maha Uparat, Prince Porn, thus won the throne, bearing the title of King Maha Tammarajatirat, but he was subsequently known as King Boromakot. Under his rule of twenty five years (1733-1758), the country enjoyed peace and tranquillity, the people were happy and contented, and the arts and letters flourished for the last time before the most terrible catastrophe which befell Siam, ending for ever the glory of Ayutthaya as the Thai metropolis. Among the outstanding poets were the King's son, Prince Tammatibet, as well as the King's daughters, Princess Kunthon and Princess Mongkut. Prince Tammatibet, who bore the title of Krom Khun Senabhitak, but is usually referred to as Chao Fa Kung (meaning shrimp), won fame in lyric poetry. One of his poems is *Kap Hokhlong Prapat Tantongdang*, in which the poet sings the praise of his ladylove against the background of the beauty of nature, while another poem is *Kap Hokhlong Herua*, composed as a song for the crew of a royal barge to sing in a procession. The two Princesses selected as the theme for their literary works an episode of the history of Java which was widely known in Siam in the eighteenth century, but as they did not collaborate in their work, they produced two different versions of the same story, namely, *Inao Yai* or *Dalang* and *Inao Lek*, dealing with a Javanese romance in Thai poetry. Parallel to the extraordinary progress made in the field of arts and letters was the thriving state of the Buddhist Church which enjoyed the King's patronage and devotion. He was strict in requiring the moral and educational training of government officials, and would not confer a title of nobility on a person who had not been ordained as a monk, thus originating in all probability a custom for a young man aged twenty one to take a monk's vow at least temporarily. In 1750, King

Boromakot was greatly elated with a request of King Kirti Srirajasih of Ceylon, brought to Siam by a Singhalese embassy, for a mission of Buddhist Thai monks to purify the Buddhist Church in his realm. *An Account of King Kirti Sri's Embassy to Siam in Saka 1672 (1750 A.D.)*, translated from the Singhalese by P.E. Pieris, records that "There King Kirti Sri Raja Sinha, the great reformer, had succeeded to the Crown; he applied himslef vigorously to sweeping all the abuses that had crept into priesthood, ably and zealously supported by Saranankara Uranse and his Minister Ehelapola. His crowning work was the re-institution of the Upasampadawa in Lanka." The embassy was received in a grand style. With regard to an audience which Boromakot granted to the Singhalese embassy *An Account of King Kirti Sri's Embassy to Siam in Saka 1672 (1750 A.D.)* says that "On the morning of Thursday two officers came and took us to the palace. We halted for a short time at a madapé while our arrival was being announced, after which we were presented and received with great kindness by his majesty the king, the prince, and the sub-king; we were informed that the presents destined for Ceylon would be ready to start in a short time and then were given permission to withdraw, when we returned again to the same mandapé for a short interval." A group of fifteen monks under Pra Upaliwong was sent to Ceylon in 1753. The Thai monks achieved such gratifying and durable results that they founded a new sect known as the Upaliwong or Sayamwong.

Nevertheless the other side of the picture of Boromakot's reign should not be neglected or forgotten. The civil war, immediately preceding his accession to the throne, contributed considerably to the weakening of the Kingdom but fortunately for Siam, Cambodia and Burma, which might imperil her position, found themselves in a similar plight.

Cambodia was in a chaotic condition, due to the disputed succession to the throne, and in 1750, King Boromakot intervened to settle it by placing on the Cambodian throne once more his nominee, Ramatibodi, who had previously been expelled from his capital. Thus the Thai suzerainty was re-asserted. In Burma, the Mons successfully rebelled in 1742, and two years later, they unanimously raised their leader, Sala, to the throne of independent Pegu, with the title of Sming Toh or Smim Htaw. He had been a Shan monk before he discarded the yellow robe for the throne, and relying on his claim of being related to the Burmese royal family and of possessing such magical powers that rendered him invulnerable, he had gathered a large force. So the revival of the Mon kingdom barred the return of the Burmese governor of Pegu to Ava, the new Burmese capital set up in 1734, and forced him to leave his headquarters at Martaban together with three hundred followers for Ayutthaya, where they sought asylum. Kind assistance was bestowed on them by King Boromakot, an instance of which was the proper arrangement for their housing. The Burmese King was so pleased with the good treatment given to the Burmese fugitives that in 1744, for the first time in over a century, he sent an embassy to Ayutthaya with a mission to express his thanks to King Boromakot and to secure his help in quelling the Peguans or at least to ask him to be neutral. In reciprocating the good will of the Burmese King, a Thai embassy, comprising Phya Yomarat, Pra Thonburi and Pra Sutammaitri, went to Ava in 1746 at King Boromakot's command and Siam adopted the policy of neutrality in the Burmese-Peguan imbroglio.

But Sming Toh did not remain long on his throne. Taking advantage of his absence at an elephant hunt, a leading official named Phya Dala seized the power and proclaimed himself King of Pegu in 1746. Saming Toh fled to Chiang Mai, and after a fiasco in regaining the throne, he proceeded to Ayutthaya. Instead of obtaining aid from King Boromakot, he was exiled to China, but he was released on the coast of Annam. In 1756, he managed to raise a small contingent at Chiang Mai and offered his services to Alaungpaya in Burma. Distrusting him, Alaungpaya permitted him to live under surveillance until his death two years later.

In the meantime, Phya Dala of Pegu continued to fight the Burmese, and in March 1752, his army captured Ava, thus ending the Taungu dynasty with the deposition of its last king. A liberator of Burma by name of Aungzeya appeared on the scene immediately. Besides being a hunter, he was the headman of the village of Moksobo (now called Shwebo). Having collected his followers and organized them into an army of five thousand men, he led them against the Peguans, and during that time he styled himself Alaungpaya, meaning "embryo Buddha." He won victories one after another; he retook Ava in December 1753 and conquered Hanthawadi in May 1757, putting an end to the Peguan Kingdom. The whole of Burma, therefore came to be under the rule of Alaungpaya, and, reunited once more, she soon became a threat to Siam which was in the throes of internal dissensions. Having suffered defeat at the hands of the Burmese, the Peguans fled to Siam for protection and were, by order of King Boromakot, given land just outside the capital on which to build their dwelling places.

Prince Tammatibet, who was Boromkot's eldest son of the Chao Fa or celestial rank was the Maha Uparat, but he predeceased him, while suffering from heavy punishment by beating because he had committed adultery with Chao Fa Sangwal, one of the King's consorts. The other two sons of the same rank were Prince Ekatat and Prince Utumporn who bore the title of Krom Khun Anurakmontri and Krom Khun Pornpinit respectively, and they were at loggerheads with three of their half-brothers, namely Prince Chitsuntorn, Prince Suntorntep and Prince Seppakdi. In Boromakot's opinion, Ekatat lacked intelligence perseverance and ruling capabilities; so he was passed over as his successor and by royal command, he entered the monkhood. The King then selected as the Maha Uparat Prince Utumporn in spite of his entreaty. Due to his upbringing in a monastery, this Prince showed no high ambition, though he was clever and studious.

UTUMPORN (1758). In 1758, King Boromakot died at the age of seventy eight, and was succeeded by the Maha Uparat who was known as King Utumporn. The fact that the new King had been the Maha Uparat proved to be a great help to him, as most of the people in the capital had rallied around him; otherwise he would have faced a possible civil war. However, he was fully aware of the preparations being made by his opposing three half-brothers for an action against him, and therefore his first act was to order their arrest and execution which was carried out accordingly.

Still imbued with an unsatiable ambition, Prince Ekatat left the monkhood and installed himself at the Suriyamarin Hall in the royal palace. King Utumporn realized at once that his brother still cherished a strong desire for the throne, and if he took any measure to remove him, he might hurt the feelings of the Queen Dowager whom he respected. In order to avoid any incident which might cause him trouble, he ceded the crown to him. He himself retired to the monastery called Wat Pradu, after a reign of more than one month only, and soon he acquired the popular name of Khun Luang Ha Wat meaning "a king seeking a monastery" or Khun Luang Wat Pradu Rongtham, meaning "a king of the Pradu Rongtham monastery."

EKATAT ( 1758-1767 ). Prince Ekatat's accession was a catastrophe for Siam. King Boromakot's estimate of his abilities proved in the end to be absolutely correct, as he was extremely incompetent and too fond of female company. King Ekatat took upon himself the official title of Boromarajatirat, but the Thai people called him King Ekatat, King Suriyamarin, after the name of his favourite hall, or the leprous King, though he suffered from a kind of eczema and not from leprosy.

King Ekatat's reign opened with a conspiracy, hatched by his half-brother, Prince Teppipit, in collaboration with Chao Phya Apairaja, Phya Yomarat and Phya Petburi. The plotters wanted to restore the ex-King Utumporn to the throne, but being loyal to the King and possessing no ambition for power, he revealed their design to him, after securing a promise that their lives should be spared. As a punishment for being the ringleader, Prince Teppipit was exiled to Ceylon, while the other conspirators were imprisoned.

Hardly had the officials recovered from excitement and restlessness arising from the premature plot when they were confronted with a Burmese invasion. The main reason for this Burmese aggression was that Alaungpaya was to all intents and purposes aspiring to revive the glories of Burengnong's reign. Evidently the rise of a great King in Burma constituted a real danger to the Thais. After a show of force, he induced most of the northern towns such as Nan, Payao and Chiang Saen to acknowledge his overlordship. In his opinion, Chiang Mai and Siam still challenged his might. In 1760, he utilized the Thai refusal to hand over to him the Mon rebels who had taken refuge in Siam as a pretext for an attack on the country.

Alaungpaya's army marched southwards, took Tavoy, Mergui and Tenesserim, and crossed the mountain range through the Singkhorn Pass. Meeting with weak opposition, he made a rapid advance towards Ayutthaya, capturing Phetchaburi, Ratchaburi and Suphan Buri on the way. Having been reinforced with new troops in sufficient numbers, his army laid siege to the Thai capital in April 1760. Unable to cope with the chaotic conditions which might develop into riots, King Ekatat sent for the ex-King Utumporn who resided quietly at his monastery. In compliance with the King's wishes, he doffed the yellow robe and reassumed absolute power in organizing the defence of Ayutthaya. After one month's siege, the Burmese were still outside its walls, and bombarded the city with cannons. One day Alaungpaya himself superintended the firing of such a cannon, but it burst accidentally and he was severely wounded in consequence. With their King being unable to direct command, the Burmese withdrew to their country by way of the Melamao Pass, and Alaungpaya died during the retreat in May 1760.

Only the necessity of survival held the people of Ayutthaya together. Once the Burmese danger was over and they were again disunited. It is true that a large programme for the repair of the fortifications and the acquisition of weapons and military supplies was undertaken. Hoping to regain their lost power, the officials who opposed King Utumporn constantly aroused King Ekatat's suspicions against him. On seeing Ekatat with a long sword on his lap one night, Utumporn took the hint at once. If he continued to govern the Kingdom, a fratricide was bound to occur. For this reason he returned to his monastery Wat Pradu Rongtham, and a number of officials who had supported him followed suit. Having learnt a bitter lesson, he refused to assume the role of the defender when the Burmese pounded the walls of Ayutthaya again six years later.

In Burma, Manglok or Naungdawgyi, Alaungpaya's son and successor, had a short reign of three years (1760-1763), and he was succeeded by his brother, Mangra or Hsinbyushin, who ruled the country from 1763 to 1776. His father, Alaungpaya, had established his capital at Shwebo on which he gave the name of Ratanasingha, but King Mangra moved it back to Ava, probably due to its conveniences. In his relations with the neighbouring states, however, he consistently followed Alaungpaya's policy. He subdued Manipur, Chiang Mai and Luang Prabang. In 1765, he commenced the operations against Siam. One Burmese army moved down from Chiang Mai, while another pushed its way through Suphan Buri, and by February 1766, the Burmese besieged Ayutthaya once more. The siege caused terrible hardship to the defenders, as it lasted one year and two months. During that time, the men of the Bang Rachan village in the province of Sing Buri committed a series of memorable deeds of bravery in harassing the Burmese invaders with guerrilla tactics, but to the disappointment of the Thai people, they were outnumbered and finally crushed. Seeing no hope of holding the capital any longer, King Ekatat offered to lay down his arms and become a vassal of Burma, but the Burmese insisted on unconditional surrender, which he could not agree to for obvious reasons. Having gathered together all the available forces, the Burmese generals threw them into a great onslaught against the city. Ayutthaya fell into the enemy's hands on the night of April 7,1767. Showing no mercy whatever to the Thai people, the Burmese put city to the fire and sword. They carried off to Burma an incalculable amount of booty and about 30,000 inhabitants including the ex-King Utumporn, most of the members of the Royal Family, government officials, soldiers, peasants, and even monks and novices who could not escape from them. The unfortunate monarch went into a hiding place near a monastery outside the city walls, but he was found in a very weak condition by some Burmese troops, and soon afterwards he died of exhaustion.

The Burmese sack of Ayutthaya in 1767, which ended its existence as the Thai metropolis, was the most terrible blow to Siam, as most of her treasures both material and cultural, were lost forever. *An Outline of Siamese Cultural History* by His Highness Prince Dhani Nivat says that "Speaking generally the age of Ayutthaya which lasted from 1350 to 1767 was rich in cultural attainments, developed internally without much outside influence." According to *An Account of Ayutthaya by Khun Luang Wat Pradu Rongtham*, which has recently been discovered, Ayutthaya was really a thriving city, with bustling trade and containing 30 markets, where people of different nations such as the Chinese, the Indians, the French, the English, the Dutch and the Portuguese congregated. So long as they did not interfere in the internal politics of Siam, they were permitted to pursue their occupations without any hindrance. In his *Diplomatic History of Thailand*, Prince Wan Waithyakorn commented on the Portuguese in the following words: "Both the Portuguese merchants and missionaries continued to live freely, thus showing that although they had a different civilization and intended to trade and propagate their religion only, not interfering in the politics, the Thais were broadminded and willing to give them facilities. They had no prejudice against any other religion nor did they close their door to the trade like other countries." This comment applied equally appropriately to people from other countries. With regard to the history of the country, although most of the records were destroyed, the later Kings undertook a most laudable task in collecting the scattered fragments and noting down recollections from the old people. They had them pieced together and compiled to form the history, or Pongsawadan, of the Kingdom. At present several versions of the Pongsawadan are printed, including the Pongsadawan of the *Royal Autograph Edition* which was revised by King Mongkut or Rama IV. All of them contain inaccuracies, while the *Luang Prasoet's History* written in King Narai's reign is generally relied upon for the dates down to the demise of King Naresuan the Great. Another useful piece of historical evidence is a memoir, which the ex-King Utumporn related during his captivity in Burma. It is entitled the *Evidence of Khun Luang Ha Wat* or *Evidence of the Krungkao (Ayutthaya) Inhabitants*, and traces the history as well as the royal ceremonies, customs and practices of Ayutthaya to its destruction by the Burmese in 1767. A new version of the memoir has just come to light.

In summary, the fall of Ayutthaya may be attributed to the policy of the first and the third Kings of the Alaungpaya dynasty who ruled a strong and united Burma and were at the same time in search of glories for the country. The Burmese would not have dared to advance to the gates of Ayutthaya, if the Thais had not exhibited weaknesses in opposing them. Since the termination of King Prasattong's rule, Siam had unfortunately been plunged into internecine struggles for the throne between the members of the Royal Family and the partisans of the losing side had suffered death, imprisonment, exile, confiscation of property or at least deprivation of offices accordingly. A long period of peace which resulted in the lack or inadequacy of warlike preparations and military training had apparently sapped the vitality and energy of the Thais. When they were at grips with the enemy, they were often conspicuous by their cowardice or inefficiency, but exceptions to this generalization were of course numerous such as the episode of the Bang Rachan resistance to the invaders. Finally, it cannot be denied that King Ekatat bore the brunt of responsibility for the loss of Ayutthaya. Evidently the events which occurred during the siege of the city confirmed his proverbial incompetence, an instance of which was that in his efforts to drive out the Burmese, Phya Tak took the initiative in bombarding them without proper permission. He would have suffered severe punishment in consequence, but for the fact that he had previously rendered good services to the King; as it was, he was censured. However, he was completely discouraged from taking any further action for him. Subsequently he was ordered to fight the Burmese, and availing himself of the opportunity, he made a brave sortie, cut across the Burmese lines and escaped from the besieged city with his 500 followers who were fully prepared to face all the eventualities with him. It should, without any hesitation, be stressed that his flight was not in any way motivated by selfish interests. Actually it was a blessing in disguise, as he soon organized an army and liberated Siam from the Burmese, and in doing so, he exemplified supreme patriotism, praiseworthy valour and fearless decisiveness.

# CHAPTER IX

# TAKSIN OF THON BURI

TAKSIN OF THON BURI (1767-1782). There used to be in Siam a common saying that Ayutthaya never lacks good men. When the fortune of the country was at a low ebb, some Thai people would recall this saying in order to raise a bright hope for their own welfare and for the safety of their fatherland. Most probably their compatriots who were fortunate enough to slip through the Burmese clutches in the transplantation of prisoners of war would have prayed for such a good man to make his appearance, and they did not have to wait long, since Phya Tak was undoubtedly the saviour who answered the call.

Phya Tak was born in 1734 at Ayutthaya, where his Chinese father, Haihong, who married a Thai woman, was earning his living as a tax-farmer of gambling houses. Greatly impressed with the boy's smart appearance, Chao Phya Chakri who was the Samuhanayok in King Boromakot's reign adopted him and gave him the Thai name of Sin meaning "money or property." At the age of nine, the boy Sin was assigned to a monk named Tongdee in the monastery called Wat Kosawas, where he received his education. By the nobleman's recommendation, the boy entered the royal service as a royal page, when he was thirteen years of age. He studied Chinese, Annamese, and one of the Indian languages with diligence and soon he was able to converse in them with fluency. After taking the vows of a Buddhist monk for about three years, he rejoined the service of King Ekatat who appointed him as Luang Yokkrabut assisting the Governor of Tak near Kamphaeng Phet. Later he succeeded the old Governor on his death and was thus known as Phya Tak. He and his men were drafted to help in the defence of Ayutthaya which was facing the full blast of the Burmese siege. Due to his courage and skill in fighting the enemy, he was promoted to be the governor of Kamphaeng Phet with the title of Phya Wichienprakarn, but he was popularly referred to as Phya Tak. He carried out the defence of Ayutthaya to the best of his ability. Once in repelling the attack of the Burmese he fired the cannon without having obtained permission from the proper authorities who then proceeded to reprove him, causing him sorrow and discouragement. So before the end of Ayutthaya came, he cut his way out from the city and travelled first to Chon Buri and then to Rayong where he raised a small army and his supporters began to address him as Prince Tak. With his soldiers, he moved to Chanthaburi, and being rebuffed by the Governor of the town for his friendly overtures, he made a surprise night attack on it and captured it in June 1767, only two months after the sack of Ayutthaya. His army was rapidly increasing in numbers, as men of Chanthaburi, Trat and other towns flocked to his standard. Lying on the eastern coast at a great distance from Ayutthaya, the towns of Chon Buri, Rayong, Chanthaburi and Trat, which had not been plundered and depopulated by the Burmese, naturally constituted a suitable base for Phya Tak to make preparations for the liberation of his motherland.

Having thoroughly looted Ayutthaya, the Burmese did not seem to show serious interest in holding down Siam, since they left only 3,000 troops under General Suki to control the shattered city. They turned their attention to the north of their own country which was soon threatened with a Chinese invasion. In October 1767, having mastered 5,000 troops and all in fine spirits, Phya Tak sailed up the Chao Phya river and seized Thon Buri opposite present day Bangkok, executing the Thai governor, Tong-in, whom the Burmese had placed over it. He followed up his victory quickly by boldly attacking the main Burmese camp at Posamton near Ayutthaya. The Burmese under the command of Suki were utterly defeated, and Phya Tak won back Ayutthaya from the enemy within seven months from its holocaust.

Phya Tak took important steps to show that he was a worthy successor to the throne. He accorded appropriate treatment to a few members of the ex-Royal Family, arranged a grand cremation of the remains of King Ekatat, and tackled the problem of locating the capital. Many factors militated against his intention to re-establish Ayutthaya as the capital. It had suffered such vast destruction that to restore it to its former state would undoubtedly have strained his resources. The Burmese were quite familiar with the various routes leading to Ayutthaya and in the event of the renewal of a Burmese attack on it, the troops under the liberator would be inadequate for the effective defence of the city. With these considerations in mind, he established his capital at Thon Buri, nearer to the sea than Ayutthaya. Not only would Thon Buri be difficult to invade by land, it would also prevent an acquisition of weapons and military supplies by any one ambitious enough to establish himself as an independent prince further up the Chao Phya river. As Thon Buri was a small town, Phya Tak's available forces, both soldiers and sailors, could man its fortifications, and if he found it impossible to hold it against an enemy's attack, he could embark the troops and beat a retreat to Chanthaburi.

A concourse of the leading officials who had rallied to him offered the crown to him, and then he assumed the official name of King Boromaraja IV, but is known in Thai history as King Taksin, being a combination of his popular name, Phya Tak, and his first name, Sin, or the King of Thon Buri, being the only ruler of that capital. He never had time to build Thon Buri into a great city, as he was fully occupied with the suppression of the enemy, both internal and external, almost throughout his reign. At the sack of Ayutthaya, the country had fallen apart, due to the disappearance of the central authority. Besides King Taksin, who had organized his forces in the south-eastern provinces, Prince Teppipit, Boromakot's son, who had been unsuccessful in a diversionary action against the Burmese in 1766, had set himself up as the ruler of Phimai holding away over the eastern provinces including Nakhon Ratchasima or Khorat, while the Governor of Phitsanulok, whose first name was Ruang, had proclaimed himself independent, with the territory under his control extending to the province of Nakhon Sawan. North of Phitsanulok was the town of Sawangburi (known as Farng in the province of Uttaradit), where a Buddhist monk named Ruan had made himself a prince, appointing his qualified fellow monks as army commanders. He had himslef pursued the Buddhist studies at Ayutthaya with such excellent results that he had been appointed the chief monk of Sawangburi by King Boromakot. In the southern provinces up to Chumphon, a Pra Palad who was the acting Governor of Nakhon Si Thammarat declared his independence and raised himself to the princely rank.

Having firmly established his power at Thon Buri, King Taksin set out to crush his rivals so as to effect the reunification of the Kingdom. After a temporary repulse by the Governor of Phitsanulok, he concentrated on the defeat of the weakest one first. Prince Teppipit of Phimai was quelled and executed in 1768. In dealing with the Prince of Nakhon Si Thammarat, who was taken prisoner by the loyal Governor of Pattani, the King not only pardoned him but also favoured him with a residence at Thon Buri. Chao Narasuriya- wongse, one of Taksin's nephews, was substituted for him as Governor. The last so-called ruler who still challenged the King was the Prince of Sawangburi or Chao Pra Fang, as he had just annexed Phitsanulok on the death of its Governor. King Taksin himself led an expedition against him and took it, but the Prince disappeared and cound not be found again.

The successes against the competitors for power were due to King Taksin's fighting ability as a warrior, splendid leadership, exemplary valour and effective organization of his forces. Usually he put himself in the front rank in an encounter with the enemy, thus inspiring his men to brave danger. Among the officials who threw in their fate with him during the campaigns for the recovery of national independence and for the elimination of the self-appointed local princes were two personalities who subsequently played excep- tionally important roles in Thai history. They were the sons of an official bearing the title of Pra Acksonsuntornsmiantra, the elder of whom named Tongduang (or just plain Duang) was born in 1737 at Ayutthaya and was destined to be the founder of the Chakri Dynasty, while the younger one, Boonma, born six years later, assumed the power second to him. The two brothers joined the royal service; Tongduang was soon ennobled as Luang Yokkrabut serving the Governor of Ratchaburi, and Boonma had a Court title conferred upon him as Nai Sudchinda. Luang Yokkrabut (Tongduang) was therefore not in Ayutthaya to witness the horrors arising from the fall of the city, while Nai Sudchinda (Boonma) made his escape from Ayutthaya. However, while King Taksin was assembling his forces at Chanthaburi, Nai Sudchinda brought his retainers to join him, thus helping to increase his fighting strength. Due to his previous acquaintance with him, the liberator was so pleased that he promoted him to be Pra Mahamontri. Just after his coronation, Taksin was fortunate to secure the service of Luang Yokkrabut on the recommendation of Pra Mahamontri and as he was equally familiar with him as with his brother, he raised him to be Pra Rajwarin. Having rendered signal services to the King during his campaigns or their own expeditions against the enemies, Pra Rajwarin and Pra Mahamontri rose so quickly in the noble ranks that a few years after, the former was created Chao Phya Chakri, while the latter became Chao Phya Surasih.

Simultaneously King Taksin was deeply engaged in restoring law and order in the Kingdom and in administering a programme of public welfare to his people. Abuses in the Buddhist Church and among the public were duly rectified and food and clothes as well as other necessities of life were hastily distributed to those who needed them, thus bringing respect and affection to him.

Needless to say, King Mangra of Burma never abandoned his plan to force Siam to her knees, and as soon as he had been informed of the foundation of Thon Buri as King Taksin's capital, he commanded the Governor of Tavoy to subjugate him in 1767. The Burmese army advanced to the district of Bangkung in the province of Samut Songkhram to the west of the new capital, but it was routed by the Thai King himself. Peace having been concluded with China, the Burmese King sent another small army of 5,000 to attack

Siam in 1774. It was completely surrounded by the Thais at Bangkeo in the province of Ratchaburi, and eventually starvation compelled the Burmese to capitulate to King Taksin. It would be no exaggeration to say that he could have massacred all of them if he wished to do so, but the fact that he took them alive was to promote the morale of the Thai people. The Burmese soldiers were not invulnerable nor were they better than Thai troops in any way. The Burmese reinforcements who had encamped themselves in the province of Kanchanaburi were then mopped up. Undaunted by this defeat, King Mangra tried again to conquer Siam, and in October 1775 the greatest Burmese invasion which occurred in the Thon Buri period began under Maha Thihathura known in Thai history as Azaewunky. This man had distinguished himself as a first rate general in the wars with China and in the suppression of a recent Peguan rising. After crossing the Thai frontier at the Melamao Pass, the Burmese marched towards Phitsanulok, capturing Pijai and Sukhothai on the way. In his interrogation of two Pijai officials, Azaewunky referred to Chao Phya Surasih who was the Governor of Phitsanulok as "Phya Sua" or "The Tiger", thus testifying to his boldness and decisiveness. The Burmese then besieged Phitsanulok which was defended by the brother generals, Chao Phya Chakri and Chao Phya Surasih, and as the result of the stubborn resistance on the part of the Thai soldiers, they were checked outside the city ramparts for about four months. Hearing about Chao Phya Chakri's successful assaults which drove back the Burmese to their well fortified camp, Azaewunky arranged a meeting with him, in the course of which he extolled his generalship and advised him to take good care of himself. He prophesied that General Chakri would certainly become king. Was he really honest in his prediction? No definite answer has been found for it. Anyhow he was at that time seventy two years of age, while his opponent was only thirty nine. Any doubt about Azaewunky's stratagem to sow discord between King Taksin and Chao Phya should be dismissed, since they collaborated closely in subsequent military expeditions.

In spite of King Taksin's endeavour to attack the Burmese from the rear, Chao Phya Chakri and Chao Phya Surasih could not hold Phitsanulok any longer, due to lack of provisions. Having collected most of the inhabitants, they successfully fought their way through the enemy lines and made Phetchabun their headquarters. Azaewunky led his army into the deserted city at the end of March 1776, but was presently confronted with the same problem of the shortage of food supply. At this juncture he was instructed by the new Burmese King, Singu Min or Chingkucha (1776-1782) to evacuate Thai territory. So Azaewunky's army left Siam, but the remnants of the Burmese forces continued the war until they were pushed out of the country in September of that year.

In King Taksin's opinion, so long as Chiang Mai was ruled by the Burmese, the north of Siam would be constantly subject to their incursions. The prerequisite for the maintenance of peace in that region would therefore be the complete expulsion of the Burmese from Chiang Mai. In 1771, the Burmese Governor of that city moved his army southwards and laid siege to Pijai, but he was driven out. Taksin followed the Burmese with a view to studying their strength, and his army was thus not prepared for a direct assault on their city fortress. After meeting with a stubborn resistance, he retired, presumably believing in an ancient prophesy to the effect that two attempts were required for the capture of Chiang Mai. King Narai had tried twice to seize it before it fell into his hands.

The Burmese failure to take Pijai formed a prelude to Taksin's second-expedition to Chiang Mai. In 1773, a Burmese army which threatened Pijai was drawn into an ambush and was heavily routed. Phya Pijai, who was the Governor of the town engaged the Burmese in a hand to hand fight until his two long swords were broken, and thus won the epithet of the "Broken Sword." When a Thai army under the command of Chao Phya Chakri and Chao Phya Surasih reached Lampang, Phya Chaban and Phya Kawila, the two leading officials who had deserted the Burmese joined him in laying siege to Chiang Mai and soon King Taksin arrived on the spot. The city fell to the Thai armies in January 1775, but the Burmese Governor and the Commander managed to escape with their families. Before his departure for Thon Buri, the King conferred honours and distinction on those who had contributed to the success of his campaign. Phya Chaban was made Governor of Chiang Mai with the title of Phya Wichienprakarn, while Phya Kawila and Phya Waiwongsa governed Lampang and Lamphun respectively. Chao Phya Chakri was directed to prolong his stay in order to assist them in the pacification of the north, which included the Laotian states. However, the Burmese King considered that as the Laotian states constituted his base for the maintenance of Burmese power in the territory further east, namely, Luang Prabang and Wienchan (Vientiane), Chiang Mai must be taken back, and so a Burmese army of 6,000 men was sent there to carry out its mission in 1776. The Burmese entered the city, but were forced out by a Thai army under Chao Phya Surasih which had marched to its relief. Chiang Mai had suffered from the recent campaigns so badly that its population was greatly reduced and impoverished, and in the event of a new Burmese attack, it could not defend itself. For these reasons, King Taksin abandoned the city and its remaining inhabitants were transplanted to Lampang. Chiang Mai thus became a deserted city and continued to be in this state for fifteen years.

The annexation of Champasak or Bassac led King Taksin indirectly to send an expedition against Wiengchan. In 1777, the ruler of Champasak, which was at that time an independent principality bordering on the Thai eastern frontier, supported the Governor of Nangrong near Khorat, who had rebelled against the Thai King. A Thai army under Chao Phya Chakri was ordered to move against the rebel, who was caught and executed, and having received reinforcements under Chao Phya Surasih, he advanced to Champasak, where the ruler, Chao O and his deputy, were captured and were summarily beheaded. Champasak was added to the Kingdom of Siam, and King Taksin was so pleased with Chao Phya Chakri's conduct of the campaign that he promoted him to be Somdech Chao Phya Mahakasatsuek Piluekmahima Tuknakara Ra-adet (meaning the supreme Chao Phya, Great Warrior-King who was so remarkably powerful that every city was afraid of his might)—being the highest title of nobility that a commoner could reach. It would be equivalent to the rank of an English duke.

In Vientiane, a Minister of State, Pra Woh, had rebelled against the ruling Prince and fled to the Champasak territory, where he set himself up at Donmotdang near the present city of Ubon. He made formal submission to Siam, when she annexed Champasak, but after the withdrawal of the Thai army, he was attacked and killed by the Vientiane troops. This action was instantly regarded by King Taksin as a great insult to him, and at his command, Somdech Chao Phya Mahakasatsuek invaded Vientiane with an army of 20,000 men in 1778. It would be useful here to briefly summarise the history of Laos which had been separated into two principalities of Luang Prabang and Vientiane since the beginning of the eighteenth century. The Prince of Luang Prabang, who was in enmity with the Prince of Vientiane, submitted to Siam for his own safety, bringing his men to join Somdech Chao Phya Mahakasatsuek in besieging the city. After a siege of about four months, the Thais took Vientiane and carried off the image of the Emerald Buddha to Thon Buri. The Prince of Vientiane managed to escape and went into exile. Thus Luang Prabang and Vientiane became Thai dependencies.

Nothing definite is known about the origin of the celebrated Emerald Buddha. It is believed that this image was carved from green jasper by an artist or artists in northern India about two thousand years ago. It was taken to Ceylon and then to Chiang Rai, a town in the north of Siam where it was, in 1434, found intact in a chedi which had been struck by lightning. As an object of great veneration among Thai Buddhists, it was deposited in a monastery in Lampang, Chiang Mai, Luang Prabang, Vientiane, Thon Buri, and eventually in Bangkok at the beginning of the reign of King Yodfachulaloke or Rama I (1782-1809).

In 1769, Cambodia was in turmoil again, due to the rivalry for the throne by two royal brothers, the elder of whom was King Ramraja (Non). Having suffered defeat at the hands of his brother (Ton) who was aided by the Annamite troops, he sought shelter in Siam. Prince Ton proclaimed himself as King Narairaja. This struggle afforded an opportunity to King Taksin to resuscitate Thai suzerainty over Cambodia as in the days of Ayutthaya. An army was despatched to assist the ex-King Ramraja to regain his power, but met with no success. In 1771, however, the Thai forces won back the Cambodia throne for him, but Narairaja retreated to the east of the country. In the end, Ramraja and Narairaja came to a compromise, whereby the former became the first King and the latter was the second King or Maha Upayoraj, and Prince Tam was Maha Uparat or Deputy to the first and the second King. This arrangement proved to be unsatisfactory. Prince Tam was murdered, while the second King died suddenly. Believing that King Ramraja was responsible for their deaths, many prominent officials under the leadership of Prince Talaha (Mu) revolted, caught him and drowned him in the river in 1780. Prince Talaha put Prince Ang Eng, the four year old son of the ex-King Narairaja, on the throne with himself acting as Regent, but he soon leaned too much on Annam, thus coming into conflict with King Taksin's policy to support a pro-Thai prince on the Cambodia throne. The Thai King therefore decided on an invasion of Cambodia. A Thai army of 20,000 under Somdech Chao Phya Mahakasatsuek moved into Cambodia, and in the event of his success in subduing the country, he was to assist in crowning Taksin's son, Prince Intarapitak, as King of Cambodia. With the aid of an Annamite army, Prince Talaha was prepared to take his stand against the Thai forces at Phnompenh, but before any fighting started, serious disturbances which had broken out in Siam made Somdech Chao Phya Mahakasatsuek decide on a hasty return to Thon Buri, after handing the command of the army to Chao Phya Surasih.

In Thon Buri, King Taksin became insane. He had, in fact, been eccentric for a few years, probably due to the war strain and overwork arising from absolute rule. When he was out of his mind, he inflicted cruel punishment on those who would not comply with his wishes, an instance of which was the flogging of many monks for their refusal to make obeisance to him as a self-styled incarnation of the Buddha. A revolt against him broke out at Ayutthaya and was led by Phya San who was so successful in his venture that he held the King and the senior princes in captivity. As soon as Somdech Chao Phya Mahakasatsuek had arrived at the capital in April 1782, he consulted all the principal officials as to the punishment to be meted out to the mad King. Their unanimous counsel was death for him.

Taksin was accordingly put to death. The rebellious Phya San and his chief collaborators suffered the same fate. For the peace and tranquillity of the Kingdom, they humbly offered the crown to Somdech Chao Phya Mahakasatsuek who thereupon ascended the throne as King Ramatibodi at the age of forty five. He inaugurated the Bangkok period under the Chakri dynasty, named after his title of Chao Phya Chakri.

# CHAPTER X

# SIAM UNDER RAMA I (1782-1809),
# RAMA II (1809-1824) AND RAMA III (1824-1851)

KING RAMATIBODI who founded the present Chakri dynasty was given the posthumous title of Pra Buddha Yodfachulaloke by his grandson and that of Rama I by his great-great-grandson. For the sake of convenience, all the Kings, or at least the first six Kings of this dynasty will be referred to as King Rama I, King Rama II, etc. King Rama I raised his brother, Chao Phya Surasih, to the exalted position of the Maha Uprat (Deputy King), commonly known as the Wang Na - the Prince of the Front Palace, and promoted his nephew, Prince Anurak-devesr to be the Prince of the Rear Palace (Deputy Maha Uparat) generally called the Wang Lang. These two Princes predeceased the king who in 1806 appointed as the Maha Uparat his eldest son, Prince Isarasuntorn, who was born of his Queen.

The succession to the throne in Siam from the Sukhothai period to the reign of King Rama V or Chulalongkorn (1868-1910) might be a source of confusion to those who are not familiar with the Thai Royal Family. It was not systematically regulated, as the King, being the Lord of Life, could alter the order of succession at his will. The Palace Law, proclaimed by King Boromtrailokanat was not clear about this matter. This was one of the causes of the struggle for the throne in the Ayutthaya period. The normal practice seemed to be that the King appointed his brother to be the Maha Uparat so as to prepare him for the throne, but he could install or nominate his son as his successor.

King Rama I had 42 children, 17 sons and 25 daughters, when he died in 1809 at the age of seventy two. He pas succeeded by the Maha Uparat, Prince Isarasuntorn, as King Rama II or Pra Buddha Loethlahnaphalai, another posthumous title created by his son, Rama III. At his accession, the new King was forty two years old, having acquired considerable experience in the civil and military affairs of the Kingdom, as he had been associated very closely with his father in the government and had accompanied him on most of his military expeditions. Like his father, he had taken the temporary vows of a monk. At the very beginning of Rama II's reign, Prince Kasatra, who was King Taksin's son, conspired against him. He and his adherents, including his sister, were arrested and executed. The King proceeded to fill the office of the Maha Uparat with his half brother, Prince Senanurak, but he outlived him. After the death of this Prince in 1817, this exalted position was left vacant.

King Rama II had a larger family than his predecessor, since he begot 73 children, 38 boys and 35 girls from 38 different mothers. When he died in 1824 at the age of fifty seven, he left a vacant throne with no designated heir. With the consent of the Accession

PAINTING OF KING RAMA I'S RETURN FROM CAMBODIA
TO RESTORE PEACE AND ORDER IN SIAM

Council, which consisted of leading princes and senior officials, Prince Chesdabodin became King Rama III or Nangklao.  He was Rama II's eldest surviving son by a minor wife who was a commoner, and his real name was Tub.  When he succeeded to the throne, he was in his middle age of thirty seven and was well versed in the government of the realm, as he had been in charge of the Treasury, Foreign Trade, Foreign Affairs, Justice and Palace Police and had also represented the King on a military expedition in Kanchanaburi.

King Rama III created his uncle, Prince Sakdipalasep, as the Maha Uparat.  When the Maha Uparat died in 1832, no successor was appointed.  There was, however, another uncle of the King by name of Prince Raksaronnaret who thought that as the senior member of the Royal Family, he would be promoted to that high post.  As he superintended the Royal Household, he was entrusted with many responsibilities and thus wielded much power.  Apparently being disappointed with the King, he began to abuse his office to such an extent that frequent complaints were made against him.  It also transpired that he was plotting against Rama III.  Consequently he was accused of high treason, bribery and embezzlement.  Since the charges against him were proved in a special court, he was put to death in the royal manner in 1848.  Although Rama III had 51 children, none of his 22 sons was a prince of the Chao Fa or first rank, because he did not raise any wife to be his queen.  Furthermore, he did not designate any of his sons as the heir to the throne, probably thinking that their mothers had no blue blood.  He had ruled the country for twenty seven years before he became gravely ill. He requested the Accession Council to choose a suitable prince for the throne. On his death in 1851, the Council offered the crown to Prince Mongkut, as he was Rama II's son of the first rank. Thus Mongkut became King Chomklao, but foreigners have since then been calling him King Mongkut.

Regarding the reconstruction and consolidation of the Kingdom, Rama I began by moving in 1782 the capital from Thon Buri to Bangkok for strategic, geographical and religious reasons.

Generally speaking, foreigners know the capital of Thailand by the name of Bangkok. According to Seidenfaden's *Guide to Bangkok*, "no other city in Southeastern Asia compares with Bangkok in the gripping and growing interest which leaves a permanent and fragrant impression on the mind of the visitor. It is difficult to set down in words, precisely whence comes the elusive fascination of Bangkok. With a wealth of imposing temples, beautiful palaces, other characteristic buildings and monuments, Bangkok offers a vista of fascinating views." In Thai, Bangkok is made up of two words: namely, "bang" and "kok," signifying a "district," or "village" on the river and a "hog plum" respectively; therefore it means the "village of hog plum." Usually the Thai people refer to their metropolis in its abbreviated form as Krungtep, meaning the city of gods or angels just like Los Angeles in California, U.S.A. As a matter of fact, its full name is "Krungtep, Maha Nakorn, Amorn Ratanakosindra, Mahindrayudhya, Mahadilokpop Noparatana Rajdhani, Burirom, Udom Rajnivet Mahastan, Amorn Pimarn Avatarn Satit, Sakkatuttiya Vishnukarm Prasit," which may be translated into English as follows: "The city of gods, the great city, the residence of the Emerald Buddha, the impregnable city (of Ayutthaya) of God Indra, the grand capital of the world endowed with nine precious gems, the happy city, abounding in enormous royal palaces which resemble the heavenly abode where reigns the reincarnated God, a city given by Indra and built by Vishnukarm."

Bangkok was a small fishing village situated on the left bank where the Chao Phya river or the River Menam formed a huge bend about 25 kilometres from its estuary (as the crow flies), when King Ramatibodi I (Utong) founded Ayutthaya as the second capital of Thailand in 1350. King Prajai (1534-1546) caused a channel to be dug across this neck of land (the narrowest part of the bend), which in a few years became the main waterway, which flows past the present Grand Palace. During the reign of King Mahachakpat (1549-1569), the status of Bangkok was raised to that of a town known as Thon Buri, but the new name failed to acquire popularity among the Europeans who continued to record it by the old name. The town gradually attracted an increasing number of people who settled there, since it was a convenient stopping place from the sea to Ayutthaya, and by the time of King Narai (1656-1688) it was a flourishing trading centre.

Foreign merchants and missionaries who maintained intercourse with Siam did not adopt Thon Buri for Bangkok, nor did they begin to regard the land on the eastern bank of the Chao Phya river as a separate district. To them, Bangkok covered both Thon Buri and its surroundings.

Again Thon Buri appeared on the scene of Thai history, when it reached its zenith as the capital of King Taksin. As Thon Buri was a small town, Taksin's available forces, both soldiers and sailors, could man its fortifications, and should he find it impossible to hold it against an enemy's attack, he could collect and embark his troops and beat a hasty retreat to Chanthaburi, a town on the east coast, which was his first stronghold in the hard-won fight against Burma. Thon Buri served as his seat of government for a period of fifteen years, during which he did not fail by any means to strengthen its defence. A huge wall of brick and mortar was erected along the Lawd canal on the eastern bank of the Chao Phya river, so that the stretch of the river flowing through Thon Buri could safely be converted into a base for warships. It is now a general consensus of opinion that Rama I was certainly justified in making Bangkok his capital. With the river flowing through its centre, Thon Buri was difficult to defend in case of a direct assault, as he had learned this from his bitter experience in fighting the Burmese at Phitsanulok. The palace in this city stood at the bend of the river which might be subject to constant erosion. Besides, it was not possible to extend its precincts, as it was sandwiched by two monasteries. Perhaps King Rama I entertained a strong desire to start a new life for both the country and the people, when he ordered the transfer of the capital. The site for the Grand Palace at Bangkok occupied a built-in area, being a Chinatown, whose magistrate, Phya Rajasethi, was a rich merchant. The Chinese community was removed to the district of Sampeng, about three kilometres to the south of the Palace, which now constitutes the prosperous Thai-Chinese business quarter. The wall along the Lawd canal which had been built by command of King Taksin was demolished, since it was only 300 metres from the Royal Palace, thus obstructing the extension of the city area towards the east. A new canal at the distance of less two kilo- metres from the Royal Palace was dug from one end to the other end of the Chao Phya river, covering a length of 7.2 kilometres, and it is to-day called Klong Banglampoo and Klong Ong Ang. Strong and solid walls were laid down along the inner side of this cannal, being 3.6 metres high and 2.70 metres thick and dotted with 16 main gates and 16 forts, two of which now remain as historic places on the 200 metre wall, namely, Fort Mahakal and Fort Prasumeru. The construction of the Grand Palace including the Temple of the Emerald Buddha within its compound having been completed in 1785, Bangkok was given the official long name of Krungtep etc., as has already been mentioned. It is interesting to note that the new capital was built in such a way as to be an exact replica of Ayutthaya, many of the old city's monuments being restored in name. Though it was small in area, it formed the genesis of the Bangkok which we so much admire to-day.

Some accounts of Bangkok, written by foreign visitors, are really note-worthy. In his *Journal of an Embassy to the Courts of Siam and Cochin-China*, Dr. John Craw- furd whom the Governor-General of India, the Marquess of Hastings, had appointed as a British envoy to Siam in 1822, described her capital thus: "Bangkok extends along the banks of the Menam, to the distance of about two miles and a half; but it is of no great breadth, probably not exceeding one mile and a half. The principal portion of the town is on the left bank of the river, where the palace is situated. The accounts which we received of its population were very vague and little to be relied on. Some of them made it amount to so much as one hundred and fifty thousand. Judging by the extent of ground on which it stands, I should not be disposed to estimate the inhabitants at more than one-third of this number."

According to Bishop Pallegoix, who was engaged in the propagation of the Catholic faith in Siam in the middle of the nineteenth century, "Bangkok (village des oliviers sauvages), est devenu le siège du gouvernement depuis la ruine de Juthia. Cette ville n'a pas encore quatre-vingt-dix ans d' existence, et compte deja plus de 400,000 habitants.

Bangkok a inherité du nom de Juthia, aussi l'appelle-t-on Krungthèpha-maha-nakhon-si-ajutthaja-maha-dilok-raxathani, etc., c'est-à-dire, grande ville royale des anges, belle inexpugnable, etc. Elle est située sur les deux bords du fleuve Me-Nam, à huit lieues de la mer. La ville proprement dit forme une île de deux lieues de tour; elle est entourée de murailles crénelées et flanquée de tours ou bastions de distance en distance. Située au milieu d' immenses jardins ornés d' une verdure luxuriante et perpétuelle, elle offre un aspect très-pittoresque; des navires et une mulitude de jonques pavoisées sont à la file sur les deux bords; on voit s'élever dans les airs des flèches dorées, des dômes, de hautes pyramides d' une structure admirable, garnies de dessins en porcelaine de toutes couleurs; les toits étagés des pagodes, ornés de belles dorures et couverts en tuile varnissée, qui réfléchissent les rayons du soleil; deux rangées de plusieurs milliers de boutiques flottantes sur des radeaux, qui se déroulent devant vous, en suivant les sinuosités d'un fleuve ma-jestueux, sillonné en tous sens par des milliers de barques, dont la plupart sont très-élégants; la forteresse blanche comme neige, la ville avec ses tours et ses nombreuses portes; les canaux alignés qui traversent la cité, la flèche dorée du palais étagé à quadruple façade, la variété des édifices à l' indienne, à la chinoise, à l' européenne; les costumes singuliers des diverses nations, le son des instrument de musique, les chants des comédies, le mouvement et la vie qui animent cette grande ville, tout cela est pour les étrangers un specatcle qui leur cause une agréable surprise.

Il n'y a pas une seule voiture dans la capital, tout le monde va en barque: le fleuve et les canaux sont presque les seuls chemins fréquentés. Ce n' est guère que dans l' intérieur de la cité et aux bazars ou marchés qu'on trouve des rues pavées en larges briques.

Ce qu'il ya de plus remarquable à Bangkok c'est le palais et les pagodes royales. Le palais est une enceinte de hautes murailles, qui a plus d' un quart de lieue de tour.

Les pagodes royales sont d'une magnificence dont on ne se fait pas une idée en Europe; il y en a qui ont coûté jusqu'à 200 quintaux d' argent, (plus de quatre millions de francs). On en compte onze dans l' enceinte des murs de la ville; et une vingtaine en dehors des murs.

Les habitations à Bangkok sont de trois sortes; les unes sont en briques et fort élégantes; d' autres en planches, et celles du pauvre peuple en bambous. Aussi arrive-t-il que les incendies sont fréquents et désastreux; il n' est pas rare de voir le feu consumer quatre ou cinq cents maisons; mais dans sept ou huit jours tout est rebâti â neuf, grâce aux parents et amis qui viennent en aide aux incendiés."

Although the absolute monarchy was the form of government, Rama I's rule was endowed with the ten kingly virtues. He devoted himself to a thorough reorganisation of the administration which had fallen into a chaotic condition since the destruction of Ayutthaya. The administrative system, as created by King Boromatrailokanat and strengthened by King Ramatibodi II of Ayutthaya, was adopted and supervised at a close range. The Praklang came to control the Harbour Department and the sea-ports and thus he shared the provincial administration with the Samuhanayok and the Samukalahom. In addition to his regular post of the Minister of Finance, he also acted as the Foreign Minister, the Minister of Foreign Trade, and the Minister of Sea-port Government. Later, a practice grew up, whereby senior or outstanding princes received appointments as superintendents of certain ministries or departments. It may therefore be repeated that Rama I's government was still highly centralized with officials whom he could trust to the fullest measure in charge of the various offices. It was without doubt suitable for the country and the people of that period, since education was practically non-existent for the common people. He then undertook a reform of the Buddhist Church. The Buddhist hierachy was reorganized, and only prelates whose unblemished conduct commanded respect were appointed to high posts in the Church, an instance of which was the reinstatement of the Supreme Patriarch, Somdech Pra Buddhacharn, and Pra Pimontam who had been demoted by King Taksin to be ordinary monks. The monks' discipline was tightened in order to maintain the respectable standard of their behaviour; 128 profligate monks were by King Rama I's decree unfrocked due to drinking intoxicants, wandering out at night to see entertainments, rubbing shoulders with women, engaging in loose talk, and boarding Chinese junks in order to obtain fanciful objects of merchandise. The Buddhist Scripture or the Tripitaka was assiduously revised at the royal expense, for most of the authoritative books on the subject had been scattered or lost in the conflagration of Ayutthaya. A Council of the Church consisting of 250 learned monks and laymen was summoned in 1788 to collect and collate reliable texts for the compilation of a new edition of the Buddhist Scripture which was completed in five months. The King built and restored twelve monasteries, in addition to a monastery called Wat Prajetubon or Wat Po at the rear of the Royal Palace.

Essentially a good government depends on well arranged, correct and just laws. King Rama I was fully alive to the need of such laws, for most of the law texts had suffered the same fate as the Buddhist Scriptures in 1767. The laws which were recovered and put in book form at the beginning of his reign were not satisfactory, since they were written from memory of judges or lawyers who were survivors of Ayutthaya. A commission of legal experts was therefore set up to revise the laws in 1805, and the result of its work was the Laws of Three Seals (Lion, Elephantine Tiger, and Glass Lotus Flower) or the Law Code of 1805-1808.

Rama I's reign was a literary renaissance after the ransacking of Ayutthaya. Inspite of such pressing matters as the war with Burma, he found time to uplift the dignity of Thai literature. In connection with this matter, Prince Dhani Nivat stated in his book on *The Restoration of Culture by Rama I* that the cultural restoration dealt largely with Liberal Arts, especially Arts, as understood in the English sense. Not only did he encourage the writing of prose and poetry, but he himself composed poems so well that he is now accepted as a poet in the history of Thai literature. He took upon himself the task of rewriting and revising the *Ramakien* and the *Inao*. The *Ramakien* is the Thai version of the Ramayana which is a great epic of Hindu inspiration; it ranks as a literary work of enormous popularity and is the only one used in the classical masked play called "Khon." One great author who lived in Rama I's reign was Chao Phya Praklang (personal name-Hon), his Minister of Finance, who wrote both prose and poetry. Among his well-known works are the *Sam Kok* which he translated from the San Kuo, being an episode in Chinese history during the age of the three kingdoms, and the *Rajadhiraj* for which he obtained material from an episode in Peguan history. These two books are prescribed as School Readers of Thai language, and every boy and girl who finish their high school are familiar with them.

Rama II was a greater poet than his father, who cultivated his love of versification. He wrote seven epic poems for the Thai classical ballet, two of which stand out prominently, namely, the Inao and the Ramakien. The Inao, which covered forty five volumes of the old type of Thai books (accordion-pleated books), was the product of his own effort,

STATUE OF SUNTORN POU, FAMOUS POET
IN RAMA II'S REIGN AT THE TOP
AND
STATUE OF PRA APAIMANI, HERO OF HIS
ROMANTIC EPIC AT THE BOTTOM

while the other poems were composed in collaboration with his eldest son, Prince Chesda-bodin, Prince Pitakmontri and other poets such as Pou or Suntorn Pou (1787-1855). Indeed the King enjoyed their company when they met to compose poems. Pou became his favourite because of his sharp wit and great artistry, and he was ennobled as Khun Sun-thornvoharn. In King Rama IV or Mongkut's reign, he was promoted to be a Pra of the same name. Due to the excellent quality of his numerous works, he is to-day recognized as "one of the giants of Thai literature." His statue has been unveiled at his birthplace in Amphoe Klaeng in the province of Rayong. His popular work of Pra Apaimani may be regarded the acme of his wonderful ability in making the Thai language worth a profound study; it is a romantic epic which records the adventures and love affairs of Pra Apai, the hero, and his brother.

Another aspect of Rama II's internal activities was the restoration and construction of Buddhist monasteries which had been initiated by his august father, the most famous of

PAINTING OF KING RAMA III IN A ROYAL PROCESSION
TO A MONASTERY, ON THE CEILING OF THE ANANTA SAMAKOM HALL,
PRESENT SEAT OF THE NATIONAL ASSEMBLY

which was Wat Arun, generally known as the Temple of the Dawn. The magnificent central phraprang at Wat Arun—the tallest religious building in the Bangkok area to-day —was built during the Third Reign. The temple was begun by Rama II, but Rama III replaced the 52-feet central phraprang put up by his predecessor by a tower 227 feet tall. He himself displayed his artistic skill in religious work when he carved the doors of the vihara or prayer house of the Sutat monastery. His pious interest in Buddhism led him to send a religious mission on a study tour of Ceylon which had just become a British colony in 1815.

Rama III outdid his predecessor in the support of the Buddhist Church. He built three new monasteries and restored thirty five monasteries. Most of these monasteries were decorated with porcelain pieces in the Chinese architectural style, since Siam and China traded on a much larger scale than before in his reign, and porcelain was one of the imports which were loaded on Chinese junks bound for Bangkok. As steamships were coming into use, it seemed inevitable they would push Chinese junks out of business. The King therefore had a chedi at Wat Yannawa erected in the shape of a Chinese junk, so that later generations could see the means of transportation which helped to enrich and beautify the city of Bangkok and contributed in some degree to the progress of the country. Mention must be made of a chedi on an island at the entrance of the Chao Phya river as well as the huge image of the reclining Buddha and the mural pictures in the main building of Wat Po. The chedi on an island was constructed to emphasize to newcomers that

Siam was a Buddhist Kingdom, while the reclining Buddha, which is 160 feet long, built of brick and mortar and covered with gold leaf, was an act of merit. Since knowledge was not widespread and the rate of illiteracy was very high, the King aimed at converting this monastery into an institution of higher learning, where the wall paintings and inscriptions on small stone slabs dealt with Medicine, Osteopathy, Astrology, and other branches of study. Such visual representations would be a boon to those who were eager for professional knowledge. Simultaneously Rama III gave an impetus to the Buddhist studies, in which examinations for the various grades were held in the Royal Palace, and a monk who passed the parien or qualifying examination for Buddhist discipline would be supported at the royal expense. Besides presiding over the Buddhist Church, the Prince Patriarch Paramanujit achieved fame as the foremost literary luminary of the day. Among the great works of which he was the author were the *Pathamasombodhikatha, the Talaing Phai, Krisna's Exhortations to Her Sister*, and a History of Ayutthaya, and he also wrote the last part of the *Samuthakhot*, thus completing the book relating a Jataka tale about the Lord Buddha. *The Pathamasombodhikatha* narrates the life of the Lord Buddha. The *Talaing Phai* is a poetical glorification of the heroic exploits of King Naresuan the Great; *Krisna's Exhortations to Her Sister*, which deals with the duties of a wife towards her husband, seems to be out of date in view of the modern evolution of Thai womanhood. All these books are still prescribed for a thorough study at the school or the university level. In the field of literature, Rama III kept up the royal tradition of composing poetry, perhaps as a relaxation after the arduous state duties, and his chief contribution is a dramatic poem called *Sangsiljai*.

Burma still loomed large as an enemy of Siam in King Rama I and Rama II's reigns, since her powerful monarch, Bodawpaya or Padung (1782-1819), nourished his high ambition to extend his dominions in the same fashion as his renowned father, Alaungpaya. During the first three years on the throne, he was fully occupied in the restoration of peace and order in the Kingdom, and transferred his capital to Amarapura about six miles or nine kilometres northeast of Ava. Contemporaneously he thought that the change of the reign and dynasty would create chaos in Siam, and thus was an opportunity for him to invade the country.

In 1785, Bodawpaya launched a full scale invasion of Siam and his nine armies of 144,000 men crossed the Thai boundaries at five different points—at Chumphon for an attack of the southern provinces, through the Bongtee Pass against Ratchaburi and Phetchaburi, through the Three Pagodas' Pass against Bangkok, through the Melamao Pass against Tak, and from Chiang Saen for the capture of Phitsanulok. King Rama I could master only 70,000 troops, but he fearlessly stood up against the enemy, relying on newly devised tactics, the main principle of which was to deploy a large army at the frontiers in order to repel the invaders instead of fighting them on their march towards the capital or concentrating all the forces that could be mobilised in the capital. The Burmese King led the main attack against the Thai territory through the Three Pagodas' Pass, but he proved to be an incompetent commander, lacking even in basic principles of logistics. On approaching Kanchanaburi, he found that a Thai army had already established itself strongly on the plain of Lardya. For this reason, he had to set up his camp on the mountains which were bare of food supply, and the deliveries of provisions which were transported from Burma were subject to frequent attacks of the Thai guerrillas. After a siege of about two months, the Thai soldiers took the Burmese camp by a direct assault, forcing Bodawpaya to escape in a great hurry.    The other Burmese armies suffered a similar fate and their remnants were compelled to withdraw.

After their initial victories in the southern provinces in 1785, the Burmese besieged the town of Thalang on the island of Phuket. During that time, the Governor of the town died, but with the co-operative efforts of the officials and the people, his wife, Chan, and her sister Mook organized a very effective defence against the Burmese and held them off for more than a month.   Eventually starvation forced the Burmese to retire from the island. As a reward for their exemplary services, Rama I conferred a title of nobility on Chan as Tao or Lady Tepsatri, while Mook was ennobled as Tao Srisuntorn.   The Burmese were then mopped up by Rama I's Maha Uparat who followed up his successful expedition by regaining control over Pattani.   There he captured a siege gun nine foot long which, at his order, was brought to Bangkok. Fearing Rama I's might, Kedah, Perlis, Kelantan and Trengganu again submitted to Siam as her vassal states.   Before doing so, however, the Sultan of Kedah or Saiburi had in 1786 leased the island of Penang to Captain Francis Light and the British Government at a nominal sum, in the hope of getting British support to guarantee his independence.   Fourteen years later he ceded the province of Wellesley to Great Britain apparently without a protest from Siam.

In this book on *The Restoration of Thailand under Rama I, 1782-1800*, Klaus Wenk asserted that "Thai pretensions to control over the regions were not based on legal title voluntarily accepted by the Malayan states but simply on the claims of the stronger to extend its boundaries at the expense of the weaker, together, perhaps, with declarations of loyalty made under compulsion at the time of earlier conquests."

King Bodawpaya persisted in his attempt to overwhelm Siam, but his army was, in 1786, utterly defeated at Tadindang, a district in Kanchanaburi, thus ending henceforth any plan to advance to Bangkok.    In 1787, the Burmese who still held Chiang Rai and Chiang Saen made an attack on Lampang and Pasang, but they were again heavily routed.  Meanwhile Rama I had designated Prince Kawila of Lampang to re-establish Chiang Mai as a city with the assistance of the Maha Uparat. He thus became Prince Kawila of Chiang Mai, while his younger brother, Kamsome, was appointed Prince of Lampang.  Chiang Mai therefore recovered its status as an important city of Siam.   Their descendants continued to rule these two cities as vassals until their power began to be gradually whittled down in King Chulalongkorn's reign, and the status of vassal princes was definitely suspended in King Prajadhipok's reign.   On his return from Chiang Mai, the Maha Uparat brought with him an ancient bronze image called Pra Buddha Sihing which is now housed in the National Museum.  Cast in Ceylon and taken over to Nakhon Si Thammarat, it went on its peregrinations to Sukhothai, Ayutthaya, Kamphaeng Phet, Chiang Rai and Chiang Mai. The reason why it is popularly worshipped is that it is supposed to bring peace, prosperity and happiness to the people.

It now became King Rama I's turn to take the offensive against the Burmese for the purpose of demonstrating the strength of the country and furthering the morale of the people.  In 1787, he attempted to take Tavoy, but had to retire, due to shortage of food supply. Subsequently, in 1791, the Governors of Tavoy, Mergui and Tenesserim overthrew their allegiance to the Burmese King and requested protection from Rama I.  This led him to undertake an invasion of Burma in 1793, but it failed miserably owing to the treachery of the local people and difficulties in transporting military supplies over the mountains.

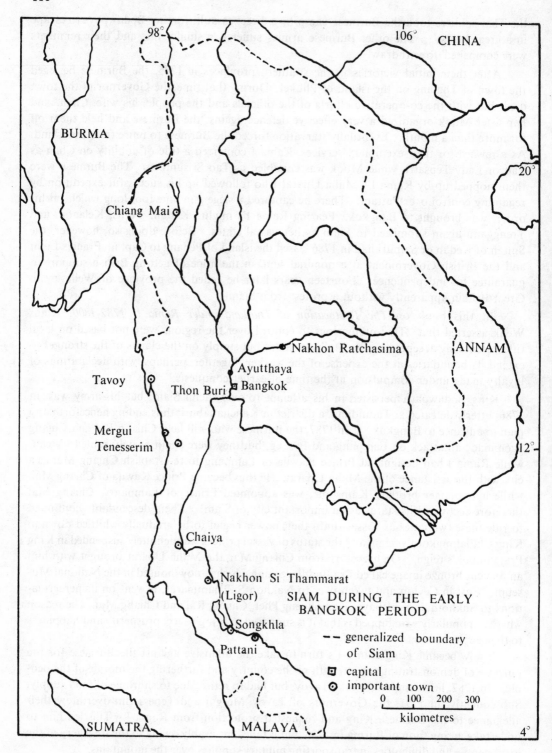

98°
106°
CHINA
20°
BURMA
Chiang Mai
Nakhon Ratchasima
ANNAM
Ayutthaya
Tavoy
Bangkok
Thon Buri
12°
Mergui
Tenesserim
Chaiya
Nakhon Si Thammarat
(Ligor)
SIAM DURING THE EARLY
BANGKOK PERIOD
Songkhla
Pattani
– – generalized boundary
of Siam
□ capital
⊙ important town
0    100   200   300
kilometres
SUMATRA
MALAYA
4°

In 1797, King Bodawpaya ordered an army to march once more against Chiang Mai, the loss of which he had felt very badly. The Burmese reached the city which had been rebuilt by Prince Kawila as his seat of government the year before, but they were repelled and fell back to Chiang Saen. Enraged at Kawila's attack on the town of Sard which was under his suzerainty, the Burmese King sent an army to besiege Chiang Mai on all sides in 1802. The Thai forces under the Deputy Maha Uparat moved up to the relief of the city, drove back the Burmese and cleared them out of Chiang Saen, their last stronghold on the Thai territory. Subsequently in 1804, they chased them out of the eastern part of the Shan states including Chiang Rung, Lua, Khern and Sibsongpunna, which then recognized Rama I as their overlord.

The Burmese were still Siam's chief enemy in King Rama II's reign. They captured the island of Phuket and attacked Chumphon, but their enterprises were failures, as they were expelled from the southern provinces in 1810. Hearing about an outbreak of cholera which had caused havoc with the Thai people, the Burmese King, Bagyidaw, entered into an intrigue with the Sultan of Kedah to invade Siam just like his predecessor in 1820. Rama II took no chance to be taken unaware, and so commanded Prince Chesdabodin and Prince Sakdipalasep to undertake the defence of the west of the country against any hostile move on the part of the Burmese, but nothing came out of it, due to a rebellion in Manipur. Soon after the Burmese were deeply involved in a frontier dispute with Great Britain which ruled India at that time, and this led to the first Anglo-Burmese war (1824-1826). Thus the Burmese ceased to cause trouble to Siam, nor did the Thais seek to revenge themselves on them. The beginning of the war coincided with Rama III's accession to the throne, and although Siam was approached by Great Britain as a possible ally, she preferred to pursue the policy of neutrality. True, three Thai armies, one of which was under the command of Chao Phya Mahayota (Toria), moved into Lower Burma, but they soon withdrew to avoid any misunderstanding with Great Britain.

In connection with Cambodia, King Rama I, as Taksin's general, had been entrusted with the task of getting rid of Prince Talaha, but before he could take any step in this direction, he had to return to Thon Buri to restore order and solve his master's problem. Subsequently a Cambodian named Ban, who had served Rama I with the title of Phya Yomarat overthrew Prince Talaha and installed himself as Regent for Prince Ang Eng. However, he held power only for a short time, and as he was unable to repel the inroads of the Chams from Annam, which was in the throes of a civil war, he evacuated his protégé, Prince Ang Eng, together with his younger brother and sister to the Thai Court at Bangkok. Phya Yomarat was promoted to be Chao Phya Apaipubet as a reward for his service, while Prince Ang Eng was brought up as an adopted son of King Rama I. With the suppression of the Chams, Chao Phya Apaipubet became Regent for a second time. In 1794, Rama I enthroned Ang Eng as King of Cambodia after he had been ordained a monk for a short period, and in the following year he sent him back to rule the country as King Narairamatibodi. Battambong and Siemrap were sequestered from Cambodia and came under the direct rule of Siam with Chao Phya Apaipubet as governor. They were perhaps the price which Ang Eng paid for his restoration, but after occupying the throne for three years, he died and was succeeded by his son as King Utairaja. Both the father and the son recognized Rama I as their master, but not for long.

At the beginning of Rama II's reign, the Cambodian nobles were divided into the pro-Thai and the pro-Annam parties. As Utairaja alleged that he had been offended by Rama I, he refused to pay respects to his remains nor did he send Cambodian troops to defend the Thai Kingdom against any possible invasion. He therefore turned to Annam or Vietnam for protection, but through the mediation of the Vietnamese Emperor Gialong, who was grateful to the memory of Rama I, Siam agreed to permit him to resume his rule with a Vietnamese commissioner as his adviser in 1812. King Utairaja was again hostile to Rama II, when his army tried unsuccessfully to recover Battambong in 1815. The Thai King, however, pardoned him, for he did not wish to face at the same time trouble from Cambodia in the east and Burma in the west.

In Vietnam a Tayson rebellion had broken out and by 1777 had captured Saigon. A Vietnamese prince, Nguyen Anh (known in Thai history as Ong Chiengsue), who was the rightful heir, went to Bangkok in 1785, where he sought protection and assistance of Rama I, which were granted without any delay. The Thai soldiers made two attempts to regain the Vietnamese throne for him, but all to no avail. With no prospect of large scale support from Rama I due to the Burmese war, he escaped by boat from Bangkok for Cochin-China, where he organized his loyal followers into a powerful army. The King had reasons for not being angry with him, as he understood very well that he was not in a position to render effective assistance to him. On the contrary, he made an alliance with Nguyen Anh, who then received the Thai aid against the Tayson rebels. Finally, he succeeded in crushing the rebels, extended his power throughout the length and breadth of Vietnam, and established himself as the Emperor Gialong (1802-1820) with Hué as his capital.

Luang Prabang, Vientiane and Champasak remained as peaceful vassal states of Siam in Rama I's reign. However, in 1819, a fanatic or magician by name of Ai Sakiet-ngong revolted against the Prince of Champasak and compelled him to leave his capital. At his urgent appeal, the Thai forces under the Governor of Nakhon Ratchasima and Prince Anu-wongse of Vientiane were ordered to march against the rebel who was caught and imprisoned. As a reward, Rama II appointed Chao Yo, son of Prince Anuwongse, as Prince of Champasak.

Chao Anuwongse, more conveniently called Anu, was a man of great ability, whose aim was to free Vientiane from subordination to Bangkok. In 1827, he rebelled against Rama III and took Nakhon Ratchasima, while his forward troops ransacked Saraburi. During his return journey, he was one day suddenly attacked by the inhabitants of these two towns whom he was carrying off. Led by the Deputy Governor of Nakhon Ratchasima and his brave wife named Mo, the Thai prisoners killed 2,000 Vientiane troops and freed themselves. Two Thai armies went in pursuit of Chao Anu, routed him in battle and occupied Vientiane in May 1827, but he escaped to the Vietnamese Court of Minh-Mang (1820 - 41). With Vietnamese aid, he recovered Vientiane, but was decisively defeated and brought down as a prisoner to Bangkok in January 1829, where he died of a chronic disease which he had contracted earlier. Appropriately enough Rama III raised the liberator of Nakhon Ratchasima, Mo, to be Tao Suranari.

Rama III was bitterly angry with the Vietnamese Emperor who had considerably reduced the Thai influence in Cambodia and had supported Prince Anu. For these reasons, he directed Chao Phya Bodindeja, the conqueror of Vientiane, to lead an army to Cambodia in 1833, where he was to clear the country of the Vietnamese troops. His next objective was Saigon where he was to help the rebels against the Emperor Minh-Mang and to be reinforced by a Thai fleet. The Thai forces encountered a stiff defence put up by the Vietnamese, as they were approaching Saigon. The Thai-Vietnamese war soon became a stalemate, since it dragged on for fourteen years, and eventually both sides made peace. The result was, however, favourable to Siam as far as Cambodia was concerned. King Utairaja who had thrown in his lot with Vietnam died in 1834. Rama III availed himself of the opportunity to crown the pro-Thai prince, Ang Duang, who had been brought up and educated in Bangkok as King Harirakramatibodi of Cambodia. Nevertheless one curious fact is that the Cambodian King continued to present his customary tribute to the Vietnamese Emperor, and this was to complicate the relations between Siam and Cambodia, when France pursued an aggressive policy in Vietnam in the middle of the nineteenth century.

Rama II's reign saw the resumption of the relations with the West which had lapsed with the end of Ayutthaya. Most of the European culture which had been introduced into Siam was lost at the destruction of the city. Only a few things survived at the beginning of the Bangkok period. They were the casting of cannon, the use of firearms and fortifications for the defence of the realm and some ointments and medical prescriptions. Curiously enough, a few dessert dishes which had been copied from the Europeans in the Ayutthaya days still remain such as the eggs' net in syrup (filet d' oeuf in French or foitong in Thai) and the sponge cake (kanom farang).

The reason why Thai intercourse with the West was not revived sooner than Rama II's reign was that the European powers were preoccupied with their own affairs. The period from the reign of King Taksin to the first few years of King Rama II's reign coincided with the British expansion in India, the American Revolution or War of American Independence, the French Revolution and the Napoleonic war. Great Britain emerged from the war with France as the victor in 1815. She began to spread to the Far East where she soon became the predominating Power, having acquired Singapore in 1819 and Malacca in 1824. She was backed up by her increasing industrial might, for she was the birthplace of the Industrial Revolution. The Portuguese were a firm and faithful ally of Great Britain and consequently they could, during the Napoleonic war, pursue their trade in Asia with Goa still serving as their headquarters and Macao as their centre for China. According to the *Collected History of Siam*, (Part 62), a sloop arrived at Bangkok with a Portuguese envoy on board in 1787 but it was not known for certain whether he came from Macao or Lisbon itself. He presented a letter from the King of Portugal to Rama I who then caused a reply to be conveyed to the sloop in a procession of royal barges. Nothing, however, came out of the exchange of letters between the two monarchs.

In 1818, the Portuguese Governor of Macao took the initiative in sending Carlos Manoel de Silveira to Siam with a mission to seek facilities for shipbuilding and trading at Bangkok. As he represented the Portuguese governor, he was received not as a royal envoy but as a foreign merchant. King Rama II granted his request, conferred on him a title of nobility as Luang Apaiwanit and allotted him a plot of land on the eastern bank of the river with a house which is the site of the present Portuguese Embassy. Carlos Silveira became a popular figure when he managed to sell guns and armaments to the Thai Government. Subsequently he was accepted as the resident Portuguese consul at Bangkok. It should be remembered that no special rights or privileges were accorded to the Portuguese in the renewal of their relations with Siam.

In 1821, an Englishman, John Morgan, went from Singapore to Bangkok at the expense of the English colony there in order to seek permission to trade in his name and in no way connected with the British Government or the East India Company, and he was received by the Praklang. On his return to Singapore, he reported that trade with Siam could be carried on only in treaty arrangements. In 1822, the Marquess of Hastings, the Governor-General of India, therefore appointed Dr. John Crawfurd as British envoy to Siam. Crawfurd was considered by the British official circle in India to be a suitable person to lead a diplomatic mission to an Asian country. Crawfurd had acquired a good deal of practical experience in the East, as he had been a physician in the Bengal Medical Service, had served under Sir Stamford Raffles in Java and had been British Resident at Singapore. The aim of his mission was to obtain facilities for British merchants and so he was instructed to negotiate for the reduction of customs duties, the revision of the regulations against British ships and abolition or at least the modification of the system of royal monopolies of the Thai Government. Moreover, he was to find ways and means to effect a reconciliation between the Thai Government and the Sultan of Kedah, Pra-ngarun, who had turned against Rama II and had fled to Penang on the approach of the Thai troops under Phya Nakhon Si Thammarat or Raja of Ligor in 1821. Lastly, he was to collect as much information as possible about the country and thus he was accompanied by Dr. Finlayson and Lieutenant Dangerfield. Dr. Finlayson, who acted as the surgeon and botanist of the party, was chiefly concerned with the flora and fauna and wrote an information diary of his Thai visit, while Dangerfield, who was a surveyor, gathered data for his work. Crawfurd's negotiations were carried on with great difficulty, because there were no Thais who could speak English any more than there were any Englishmen who could speak Thai. Whatever Crawfurd wanted to say, he had to tell his interpreter who translated it into Malay. The Thai interpreter translated the Malay version into Thai for the benefit of the Praklang. The answer to Crawfurd was communicated in the same manner. Besides the language problem, the British envoy was confronted with two insurmountable obstacles concerning the Thai request for a supply of arms and ammunition in return for trading facilities to be given to the British and also regarding the Thai insistence on a large sale of sugar to the British. So the negotiation between the Thais and the British broke down. However, Crawfurd was granted an audience by Rama II and he obtained a written promise that the amount of Thai duties would not be increased and that in future British merchants would enjoy the Praklang's benevolence. On July 16, 1822, he left Bangkok after a stay of four months. It is an undoubted fact that the visit to Siam was useful to him, as he acquired valuable information about the country. In 1828, he published in London *A Journal of an Embassy from the Governor-General of India to the Courts of Siam and Cochin-China*. In spite of its failure, his mission resulted in increased trade between Siam and Great Britain.

Crawfurd's mission was followed by Burney's visit to Bangkok in 1826. Captain Henry Burney was an official at Penang who spoke Thai and was well acquainted with the affairs of the Malay Peninsula, having successfully fulfilled missions to Nakhon Si Thammarat and Kedah. He was appointed a British envoy to Siam by the Governor-General of India with instructions to maintain friendly relations with Siam, to seek Siam's help in the first war between Great Britain and Burma, to persuade Siam to sign a commercial treaty, and to induce Siam to settle the questions of Kedah and other Malay States. Apparently the events in the Malay States and Burma exercised some influences on Rama III, who ordered his ministers to be friendly with Burney, thus expediting the negotiations between the two parties. On June 20, 1826, a treaty of friendship and commerce between Siam and Great Britain was signed. Curiously enough, it was made in four languages, namely, Thai, English, Malay and Portuguese, since neither the Thais nor the English knew the language of the other. According to the terms of the treaty, Siam agreed to replace all other taxes on trade by 1700 bahts' duty for each wa or every two metres of a ship's beam. There would be free trade according to the custom of the places, but the English had no right to import opium into Siam nor to export rice to foreign countries. Permission to rent land for an English factory must be obtained from the Thai authorities and mutual aid would be extended to shipwrecked seamen. English subjects in Siam must conduct themselves according to the laws of the country. Siam would not interfere with British trade in the Malay States which the British admitted as belonging to her, and recognized Penang Island and the Province Wellesley as British possessions as well as the independence of Perak and Selangor, while Great Britain accepted Kedah, Kelantan and Trengganu as being under Thai suzerainty. The conclusion of the treaty shows that Siam continued to uphold the policy of opening the country to foreigners as had been practised in the Ayutthaya period.

The Burney treaty of 1826 increased Siam's foreign trade with the British territories, but did not abolish the system of royal monopolies of the Thai Government. Two years after Burney's departure from Siam, an Englishman, James Hunter, settled at Bangkok as the first English resident merchant, and subsequently Rama III ennobled him as Luang Wisetpanich. The King, the leading princes and the high government officials continued to equip their ships for trading with China and other neighbouring countries and Asian merchants such as the Chinese and the Indians paid customs duties and other taxes under the old rate to the Thai Government without raising any complaint. On the other hand, the Western merchants such as the British and the Americans alleged that the Thai Government was competing with them in the import and export business.

American intercourse with Siam was inaugurated through the missionaries and merchants. In 1828, two Protestant missionaries arrived at Bangkok with an intention to teach Christianity to the Chinese who had already formed a large community. One was an Englishman, Jacob Tomlin, and the other was a German, Carl Gutzlaff. After the first few months in Siam, Gutzlaff became so enthusiastic about the country as a mission field that he appealed to various Western churches to undertake its evangelization. The American Baptist Mission became interested in Siam and the first batch of its missionaries travelled to Bangkok in 1833. They were soon joined by the Presbyterians among whom were Dr. Dan Beach Bradley and his wife. At first they confined themselves to propagating their religion to the Chinese, but not wishing to neglect the Thais, they began to give medical help and treatment to them. Subsequently they introduced vaccination against smallpox into the country. The Thais at that time took all the American missionaries to be medical doctors and called them "moh." Some of them were genuine medical doctors, but others might have received a doctorate in Divinity from America. Anyhow the American missionaries have been called "moh" down to this day. In addition to their medical work, they had a share in the dissemination of modern knowledge. Dr. Bradley and his associates pioneered the establishment of the first printing press in Bangkok in 1835, but had, at first, to buy the type of the Thai alphabet from Singapore where it was cast at the printing press of the London Missionary Society. As an official at Penang, Captain James Low had studied Thai and had become so proficient in it that he wrote a Thai grammar for the Europeans and published it at Calcutta in 1828. The American missionaries concentrated on printing books on Christianity, published a newspaper *The Bangkok Recorder*, and in 1839 they printed 9,000 copies of a royal edict on the prohibition of opium smoking for the Thai Government. *The Bangkok Recorder*, the first issue of which appeared in 1844, had a short life. While still a monk, Prince Mongkut, who later became King Rama IV, realized at once the advantages accruing from printing, and at his own expense, he ordered a printing press to be set up at Wat Bowonniwet where he took up residence. It was the first printing press owned by a Thai and competed with the American press in publishing Buddhist books. By Rama IV's command, a government printing press was established for its own use and in 1858 began to print the Royal Gazette or *Rajkitchanubeksa*, which has continued till to-day and is issued weekly. The printing press has in fact been one of the contributing factors to the advancement of Thai education.

In 1833, President Andrew Jackson appointed Edmund Roberts as the first American envoy, whom the Thais called "Emin Rabad" meaning "a nobleman from America." Roberts was a citizen of Portsmouth, New Hampshire. He had been to Cochin-China and broke his journey in Siam, while he was on his way to Muscat. American merchant ships had been calling at Bangkok occasionally to sell arms, hardware and cotton goods and to load sugar and timber, and the object of his mission was to place the United States of America on a basis of equality with other nations trading in Siam. Happily he met with almost no difficulty in negotiating a treaty with the Thai Ministers of State, since he made no demand for extraterritorial rights and limitation of import duties. The first treaty between Siam and the United States of America was concluded on March 20, 1833. It was a Treaty of Amity and Commerce, and its main purposes were to establish "a perpetual Peace between the United States of America and the Magnificent Kingdom of Siam," and to enable the Thais and the Americans to hold commercial intercourse "as long as Heaven and Earth shall endure." Under the treaty, American merchants trading in Siam "shall respect and follow the laws and customs of the country in all points," and American vessels "shall pay in lieu of import and export duties, etc., a measurement duty," that is, duty based on the ship's beam. It should be remarked that Siam was the first country in the Far East with which the United States entered into treaty relations. The Treaty of 1833 was signed eleven years before the Treaty of Wanghia between the United States of America and China and twenty one years before the Treaty of Kanagawa between the United States of America and Japan.

The Treaty of 1833 did not fulfill the expectations of the American merchants who wanted trading conditions similar to those in China which were accorded to them under the Treaty of 1844. President Zachary Taylor therefore commissioned Joseph Balestier as a special envoy to Bangkok. He was supposed to be well informed of the oriental way of life, since he was an American merchant and Consul at Singapore. On March 24, 1850, he arrived by a warship at the mouth of the Chao Phya river, with instructions to secure more favourable terms by a new treaty with Siam and to establish a consulate in Bangkok. Balestier tried to get quick results from the Thai authorities, but the negotiations between the two parties broke down completely. In the opinion of the Thais, he was not a polished and skilful diplomat like Edmund Roberts. Any preconceived idea about Siam which he had developed at Singapore served him no useful purpose, as he did not really understand Thai customs and manners. At the first meeting with Balestier, the Deputy Praklang, Phya Sripipat, inquired after the health of the American President and his journey. The American envoy did not care to answer these questions and demanded to get on the business immediately. According to the *History of the Reign of Rama III*, Balestier flew into a rage with the Deputy Praklang, who informed him that since he arrived at Bangkok alone without any ceremony, it was contrary to a royal custom to arrange for him to have an audience with the King.

The British policy was to demand the same privileges from Siam as those which had been obtained by the Treaty of Nanking with China in 1842 such as extraterritorial rights, and their desire was backed up by the "gunboat policy" which had been initiated by the British Government. To achieve this objective, Queen Victoria appointed Sir James Brooke the "White Rajah" of Sarawak, as an envoy to the Thai Court. Probably he was not a suitable choice to undertake the revision of the Burney Treaty with Siam, owing to his superiority complex. Accustomed as he was to the natives of Sarawak, he tended to look down on the Asians, knowing very well that he represented the greatest Power on earth in his days. On August 10, 1850, he arrived at Bangkok, where he stayed for six weeks. Although he met the Praklang, he preferred to make his request by letters, the chief points of which could be summarised thus:- The British should have the right of residence and enjoy religious freedom in Siam. They should be protected by their consul who resided at Bangkok and exercised extraterritorial rights. Most articles of import should be duty free and a limited number of articles should be subject to moderate duties, while ship measurement duties should be reduced to one third of those existing and rice should be freely exported.

The negotiations between the Praklang and Brooke were not successful, since both of them were adamant on the points at issue. King Rama III was gravely ill and as a result no decision could be made about the British proposal. Perhaps Rama III's Government unconsciously upheld the principle of equality between states. Brooke was greatly dissatisfied with the attitude of the Thai authorities and expressed veiled threats to follow up his departure with a drastic action. The Chao Phya river might be blockaded by British gunboats and fear was expressed in Bangkok that war with Great Britain might break out. Fortunately for Siam, Rama III died in 1851 and was succeeded by Rama IV or Mongkut who was an enlightened monarch and so was ready to resume negotiations with Great Britain. In fact, Mongkut had, as a monk, been closely associated with the Brooke mission, for he had translated the English correspondence into Thai for his brother, Rama III, and vice versa for Brooke. Again good fortune smiled on Siam, helping her to avoid the clutches of the British, since Mongkut ascended the throne.

To summarise, only Portugal, Great Britain and the United States of America concerned themselves with the diplomatic relations with Siam during the period under the first three Kings of the Chakri Dynasty. It is gratifying to point out that Siam did not have to grant them any special rights or privileges.

# CHAPTER XI

# MODERNIZATION OF THE KINGDOM

MONGKUT OR RAMA IV (1851-1868). On May 1, 1856, Townsend Harris, the American envoy, had an audience with King Mongkut, where he read his address as follows:

"May it please Your Majesty.

"I have the honor to present to Your Majesty a letter of the President of the United States containing a most friendly salutation to Your Majesty, and also accrediting me as his representative at your court.

"I am directed to express, on the President's behalf, the great respect and esteem that he feels for you, and his warm wishes for the health and welfare of Your Majesty, and for the prosperity of your dominions'

"The fame of Your Majesty's great acquirements in many difficult languages and the higher branches of science, has crossed the great oceans that separate Siam from the United States, and has caused high admiration in the breast of the President. The United States possesses a fertile soil and is rich in all the products of the temperate zone. Its people are devoted to agriculture, manufactures and commerce. The sails of its ships whiten every sea; its flag is seen in every port; the gold mines of the country are among the richest in the world.

"Siam produces many things which cannot be grown in the United States, and the Americans will gladly exchange their products, their gold and their silver for the surplus produce of Siam.

"A commerce so conducted will be beneficial to both nations, and will increase the friendship happily existing between them.

"I deem it a high honor that I have been selected by the President to represent my country at the court of the wisest and most enlightened monarch of the East, and if I shall succeed in my sincere wish, to strengthen the ties of amity that unite Siam and the United States, I shall consider it as the happiest moment of my life."

There is not the slightest doubt about the laudation which Townsend Harris humbly showered on Mongkut. The King was born on October 18, 1804, as a Chaofa or celestial prince of the first rank. He was the forty third child of Rama II and was born to the first queen, and so his younger brother, Chuthamani, was also a Chaofa prince. He was educated in the Grand Palace, where he studied Thai, elementary Pali, elephantcraft, and rudiments of military science. Before the end of his father's reign, he was appointed Director-General of the Royal Pages' Department, and was ordained as a Buddhist monk when he reached the age of twenty. He stayed in the monkhood throughout Rama III's reign of twenty seven years, which was a wonderful preparation for him, when after his enthronement he inaugurated the modernisation of the country along the Western lines. He resided first at Wat Samorai, later known as Wat Rajatiwas, and after the accession of his half-brother to the throne, he moved to Wat Mahathat, near the Grand Palace, which was regarded as an important seat of Buddhist learning. Possessed of a keen and inquiring mind, he made a profound study of Buddhism, so much so that he passed examinations and obtained a religious degree or parien; reportedly, he was the first member of the royal family to achieve such an academic distinction in the Thai Buddhist Church. There was at that time only one sect in the Buddhist Church. He discovered that the practices of Buddhist monks were at variance with the regulations of the Buddhist canon. Many monks neglected a serious study of the Scripture and were lax in the observance of the vinaya (rules) portion of the canon. They were content to lead a contemplative life. By the way, a Buddhist monk must keep 227 rules. For these reasons, when the Prince-Monk returned to Wat Samorai in 1829, he instituted a reform movement of the Buddhist Church, the aim of which was to expunge from Siamese Buddhism all that was not in accordance with the Hinayana canon. The movement laid considerable emphasis on a serious and profound study of Buddhism, the strict observance of the vinaya, the change of details in ritual and the wearing of the yellow robe of the Mon style. In the opinion of the Prince-Monk, the Mon monks in the country lived in conformity with the vinaya. He carried his movement to Wat Bowonniwet where he was appointed abbot in 1837, and it developed into a new sect called Tammayut Nikaya (sect for those adhering to the law). In brief, he succeeded in purifying the Thai Buddhist Church, as the Maha Nikaya soon adopted such Tammayut Nikaya practices as the translation of the Pali texts into Thai. Since then, the Maha Nikaya and the Tammayut Nikaya have been thriving side by side.

As a monk, Prince Mongkut enjoyed freedom of movement, since he did not have to worry about his own safety. His predilection for travel led him on pilgrimages and visits to many shrines and towns such as the Buddha Footprint at Saraburi and Phetchaburi, thus seeing with his own eyes the actual conditions of the people. In 1833, he visited the north of the Kingdom, where he found the Manangkasila throne at Sukhothai. It was frequently occupied by Ramkamhaeng the Great in the Sukhothai days, and the Prince-Monk caused it to be brought down to Bangkok, where it was finally installed within the precincts of the Temple of the Emerald Buddha. He learned English from his American missionary friends, the Rev.Dr.D.B.Bradley and the Rev.J.Caswell, in which he attained such proficiency that he acted as the chief translator for Rama III and Brooke. He studied Latin with the Roman Catholic bishop, Pallegoix, and in turn taught him Pali, while Western science absorbed his interest, and he specialized in astronomy and astrology. Truly he was well equipped for the throne. He was the first Asian monarch who could understand, read and write English, which had superseded Portuguese as the lingua franca in the Far East. This probably accounts for the fact that the British gave up the idea of using force against Siam under his reign.

Prince Chuthamani shared his brother's interest in the study of English with enthusiasm, and according to Townsend Harris, he spoke English very well. After his coronation, Rama IV appointed him as the Maha Uparat with the exalted position of King Pinklao. Thus his reign resembled that of Naresuan the Great in that the First King was assisted by the Second King in ruling the country.

The British followed up Brooke's mission with the appointment of Sir John Bowring

KING RAMA IV GIVING AUDIENCE TO FRENCH ENVOYS

as a British envoy by Queen Victoria. He was born at Exeter, England, on October 17,1792, and died at Claremont near Exeter on November 23,1872. As a young man, he studied modern European languages and worked for the *Westminster Review*. At the time of his assignment to Siam, he held the official post of Governor of Hong Kong, having been the editor of the *Westminster Review*, which was published as a periodical in London, a Member of Parliament for Kilmarnoch, and the British Consul at Canton as well as superintendent of British trade for China. He travelled by the ship "Rattler" to Bangkok, where he was received in a grand style like the French envoys of Louis XIV who had been sent to King Narai's Court in the seventeenth century. He had an official audience with King Mongkut on April 16, 1855, and then a private audience with the Second King, Pra Pinklao. Soon Bowring got on very well with King Mongkut and saw him privately on several occasions. The main purpose of his mission was to request from Siam extraterritoriality and other privileges to British subjects. Mongkut's foreign policy was friendship with Great Britain, as he was well aware of the fact that she would tolerate no defiance. The Burmese who had opposed her were defeated in two wars, 1824-1826 and 1852-1854, while the Chinese had learnt a bitter lesson in the Opium War. Mongkut therefore acceded to Bowring's proposal with a result that a Treaty of Friendship and Commerce between Siam and Great Britain was signed on April 18, 1855, and a Supplementary Agreement was added to it one year later, both of which provided that there would be perpetual peace and friendship. British subjects were free to trade in all Thai sea-ports, but they could reside permanently in Bangkok or in any district which could be reached by a Thai boat in twenty four hours. They were given religious freedom. They were required to register themselves at the British

Consulate and were permitted to buy land within four miles of the city walls of Bangkok. The British consul and the Thai authorities tried and decided a case involving a British subject and a Thai national as the defendant respectively. Opium, bullion and personal effects were put on the free list of imports into Siam, and a limitation of three per cent ad valorem was placed on all other imports. Exports were subject to duties according to the scheduled attached to the treaty. Great Britain was accorded the most favoured nation treatment. The Treaty could not be denounced, and its revision was subject to the approval of the two parties concerned.

Great Britain derived all the advantages from the Treaty, as Bowring commented that "my success involved a total revolution in all the financial machinery of the Government-that it must bring about a total change in the whole system of taxation, that it took a large proportion of the existing sources of revenue, that it uprooted a great number of privileges and monopolies that had not only been long established but were held by the most influential nobles and highest functionaries in the State." Siam lost judicial and fiscal autonomy, since the Thai courts ceased to exercise jurisdiction over British subjects and the Royal Warehouse Department was abolished. The Treaty had no time limit. If she did not sign the Treaty, she might be forced to do so, as Bowring had hinted at such a step. However, Mongkut recognized his ability as a diplomat, as he entrusted him with the duties of negotiating similar treaties with such Western Powers as Sweden-Norway, Belgium and Italy and conferred on him a Thai title of nobility as Phya Sayamanukunkich. During his stay in Bangkok, Bowring gathered a good deal of material for his book on *The Kingdom and People of Siam* which was published in two volumes at London in 1857.

In 1856, the United States of America closely followed the example of Great Britain by negotiating a new treaty with Siam. President Franklin Pierce appointed Townsend Harris, (1804-1874), the American Consul-General to Japan, as his envoy to Siam. The American envoy travelled by the ship "San Jacinto" which arrived off the Chao Phya river on April 15, 1856, and he left Bangkok on May 31, 1856, in order to take up his post in Japan. With regard to the attitude of the Thais towards the Americans, he recorded in his Journal as follows: "Mr. Parks informs me that I will meet a most friendly reception from the Siamese, but that I must be prepared for many and some very unreasonable delays which greatly try my patience," and he went on with his comment of the Thais, "It is an old saying here (Bangkok) that those who come here for business should bring one ship loaded with patience, another loaded with presents, and a third ship for carrying away the cargo." After his audience with King Mongkut, he was received by the second King Pinklao. Following his successful negotiations, he signed with Siam on May 29, 1856, a Treaty of Amity, Commerce and Navigation which replaced the Treaty of 1833. An American missionary by name of Stephen Mattoon was appointed the first United States Consul at Bangkok. In the opinion of Townsend Harris, "he (Mattoon) speaks the (Thai) language like a native, he knows the people well—their manners, customs, laws, prejudices, etc., having lived here nearly ten years."

The Bowring Treaty was the pattern for the Treaty which Napoleon III's envoy, M.de Montigny, signed with Siam in 1856. Identical treaties were concluded with Denmark and Portugal in 1858, with the Netherlands in 1860, with Prussia on behalf of the German Customs Union in 1862, and with Sweden-Norway, Belgium and Italy in 1868.

King Mongkut sent Phya Montri Surawong (personal name-Choom) as a special envoy on a goodwill mission to Great Britain in 1857, where he was granted an audience by Queen Victoria. Later in 1861, another Thai embassy headed by Phya Sripipat (personal name Pae) visited Great Britain on a similar mission, and continued his journey to France where he was officially received by the Emperor Napoleon III. Still no Thai envoy went to the United States of America to return the courtesy during that period; however, King Mongkut entered into correspondence with President Abraham Lincoln.

The Bowring Treaty and similar treaties gave a fillip to the foreign trade of Siam. According to Monsignor Pallegoix, there were in 1852 only three European merchants, namely, one Englishman, one Dutchman and one Portuguese. In 1856, the ships of the different nations which called at Bangkok numbered 200. During King Mongkut's reign, the exports were pepper, rice, sugar, coconut oil, tin, lead, ivory, horns, animals, resin, cotton, timber and birds' nests, while the imports consisted of hardware, arms, cutlery, Chinese silk, soap, glassware, wines, tea, opium and bibelots.

Mongkut departed from the custom of his predecessors, who kept aloof from the people. Wherever he went in the capital and the provinces, he let his people come near him, talked to them and sometimes distributed money to them with his own hands. With the Westerners, he showed particular friendliness. They were permitted to pay respects to him, standing as they would in the presence of their own sovereigns instead of going down to their knees. He was indeed a great traveller, which habit he had probably acquired while he was a monk, and he was very fond of changing his residence from the metropolis to the provincial towns. Thus at his command, an old palace at Ayutthaya was repaired and converted into a royal residence, while new palaces were built at Bangpa-in about sixty kilometres from the north of Bangkok, near the Buddha Footprint in the province of Saraburi, and at Lop Buri, Nakhon Pathom and Phetchaburi. In the capital, he added a few buildings after the European architectural style to the Grand Palace, and just outside its precincts was erected the Saranromya Palace where he planned to reside after he crowned his eldest son, Chulalongkorn, as king. But his intention was never carried out, as the Prince did not come of age during his life time. The Saranromya Palace is to-day occupied by the Ministry for Foreign Affairs.

For the sake of communications, the King promoted the construction of roads in Bangkok and the digging of canals which connected the capital with its surrounding towns such as the Pasicharoen canal to Samut Sakhon. The roads were built at the suggestion of the foreign consuls, such as the Charoenkrung or New Road in 1862, so that their people could take some exercise for their health, and commercial premises were set up on both sides of the road. People had till then been living in houses near the river or canals which served as waterways and some of them preferred to own or rent boathouses near the banks as their dwellings, since Bangkok was criss-crossed with so many canals that it was at one time called the "Venice of the East," and roads were non-existent.

For the peace and order of the Kingdom, Mongkut established a police force charged with a special duty to protect the life and property of western people in Bangkok and an international court to judge their cases with the Thais. He issued no less than 500 acts of law and decrees, some of which aimed at improving the lot of the common people such as the reduction of the corvée service. He organized a small army on the European lines, consisting of a regiment each of Infantry, Artillery and Marines. The Infantry was in the beginning trained by an English officer, Captain Impey, who gave his words of command in English, while the Artillery was in the charge of the Second King Pinklao, assisted by another English officer, Captain Knox.    For his navy, the King introduced steamships.

Like the first three Kings of the Chakri Dynasty, Mongkut allocated state funds to the construction and restoration of several monasteries and the huge chedi at Pra Pathom. He completed the Golden Mount at Wat Srakes in Bangkok, the construction of which had been initiated by Rama III.    What was of utmost significance in this aspect was his declaration of religious freedom as well as his assumption of the title of the Protector of Faiths.

Mongkut tried to maintain the prestige of Siam as a great Kingdom in South-East Asia.    In order to give effective protection to the Prince of Chiengrung or Kengrung who had submitted to Rama III and also to him, Mongkut sent an army under Prince Wongsatiratsnit to capture the barrier town of Chiengrung in 1852 and 1853, but both attempts ended in failure due to disease and difficulties in the transportation of military supplies over the mountainous terrain.    Nor did the King achieve success in holding Cambodia under the Thai sway.    With the support of Rama III, King Harirakramatibodi had mounted the Cambodian throne and had sent his eldest son, Ang Rajawadi, to serve the Thai Government at Bangkok probably with a view to demonstrating his unswerving allegiance to Siam.    During King Mongkut's reign, Ang Rajawadi succeeded his royal father as King Norodom, but a rebellion led by Okya Mahariddhirong (personal name-Sore) forced him to seek asylum at Bangkok.    A Thai army crushed the rebels, thus enabling him to re-occupy his throne at his capital, Oudong.    The rebel leader, however, crossed into Cochin-China and was given protection by the French as a political refugee.

In pursuance of her imperialist policy, France under the Emperor Napoleon III had in 1859 compelled Vietnam to recognize Cochin-China as a French colony with Saigon as its capital.    With her new colony as a base, France spread her influence to Cambodia, and in the end, the French Governor of Cochin-China, Admiral de la Grandière, successfully persuaded King Norodom to sign a Treaty on August 11, 1863, whereby he placed himself under French protection.    Thus Cambodia became a French protectorate, but the French also recognized her as a vassal State of Siam by a treaty signed on December 1, 1863.    Such was the anomalous status of Cambodia.  The French proceeded to announce that King Norodom had concluded the treaty with them of his own free will, but in his letter to King Mongkut, he informed him that he had been constrained to do so.    Whatever that might be, Siam as a small country was naturally not in a position to resist the French pressure.    On July 15, 1867, Siam signed with France a treaty whereby Siam recognized the French protectorate over Cambodia.    The treaty between Siam and Cambodia was declared null and void, and Siam undertook not to demand taxes and tribute from Cambodia.    Battambong and Siemrap belonged to Siam, while the Thais and the Cambodians could trade with one another.    If a Thai committed a crime in the Cambodian territory, he would be brought to a Cambodian court and vice versa.    French ships had a right to navigate in the Mekong river and the Great Lake (Tonlé Sap).    Siam was to render assistance to them in case of difficulty, and France would press Cambodia to abide by this treaty,    The Thai and the French versions were applicable.    Finally the treaty was to be ratified at Bangkok within five months.

King Mongkut had 82 children—43 daughters and 39 sons—from 39 wives and after 1860 some of his sons were growing up, especially Prince Chulalongkorn, who was the eldest one, born of Queen Rampoey on September 20, 1853.    It became therefore necessary to give them the best education available, so that they would be properly equipped for the government service afterwards. Realizing the usefulness of English, the King was determined that they should acquire a good knowledge of that language. At first he got the wives of the American missionaries to teach English to Chulalongkorn, and then he engaged Mrs. Anna Leonowens, an English widow from Singapore, as a teacher. She arrived at Bangkok in 1862 where she worked for five years and left Siam in 1867. Among her royal pupils was Chulalongkorn, who learnt English with her. She wrote two books, *An English Governess at the Siamese Court* and *Romance of a Harem*, which were published in 1870 and 1873 respectively. Her name has been brought to the public attention through Mrs. Margaret Landon's book, *Anna and the King of Siam*, which was published in 1944, and the popular musical play and the film, *The King and I* which have caused a controversy in Siam. The film has been banned for showing in the country. Whatever have been the impressions of Western people about the play and the film, they should be definitely looked upon as nothing more than a kind of entertainment cleverly arranged to draw money from those who wish to be amused.

Besides English, which he continued to study with an American, Dr. Chandler, and an Englishman, Francis George Patterson, Chulalongkorn was taught Thai, Pali, Royal Customs and Ceremonies, Archaeology, Government, Horsemanship, Musketry and self-defence methods. In 1866, the Second King Pinklao died and therefore Prince Chulalongkorn became the heir apparent. Mongkut's proverbial keenness for astronomy directly brought about a serious illness which finally led to his end. According to his calculations, an eclipse of the sun would be clearly visible for the first time in Siam at Wa Kaw on the sea coast near Prachuap Khiri Khan on August 18, 1868. So he proceeded there with his children including Prince Chulalongkorn and Prince Diswarakumar (later known as Damrong Rajanubhab) in order to observe the eclipse, and at his invitation, Sir Harry Ord, Governor of Singapore, and a few English and French astronomers also joined his party. Wa Kaw was situated in a malaria-infested area where Mongkut contracted the disease from which he did not recover on his return to Bangkok and passed away on October 1, 1868.

CHULALONGKORN OR RAMA V (1868-1910). Chulalongkorn succeeded to the throne with the full consent of the Accession Council, and raised the Second King Pinklao's eldest son, Prince Yodyingyos to be the position of the Maha Uparat with the official title of Prince Bowonwijaijarn. The new Maha Uparat was the last incumbent of this high position in the history of Siam. During his seventeen years' tenure of office, he shouldered light state responsibilities, and on his death in 1885 at the age of forty eight, the position was abolished.

At his accession, King Chulalongkorn was a minor, as he had just entered on his sixteenth year. For this reason, Chao Phya Srisuriyawongse (personal name Chuang) acted as the Regent for him for five years, thus affording him opportunities to make observation and study tours of Singapore, Java and India. He would have proceeded to Europe for a similar purpose, if the Regent had not opposed him on the ground that he would be subject to the rigour of a long journey. Being the monarch of a Buddhist country, Chulalongkorn observed the royal custom and entered the monkhood for a short period. On his coming of age in 1873, he performed a second coronation in order to assume his absolute power, the first one having been held at the beginning of his reign, and he assumed the direct rule of the Kingdom immediately. He rewarded the ex-Regent for his loyal and beneficial services to the throne by promoting him to be Somdech Chao Phya Borommaha-srisuriyawongse, being the last commoner to attain the highest title of nobility.

Chulalongkorn had 77 children by his 36 wives—32 sons and 44 daughters and one unborn when Queen Sunanda was drowned. His children received the best education in his days so as to keep abreast of the progressive trends of his era. The princes proceeded to Europe, where they furthered their studies in the fields which would prepare them for services to the State. To begin with, they were required to learn at least two European languages, English and French or German. Thus Prince Vajiravudh studied military science and history in England, while Prince Boribatr of Nakhon Sawan, Prince Chakrabongse of Phitsanulok and Prince Chirapravati of Nahkon Chaisi were educated for a military career in Germany, Russia and Denmark respectively. Prince Kitiyakorn of Chanthaburi, the grandfather of the present Queen Sirikit, and Prince Rabi of Ratchaburi, the founder of the Law School also pursued their studies in England. Subsequently all of them achieved the ministerial rank, except for Prince Vajiravudh, who was created Crown Prince, and Prince Chakrabongse of Phitsanulok, who became the heir presumptive and the Chief of the Army General Staff in Rama VI's reign. With the adoption of the succession order, as generally practised in the West, Chulalongkorn installed his eldest son of the Chaofa rank, Prince Vajirunhis, as Crown Prince. On the death of the Prince in 1895, this vacancy was filled by Prince Vajiravudh, who was equally of the Chaofa rank.

The foreign tours exercised an immense influence on Chulalongkorn, as they broadened his outlook and enabled him to learn on the spot the good and bad features of colonial rule. At the same time he realized to the full the vital necessity to continue the westernisation of Siam, initiated by Mongkut, so as to preserve her independence. The Kingdom was already surrounded by the two imperialist Powers, Britain and France. All his reforms originated in the Grand Palace and in the capital. For the sake of a comparison, Chulalongkorn's age of reform (1868-1910) practically coincided with the Meiji era of Japan (1868-1912), but Thailand has not achieved as much progress as Japan.

On the occasion of his second enthronement in 1873, he dramatically announced the abolition of the practice of prostration in the royal presence. At his request, princes and officials as well as their spouses set a new fashion in dressing up in a civilized manner. Men had their hair cut after the western style instead of being close cropped, donned a white cotton coat closed up at the neck with five buttons after the "raj" pattern and a blue panung with its end rolled and tucked at the back like the Indian dhoti and wore stockings and shoes, while women put on a blouse and a panung and also footgear at an important function. Apart from the official tours, the King enjoyed travelling incognito to the provinces where he mixed and conversed informally with his people, thus acquainting himself directly with their way of living. In his foreign travels, he toured Java again in 1896 and 1901, and visited Singapore in 1902. Credit was accorded to him for being the first Thai monarch to visit Europe on two occasions. In 1897, he made friends through personal contact with the various Heads of State such as the Emperor William II of Germany, the Tsar Nicholas II of Russia, the Prince of Wales who was four years later crowned as King Edward VII of Great Britain, and President Loubet of France. In 1907, he renewed and strengthened the ties of friendship with the Emperors, the Kings, the princes and the statesmen with whom he had become intimately acquainted. In brief, he succeeded in putting Siam on the map of the

PAINTING OF KING RAMA V (CHULALONGKORN) ABOLISHING SLAVERY,
ON THE CEILING OF THE ANANTA SAMAKOM HALL,
PRESENT SEAT OF THE NATIONAL ASSEMBLY

world. Amazingly he managed to find time to record his impressions of his second European tour in the form of letters to one of his beloved daughters, which have been published as a book entitled *Klaiban* or *Far from Home*, revealing his mastery of Thai prose. His scholarly work on The Royal Ceremonies of Twelve Months relates the origin, purpose and detailed procedure of the royal ceremonies and is to-day a set book prescribed for university study.

In the social uplifting of his people, Chulalongkorn did not by any means forget the slaves. On his first enthronement, he issued a royal decree that all the people born in his reign would be free, since he was determined that slavery must eventually disappear from his realm. Seven kinds of slaves were known in those days, namely, 1. Slaves obtained by purchase from owner; 2. Children born from slave parents; 3. Slaves given as presents; 4. People who sold themselves for money to pay fines after criminal conviction; 5. People who exchanged their freedom for rice during hard times; 6. Prisoners of war; and 7. Children given to gambling houses as payment for gambling losses. However, the slaves could secure freedom through monetary redemption, and as time wore on, not a few of them became freemen. In order not to create a social upheaval suddenly, the King took gradual measures to realize his intention in this respect. He continually ameliorated the lot of the slaves, and in 1905 he issued a law for the abolition of slavery. Thus the Thai people won freedom with no struggle at all.

As the supreme patron of the Buddhist Church, he reorganized, through an Act of 1902, its administration with a view to achieving closer control, greater efficiency and raising the educational standard of the monks. Nor did he neglect the restoration and construction of monasteries. He practically rebuilt Wat Benchamabopitr which is to-day recognized as a gem of modern Thai Buddhist architecture known as the Marble Temple.

With the lapse of time, the administrative structure, as established by King Borom-trailokanat, had become complicated and confusing to the uninitiated. The Samuhakala-hom had taken charge of the south of the Kingdom, while the Samuhanayok had been entrusted with the responsibility of governing the north, and the duties of the Praklang had been considerably augmented to include not only the Treasury and finance, but also foreign affairs, foreign trade and government of the towns on the sea coast. As a first step in the reform of the administration, Chulalongkorn appointed, in 1874, the Council of State, comprising 12 members who were leading high officials of the Phya rank. The following was the preamble to his proclamation concerning the Council of State :

"His Majesty wishes to remove oppression and lower his status so as to allow officials to sit on chairs instead of prostrating in his presence. His reason for founding this Council is that, as he cannot himself carry out public duties successfully, the assistance of others will bring prosperity to the country. Appointment of selected intellectuals is simply to advise the King." So the Council of State was Chulalongkorn's first advisory body.

Some three months after the appointment of the Council of State on May 8, 1874, that is, on August 15, 1874, the appointment of a Privy Council to give direct advice to the King was announced. The Privy Council, probably patterned after the English Privy Council, consisted of 49 members including 13 princes and 36 high officials. Thus was established Chulalongkorn's second advisory body. Contrary to his expectations, the Council of State and the Privy Council, which were innovations in the administrative machinery, did not function smoothly, since some members were not well acquainted with their procedure, while others did not dare to express their frank opinions at the meetings fearing to hurt the feelings of their colleagues or ministers. On April 1, 1892, the administrative set-up was therefore replaced by twelve ministries, each with the minister as its head and being directly responsible to the King as virtual prime minister, namely, 1. Defence, 2. Foreign Affairs, 3. Interior, 4. Local Government, 5. Royal Household, 6. Finance, 7. Agriculture, 8. Justice, 9. Public Instruction, 10. Public Work, 11. War and 12. Privy Seal. Later the ministries were reduced to 10, War and Privy Seal being abolished, due to the re-adjustment of ministerial functions.

The provincial administration was reformed with the division of the Kingdom into monton (circle), changwat (province), and amphoe (district), all with officials of various ranks from Bangkok to govern them. Each amphoe was in turn split up into tambons (communes), each of which consisted of a number of villages, but tambon and village heads were elected by local people and thus a basic principle of democracy was introduced into the countryside. The new system was centralized under the Ministry of the Interior and was gradually extended until it covered the whole country. Under the able control of Prince Damrong Rajanubhab, Chulalongkorn's half-brother, who held the post of the Minister of Interior for twenty three years, the first monton of Krungkao or Ayutthaya was established in 1894, and the expansion of the much improved provincial administration eventually assimilated the vassal states in the north as Thai montons. The Prince utilized his spare time on research work on history, archaeology, government, literature and Buddhism of the country, and during his life time (1862-1944) he produced no less than 200 volumes in the most readable prose style. Very appropriately he has been recognized as the Father of Thai History.

To staff the newly created ministries and administrative units outside the capital, educated men must be available. Siam's education had till then been conducted in the Buddhist monasteries which provided a narrow curriculum including Thai, some Pali and the Buddhist Scriptures. Being fully recognisant of the value of modern education, Chulalongkorn had in 1871 founded the first school in the accepted sense of the word in the Grand Palace, where sons of princes and officials learnt the Thai language as their principal subject. Later an English school was started and followed by the Suan Kularb Villa school. The year 1884 is of special significance in the history of Thai education, since it marks the opening of the first state school for the people at Wat Mahan in Bangkok and the introduction of school examinations. With the extension of education to the provinces, there arose an urgent need to organize its administration. So there was created in 1887 the Department of Education which had in due time its status raised to that of Ministry of Public Instruction. The first teachers' training college opened its doors to young men in 1892, with an Englishman as its principal. The first national scheme of education based on the English system was humbly presented to the King with a result that two levels of education—elementary education and secondary education—totalling eleven years of schooling were adopted. For higher education, Chulalongkorn founded the Military College and the Naval College in 1887 and 1907 respectively, while the Law School opened its doors to students in 1897 and the Royal Pages' School began to train provincial administrators in 1902. With the expansion of its instruction, the Royal Pages' School was converted into the Civil Service College on January 1, 1911, being the first step towards the establishment of the University of Bangkok, which was envisaged in the first national scheme of education. This scheme was humbly submitted to Chulalongkorn.

The reform of the army and the navy, inaugurated in the previous reign, was steadily continued by Chulalongkorn, who promulgated a conscription law in 1905. Towards the latter part of his reign, the army was further improved under the direction of his sons, namely, Prince Nakhon Chaisi as its commander-in-chief and Prince Nakhon Sawan in the capacity of the chief of general staff. Simultaneously judicial reform became imperative for the mitigation of the evils of extraterritoriality and in the building up of confidence in Thai justice, and Prince Rabi of Ratchaburi who took a degree in Law at Oxford University played a leading role in it. He was appointed Minister of Justice at the age of 22, and he showed outstanding ability in justifying his tenure of office. This was no startling innovation, if the assumption of the Chancellorship of the Exchequer and the Premiership by Pitt the Younger at the respective ages of 23 and 24 could be recalled. Besides supervising the administration of the Law School which he founded, he taught some courses for a few years and instituted the Bar Association which served as a centre for practising lawyers. A law on the constitution of courts of 1908 provided for the Supreme or Dika court, the Appeal Court, the Criminal and the Civil courts as well as the police court in the capital, the monton and the changwad courts in the provinces and international courts in any city where there was a need for them. Modern methods of collecting legal evidence were substituted for those of torture. The police force in Bangkok was modernised and expanded to serve the whole country and was followed by prison reform. The welfare of the people was promoted with the establishment of the Department of Public Health and Works, hospitals and a medical school. What was essential for the prevention of diseases was a supply of pure water, and the construction of the Bangkok water supply was started in 1902, but it was not completed until 1914.

Up to 1893, the waterways were the principal means of communications between the capital and the provinces. A concession for the construction of the first railway had been given to a Belgo-Danish company, and its shareholders included the King and his sons, and in that year the company train started its service, thus linking Bangkok with Paknam or Samut Prakan at the estuary of the Chao Phya river — a distance of 16 miles or about 25 kilometres. For political and strategic reasons, the State selected the railway line from Bangkok to Nakhon Ratchasima as its first enterprise, which was begun in 1892. The first section to Ayutthaya, 45 miles or 72 kilometres long, was finished in 1897, and the whole line was completed in 1900. By 1910, the eastern line went as far as Chachoengsao and the northern line served the public to the Bangdara junction in the province of Uttaradit, while the southern line linked the capital with Phetchaburi and was to be extended to the Malayan frontier. In keeping with a state policy to avoid competition with the railways, roads were built in areas which led to the railway lines. Parallel with the railways were organized the postal and the telegraph services which were placed under the control the Department of Post and Telegraph, and in 1885 the Thai delegates attended for the first time the Universal Postal Union at Berne with a result that Siam signed the Postal Union Convention.

Chulalongkorn also improved the amenities of Bangkok considerably. He allocated funds in order to continue the road and bridge building programme which had been initiated by his august father. During his forty two years' reign, Bangkok expanded to a considerable length, encroaching upon the garden land and rice-fields in its surroundings. On his return from the first tour of Europe, he caused an avenue of some five kilometres to be built from the Grand Palace to his new Dusit Palace, after the pattern of the Champs Elysées in Paris, the Mall in London, and the Unter den Linden in Berlin. The avenue is called the Rajdamnern Avenue or Royal Progress avenue.

In addition to horse-drawn carriages, other vehicles appeared on the streets of the Thai metropolis such as the rickshaw, the tram, the motor-car, the motor-cycle, and the bicycle, and on both sides of the roads stood government buildings housing the ministries and various departments, business firms, private houses, and row-houses made of wood or brick and mortar. On the anniversary of the King's birthday almost every year, a new bridge was opened for public use. About 1871, a Thai-Chinese nobleman, Pra Joduekrajsethi, introduced the first rickshaw to Bangkok and humbly presented it to the King for private use. Within one generation, the rickshaw, which became a popular means of transportation, increased in such large numbers that the Government found it necessary to promulgate an Act governing the rickshaw in 1901 for the first time, the reason being the control of this vehicle for public safety. Next in 1888 came the tram which was at first horse-drawn and was later converted into the electric one. About 1902 the first serviceable motor-car moved along the roads; it belonged to Prince Rabi, one of King Chulalongkorn's elder sons.

With a view to encouraging government officials to put their heart and soul in the performances of their duties instead of worrying about their daily expenses, a monthly salary was substituted for a small annual gratuity as a remuneration, and a pension was also paid to those who retired after a long service.  With a steady increase in state expenditures, Chulalongkorn revamped, in 1892, the financial system as part of his general reorganization of government in order to increase the national revenue to match it.  A budget system with a regular audit was introduced; the king's personal expenditures were separated from the ordinary state expenditures, and the collection of taxes was much improved, due to the reform of central and provincial administration.  Among the sources of revenue about that time were the opium and gambling farms (40 per cent), the excise taxes (15 per cent), the customs duties (12-15 per cent), the land tax and the capitation tax (8-12 per cent), the in-land-transit duties (5 per cent),  and the royalties on mining and forestry and commercial services (5 per cent).  Notice should be taken of the fact that the rates of both export and import duties were very low, since they were fixed by treaty.  The import duties, for instance, were only three per cent ad valorem.  Nevertheless with the general increase in trade and production coupled with the better collection of taxes, the national revenue which had been estimated at 8 millions bahts in 1868, stood at 15 millions bahts in 1892 and continued to rise to 39 millions bahts in 1902 and to 61 millions bahts in 1910.  The exchange rate of the Baht per Pound Sterling was as follows: In 1850-79—8.00; in 1892-12.10; in 1902-19.30; and in 1908-18-13.00.  According to Bowring's *The Kingdom and People of Siam*, which was published in 1857, the population of Siam was about 4.5 milions, and in the first census taken in 1911, it was 8.3 millions. Agriculture constituted the chief occupation of the people, most of whom cultivated rice.  The export of rice continued to increase in Chulalongkorn's reign, as is shown by the following table :

| Period | Average Volume per Year (Thousand piculs) | Average Value per Year (Thousand Baht) |
|---|---|---|
| 1870-74 | 1,870 | 5,110 |
| 1890-94 | 7,250 | 23,780 |
| 1900-1904 | 11,130 | 61,280 |
| 1910-14 | 15,220 | 81,230 |

N.B. One picul was equal to 60.48 kg (133.12 lbs)

The King encouraged the expansion of rice cultivation through the reduction or temporary suspension of the tax on rice fields, the implementation of irrigation projects and the construction of railways.  For example, no tax was levied on new lands for the first three years of rice cultivation.  The first large scale irrigation project was, with the government permission, carried out by the Siam Canals Land and Irrigation Co. which dug canals, thus greatly improving the rice fields in the Rangsit district 30 miles north of Bangkok.  The digging of canals was also undertaken by the Department of Irrigation.

The Thai Government had until 1904 managed to allocate ordinary revenue for the capital expenditures, and a foreign loan was resorted to only in case of real necessity.  This was accounted for by the government policy to leave no pretext or loophole for foreign intervention which would in turn threaten the independence of the country, as had happened to Egypt in 1882.  However, the first foreign loan was in 1905 floated in London in order to meet an urgent need for further railway construction.  The political policy of Siam was supported by the financial policy, whereby ordinary revenue exceeded ordinary expenditures, and consequently the baht acquired the fame for being a stable currency and was also backed by an adequate reserve of gold, silver and other securities. The baht or tical, which was originally a bullet-shaped lump of silver, was made into a flat coin during the reign of King Mongkut, and the silver coin was gradually replaced by the paper currency which was introduced in 1902. The decimal system for the currency was adopted in 1908, whereby one baht was divided into 100 stangs instead of 64 atts, as had previously been legal.

The services of foreigners were wisely secured on a contract basis for the reform of the Thai Kingdom. Thus Chulalongkorn engaged, in 1892, a Belgian by name of Rolin Jacquemyns as his General Adviser who proved himself to be a truly devoted and loyal servant of the country. The Adviser was about 60 years old when he entered the Thai service. He had already made a name for himself as an international lawyer and had once held the portfolio of the Interior in the Belgian government. In addition to his responsibilities for general affairs, he assisted in the judicial reform and had a share in the founding of the Law School. During the Incident of 1893 with France, he energetically advocated reliance on Great Britain. In 1896, Jacquemyns was created Chao Phya Apairaja, thus being the second European to reach that high noble rank since Phaulkon in the reign of King Narai. During King Chulalongkorn's absence in Europe in 1897, he regularly attended cabinet meetings, presided over by the Chief Queen Saowapaphongsri. Ill health and old age were the reasons that led to his retirement in 1899. The second general adviser, Dr. E.H. Strobel, took office in 1903. From that time to 1949, this post, which later had its name changed to that of adviser for foreign affairs, was reserved for an American. Strobel was followed in this position by James I. Westengaard (the first Phya Kalyamaitri), W.H. Pitkin, Dr. Eldon James, Dr. Francis B. Sayre (the second Phya Kalyamaitri), Courtney Crocker, Raymond Stevens, R. Dolbeare and Kenneth S. Patton, most of whom hailed from the Law School of Harvard University. In finance, the adviser was by tradition an Englishman, beginning with C. Rivett-Carnac (1896-1903), and this was occupied in succession by W.J.F. Williamson (1903-1924), Sir Edward Cook (1924-1930), Hall Patch (1930-1933), James Baxter (1933-35), and W.M.A. Doll (1936-1950), who all urged the Thai Government to follow a cautious policy and build up reserves in the Treasury - a highly commendable advice. The English also produced beneficial results in Education, Police, Surveying and Railways, while the Danes were employed in the Navy and Gendarmerie, the French in Law and Public Works, the Italians in Architecture and construction work, and the Germans in the railway construction of the northern line. A few names made an indelible mark in the history of Thai education. R.L. (later Sir Robert) Morant, who went to Siam in January 1887 to teach Prince Nares' three sons, soon became an English tutor to the first Crown Prince Vajirunhis as well as headmaster of the college for Chulalongkorn's sons and was the author of a *Ladder of Knowledge* series of language text-books for Thai boys who learned English. After the termination of his engagement with the Court of Siam in December 1893, he returned to England where he entered the civil service, and he rose to be the Permanent Secretary to the Board of Education and the first Permanent Secretary of the Ministry of Health. Two other Englishmen, W.G. Johnson and E.S. Smith, helped to develop Thai education along the English lines in close cooperation with the Thai teachers who had studied in English universities and teachers' training colleges, and eventually the former occupied the post of adviser in Education, while the latter was appointed Assistant Director-General of the Department of Education.

Besides his own sons Chulalongkorn sent sons of princes and noblemen as well as commoners' sons on scholarships for further studies in Europe. Most of them proceeded to Great Britain where they entered professional schools and universities such as Oxford, Cambridge, London, Edinburgh and Manchester. On their return, they gradually replaced the foreigners and participated actively in the improvement of the various services. Naturally they must have imbibed western culture and ideas, in addition to gaining modern knowledge in their particular fields of study, and thus they felt at ease, suffering from no inferiority complex in relation with western people, as had previously been the case.

The peace of the Kingdom was disturbed by the invasions of the Hos, the French blockade of the Chao Phya river and a revolt at Prae. This revolt can be described in a few words. With the help of the Shans or Ngiao, the Prince of Prae, Chao Teppawong, rebelled against Bangkok in 1902 and killed the Governor of that province and his assistants. He was quickly crushed by the victor of the Hos, Chao Phya Surasakmontri, and no new ruling prince was appointed to take his place.

Undoubtedly full credit must redound to Chulalongkorn for his wonderful success in preserving the independence of Siam. He was fully aware of the fact that the treaties which Siam concluded with the Western countries under Rama IV constituted a formidable hindrance to the progress of the country. According to Chulalongkorn's royal documents concerning the administration of Siam (Part III-Section I), published by the Committee for historical, cultural and archaeological documents under the auspices of the Office of the Prime Minister, he noted that he contemplated the expansion of the public health service to the area outside the city walls of Bangkok, but he was confronted with a financial problem and also opposed by the foreign powers enjoying their treaty rights.

As a result of the Bowring Treaty, the system of royal monopolies which had, since King Songtam's reign, been administered by the Royal Warehouse Department under the Praklang or Minister of Finance, was abolished. Foreign merchants whose governments signed the treaties with Siam, enjoyed freedom of trade, paid the maximum import duty of three per cent ad valorem, and went to their respective consuls whenever they were involved in legal proceedings.

As European merchants moved into the interior of Siam for their expanding trade, they found it inconvenient to go to their consular courts which were located in Bangkok. An appeal had to be sent abroad for consideration. In a case concerning French subjects, for instance, it had to be referred to Pondicherry and later to Saigon for a decision. Even then it was still a source of inconvenience to the parties concerned.

The consular jurisdiction gave Siam a good deal of trouble, when both Great Britain and France expanded to the Indo-Chinese Peninsula and consequently they became rivals in their colonizing activities. After winning the first war with Burma, Great Britain annexed Arakan, Martaban, Tavoy and Tenesserim in 1826; she occupied Lower Burma as the result of the second war in 1854, and after a victory in the third war with Burma, she incorporated the country in the British Empire as a province of India in 1886. At the same time Great Britain meddled in the affairs of Chiang Mai in the hope of sequestering the northern region from Siam. Luckily for Siam, owing to the praiseworthy and wise administrative policy of Chulalongkorn, the British attempt in this direction failed rather quietly. Burma lost her independence, and the British abolished her monarchy by removing King Thibaw to India.

With her foothold at Penang, the Province of Wellesley and Singapore, Great Britain had been extending her territories in the Malay Peninsula and by 1895, Johore, Pahang, Negri Sembilan, Selangor, and Perak became her protectorates.

In pursuance of the policy for her glory (la gloire), France under Louis XVIII (1815-24), Charles X (1824-1830), Louis Philippe (1830-1848) and Napoleon III (1852-1870) had been concentrating her attention on Vietnam, which was then known as Annam, since the beginning of the nineteenth century. In 1859, Vietnam had to recognize Cochin-China or South Vietnam as a French colony with Saigon as its capital. Using her new colony as a base, France spread her influence to Cambodia which was a vassal State of Siam. In the end, the French Governor of Cochin-China, Admiral de la Grandière, successfully persuaded King Norodom of Cambodia to sign a Treaty on August 11, 1863, where he placed himself under French protection. Thus Cambodia became a French Protectorate, but the French recognized her as a vassal state of Siam by a treaty signed on December 1, 1863 and ratified on January 4, 1864. It is interesting to note that the Treaty between France and Cambodia was ratified on April 14, 1864. Such was the anomalous position of Cambodia. The French proceeded to announce that King Norodom had concluded the treaty with them of his own free will, but in his letter to King Mongkut, he informed him that he had been compelled to do so. Whatever that might be, Siam was a small country and naturally she was not in a position to resist the French pressure. On July 15,1867, Siam signed a treaty with France. The terms of the treaty are as follows: 1. Siam recognized the French protectorate over Cambodia. 2. The treaty between Siam and Cambodia was declared null and void. 3. Siam would not demand taxes and tribute from Cambodia. 4. Battambong and Siemrap belonged to Siam. 5. The Thais and the Cambodians could trade with one another. If a Thai committed a crime in the Cambodian territory, he would be brought to a Cambodian court and vice versa. 6. French ships had a right to navigate in the River Mekong and the Great Lake (Tonlé Sap). Siam had to render assistance to them in case of difficulty. 7. France would force Cambodia to abide by this treaty. 8. The treaty was made in French and Thai, and both versions were applicable. 9. The treaty was to be ratified at Bangkok within five months.

Not only did the French occupy Cochin-China, but they also expanded northwards in Annam. In 1883, they conquered Tongkin, and in the following year Annam had to recognize French suzerainty. Siam thus found herself between Great Britain and France in Chulalongkorn's reign. The French conquest of Tongkin and the annexation of northern Burma brought France and Great Britain face to face in their search for access to southern China, and thus what became known as the *Siamese Question* assumed tangible form. As both countries began moving towards a focal point of penetration, Great Britain began to fear for Siam's fate. Holt Hallet, in a report submitted to the Foreign Office in April 1885, urged Great Britain to declare a protectorate over all Siam, except Laos, which could be generously left to the French. But the British Government preferred the policy of Satow, then Minister in Bangkok, which was to strengthen Siam against a possible French attack. This possibility, however, seemed to be increasingly remote when Ferry's Government fell that same year and the French perforce abandoned their interests in Mandalay. Moreover, the prolonged pacification of Tongkin seemed to put French aggression, at least temporarily, out of the question.

A difficulty arose in connection with the interpretation of a British subject and a

French subject. When Great Britain signed the Bowring Treaty with Siam, a British subject meant a British citizen born in that country. Siam did not regard the Asians in the British colonies and protectorates as British subjects, and she applied the same interpretation to French subjects, as mentioned in the French Treaty of 1856. As Great Britain and France ruled the protectorates and the colonies in the Indo-Chinese peninsula, they insisted on including the people in those territories as their subjects. For example, a Burmese, a Malay and a Straits-born Chinese were British subjects, while an Annamese was a French subject. The British and the French subjects were under their respective consuls and went to the consular courts when they were involved in legal proceedings. Again a small Power had to yield to a great Power. Siam had to accept the interpretation of Great Britain and France in this matter. However, exceptions were made to the consular jurisdiction by the two great Powers. The Treaty of 1867 between Siam and France stipulated that if a Cambodian subject committed a crime in the Thai territory, he would be tried, sentenced and punished according to the Thai laws, and so the consular jurisdiction did not protect him.

Many hundred Burmese and some Englishmen worked in the timber industry in the north of Siam and all of them were British subjects. Great Britain agreed to provide special treatment to them in order to facilitate legal proceedings. In 1883, Siam and Great Britain signed a treaty with a view to preventing crime in the area of Chiang Mai, Lampang and Lamphun and promoting the trade between British Burma and that area. Regarding the consular jurisdiction, the treaty stipulated that Thai judges were to decide civil and criminal cases involving British subjects according to the Thai laws, but a British consular officer could join them during the trial and could make suggestions for the sake of justice. If a British subject was the accused, he could ask for his case to be tried and decided in the British consular court. An appeal could be made to Bangkok where a Thai judge and a British consular officer would consider the case and if the accused was a British subject, the British consular officer had the right to give a judgement. Such was the system under which the international court functioned. Indeed it was a Thai court with a British consular officer, sitting on it, as an occasion arose.

The difficulty with which the consular jurisdiction was administered in the Thai provinces was the reason why Great Britain consented to make this treaty. In 1886, France signed a similar treaty with Siam for the area of Luang Prabang, where she aimed at developing trade with Annam. The system of extra-territoriality would not by itself cause too much trouble to Siam, but once mixed up with politics, it began to constitute a factor which threatened the independence of Siam.

Since the signing of the treaty with Great Britain in 1855, King Mongkut had taken steps to strengthen the ties of amity by sending two embassies to Great Britain and two other embassies to France. King Chulalongkorn adopted the same policy as his father and also made an innovation in Thai diplomacy by stationing resident ministers in the capitals of the Western Powers. In 1882, H.R.H. Prince Prisdang Chumsai was appointed Thai Minister to Great Britain, France, Italy, Germany, the Netherlands, Belgium, Austria-Hungary, Denmark, Sweden-Norway, Spain and Portugal. He was educated in England, where he received a B.A. degree from London University. It is generally believed that he was the first Thai to be awarded a degree by a Western university. Three years later, in 1885, H.R.H.Prince Naresvoraridhi became the first Thai Minister to the United States of America, while Phya Suriyanuwat (Kerd Bunnag) went to Russia in 1897 in the same capacity, and Phya Riddhirongronnachet (Sukh Chuto) was the Minister to Japan in 1899. It should be mentioned that the United States Government appointed John Halderman as the first Minister and Consul to Bangkok in 1882, that is to say, three years before the first Thai Minister went to Washington.

The reason for the appointment of resident ministers to the Western countries was to show that Siam was a modern State which should be a worthy member of the family of nations according to the international law. In 1885, Siam became a party to the Postal Union Convention. It is, however, argued in some quarters that the Postal Union Convention was a technical document, not a political one. Siam had to wait for fourteen years before she was recognized as a regular member of the family of nations. The Thai delegates attended the First Hague Peace Conference in 1899 and signed the Hague Convention on the Law of War. Consequently Siam joined the family of nations in that year.

The Siamese Question became increasingly important, due to the westward expansion of France from Annam. After the signing of the treaty of 1886, Siam acceded to the French request to appoint a consul at Luang Prabang. Frenchmen and French subjects who lived in the area of Luang Prabang came under the Thai court. It was organized as a special court with the French consul sitting on it. Thus the French recognized that Luang Prabang was Thai territory. As a matter of fact, Luang Prabang and the whole territory of Laos on the left bank of the River Mekong and beyond had been under Thai suzerainty since the Thon Buri period (1767-1782). The Thai northern and northeastern boundaries which covered Laos and her outlying provinces—Muang Phou-eun, Sibsong Chuthai and Huapan Tangha Tanghok—extended as far as South China and Annam, but they were not clearly delimited. Muang Phou-eun had Chiang Khong as its chief town, while Sibsong Chuthai which had Muang Lai and Muang Theng (Dien Bien Fu) as important towns, and Huapan Tangha Tanghok bordered on Tongkin and were claimed by Annam as far back as 1822. As protector of Annam, France asserted that Sibsong Chuthai and Huapan Tangha Tanghok should belong to her.

The French claim was complicated by the invasion of the "Hos" of the territory under Thai suzerainty. The "Hos" or "Haws" were the Chinese who had joined the Taiping rebellion against the Manchu dynasty and had, in 1864, fled into Tongkin, Muang Phoueun, Sibsong Chuthai and Huapan Tangha Tanghok where they remained and organized a force of their own. The area where they roamed about was mountainous. Having captured Chiang Khong, they threatened Luang Prabang, Vientiane and Nong Khai in 1872, but they were routed by two Thai armies. Later in 1883, they set up their main camp in the Chiang-Kam district in Muang Phou-eun and attacked the tributary towns of Luang Prabang. The Thai troops drove them back to their main camp where they put up a strong defence, and so they withdrew. King Chulalongkorn sent another army to Nong Khai in order to crush the Hos in the Chiang Kham district in 1885. Knowing that they were not strong enough to fight the Thai army, they burnt their camp and moved northwards. After the departure of the Thai forces, they struck at Luang Prabang which suffered badly at their hands in that year. The Thai troops under Chamuen Waiworanart (later Field-Marshal Chao Phya Surasak Montri) marched northwards again, and after inflicting a heavy defeat on the Hos, they remained to pacify the territory.

In the course of their operations against the Hos, the Thai forces spread out in Sibsong Chuthai and Huapan Tangha Tanghok. The French also sent their soldiers into the area which, they claimed, belonged to Annam. A frontier dispute between Siam and France arose. The French knew that Siam did not stand on firm ground with regard to the frontier bordering on Annam, as Dr. Harmand, who was the French Consul, at Bangkok had made a suggestion to the French Governor of Cochin-China to align their claims with those of the Annamites and to base them on their own maps which could be procured in all the citadels, choosing those which were the most favourable.

Siam and France entered into negotiations to settle their dispute in 1886-1887, and reached a provisional agreement whereby they would keep the territory occupied by their own troops. In this way, France got Sibsong Chuthai and Huapan Tangha Tanghok where the French had already controlled most of the territory. The French were by no means satisfied with the territory which had been ceded to them in 1887. Their policy was to extend their power to the River Mekong, that is to say, the whole territory on the left bank of the river from the northern point of Loas to the Cambodian frontier should come under their rule. Several French parties then undertook a survey of Laos, and also studied the possibilities of using the River Mekong for navigation and transportation of goods from the south of China. The next step the French took was to refer to the treaty of 1867 concerning French ships sailing freely in the parts of the Mekong river and the Great Lake bordering on Siam. According to the French interpretation of the treaty, the Thai frontier extended to the river and not beyond. The treaty of 1867, however, dealt with Cambodia but made no mention of Laos. The French also claimed that as Annam and Cambodia were their protectorates, Laos should similarly come under them. Annam and Cambodia used to exercise suzerain rights over Laos. Needless to say, Siam challenged the French cliam. Obviously the people who lived in Laos were Thais and not Annamese; the Annamese Cordilleras separated the Laotians from the Annamese, and the maps which were published by the French before 1893 showed that Laos formed part of Siam.

As France persisted in expanding its power towards the Mekong river, there was bound to be increasing friction with Siam. The French expansionist policy was supported by M. de Lanessan, who was appointed Governor-General of Indo-China in 1891. The matter came still further into prominence when, in January 1893, another advocate of this colonial expansion, M. Ribot, became the Head of the French Government. In the following month, Prince Henry of Orléans, who had recently returned from a tour in the East, published an article in the *Politique Coloniale*, in which, after blaming Louis XV for not having backed up Dupleix in his struggle against Clive, he went on to say:

"The Republic will be blamed equally if after having been informed by its agents, it hesitates to take definite action for the reconstruction in Indo-China of the Empire we lost in India." Frontier incidents between the two countries broke out and culminated in the Incident of 1893. On March 14, 1893, Auguste Pavie, who was the first French Minister Resident at Bangkok, made a demand on Siam to give up the left bank of the Mekong as her territory at once and to pay compensation to the French subjects who, as they alleged, had suffered at the hands of the Thais. He also informed the Thai Foreign Minister, Prince Dewawongse that the French gunboat "Le Lutin" was anchoring in front of the French Legation to support his dealings with the Thai Government. During that time, frontier troubles became very serious, particularly two incidents which broke out in Laos. A French army captain by name of Thoreux was captured, and then a French inspector of militia, M. Grosgurin, was killed together with fourteen of his Annamite soldiers. The French alleged that Grosgurin was murdered. At the demand of the French, Thoreux was released by the Thai authorities and they were ready to pay out a compensation, if it could be proved that Grosgurin's death was due to a Thai action.

It is rather sad to record that France adopted a stiff policy against Siam. The Governor of Cochin-China, Le Myre de Vilers, was despatched as a special envoy with precise instructions to withdraw the whole French diplomatic mission from Bangkok and to start a blockade of the mouth of the Chao Phya river at once, if Siam refused to recognize the French right over the left bank of the Mekong and to indemnify the French subjects who had suffered damages in the country. As the tension between Siam and French was mounting, two British warships, M.M.S. Swift and H.M.S. Pallas, arrived off the bar of the Chao Phya river, while a British gunboat, "Linnet", proceeded to Bangkok, where it anchored at the landing of the British Legation, and they were all there to protect the lives and property of the British subjects.

On July 10, 1893, the French notified Prince Dewawongse that the French gunboats, the "Inconstant" under Commander Bory, and the "Comète," would cross the bar on the way to Bangkok on July 13, in accordance with treaty rights. Despite Prince Dewawongse's protest, the French Government decided to insist on such rights and ordered its ships to anchor inside the bar. So on that day, as the "Inconstant" and the "Comète," which had a merchant ship, belonging the Messageries Fluviales de Cochinchine, the "Jean Baptiste Say," as a pilot ship, were forcing the bar of the Chao Phya river, they were fired upon by the Thai forts, namely, the Chula Chom Klao fort and the Phisuasamut fort under a Dane in the Thai service, Commodore de Richelieu, and the French returned fire. Both sides suffered casualities, as is borne out by a message dated July 16,1893, from the Commander of the "Inconstant" to the Minister of Marine and Colonies: "There were dead and wounded on both sides." The French pilot ship, "Jean Baptiste Say" and the Thai gunboat "Makutrajkumar" were heavily damaged, but the "Inconstant" and the "Comète" got through and anchored opposite the French Legation at Bangkok. M. Pavie suggested that France should take a strong action against Siam, and he sent, on July 4, the following telegraph to the French Foreign Minister, M. Develle: "We must take advantage of the strong position we have and send a squadron with troops for disembarking, if the Siamese government does not yield."

The relations between Siam and France worsened after the shooting at Paknam. Upon instructions from M. Develle, M. Pavie delivered, on July 20, 1893, at 5.30 p.m. an ultimatum to Prince Dewawongse to reply within 48 hours. If Siam rejected the ultimatum, the French Resident Minister would leave Bangkok by the "Forfait" and France would declare a blockade of the Thai coasts at once. The ultimatum contained six clauses. 1. La reconnaissance formelle par le Roi de Siam des droits de l' Empire d' Annam et du Royaume du Cambodge sur la rive gauche du Mékong et sur ses îles. 2. L'évacuation des postes siamois établis sur la rive gauche du Mékong dans un délai qui ne pourra pas excéder un mois. 3. Les satisfactions que comportent les incidents de Tong Xieng Kham, de Kammon, et les agressions dont nos navires et nos marins ont été l' objet dans la rivière du Ménam. 4. Les châtiments des coupables et les réparations pécuniaires dues aux familles des victimes. 5. Une indemnité de deux millions de francs pour les divers dommages causés à nos natinaux. 6. Le dépot immédiat d' une somme de trois millions de france en piastres pour garantir les réparation pécuniaires et les indemnités, ou à défaut, la remise, à titre de gage, de la perception des formes et revenus des Provinces de Battambong et de Siem Reap." In his telegram to the Commander of the "Inconstant", the French Minister of Marine added that "si pendant votre descente nos bâtiments étaient objet d' agression sérieuse, vous apprécierez conduite à tenir et êtes autorisé à riposter et user représailles. Cependant en raison questions internationales, il est du plus haut intérêt de pas tirer sur ville même Bangkok. Mais toujours en cas d' agression, vous devriez alors, si vous le jugez possible, annihiler flotte siamoise et réduire forts. Vous prendriez d' ailleurs telles mesures que la situation ainsi modifiée vous paraîtrait comporter. Ceci implique à la fois énergie et prudence."

The Thai Government accepted the French ultimatum on two conditions. 1. The right on Annam and Cambodia to control the left bank of the Mekong river would be recognized up to the 18th degree parallel 2. Siam would share the use of the islands in the Mekong river with France. France was not satisfied with the Thai reply. Pavie now left with the French gunboats for Koh Sichang, an island near the mouth of the Chao Phya river, and the French warships started the blockade of the Gulf of Siam.

In Paris, most of the French newspapers such as the "Journal des Débats," the "République Française," and the "Soleil" approved of the energetic actions taken by the French Government and also claimed Battambong and Angkor from Siam. On July 20, 1893, the Chamber of Deputies adopted the following motion, proposed by M. Camille Dreyfus et Deloncle: "Le gouvernement prendrait les mesures necessaires pour faire respecter les droits en Indochine et s' assurer les garanties auxquelles elle a droit." The blockade began to hurt the Thai shipping, but a few Thai statesmen thought that Great Britain would help Siam. As a matter of fact, there was, in England, a general indignation against the French actions in Siam. The London newspapers such as the Times and the Morning Post of July 14, 1893, advocated the maintenance of Thai independence, and Lord Roseberry, who was the Foreign Secretary in the Liberal Government under Gladstone (1892-1894), termed the French conduct towards Siam as being frightfully low, savage and treacherous. However, he thought that Great Britain should not be the "Knight Errant of the World" and that her main interest in the Franco-Thai dispute should be to set up a buffer state between the French frontier in Indo-China and India. Nor would Germany help Great Britain to resist France in the Siamese Question. According to a communication dated April 25, 1893, from the Minister of Marine to M. Delcassé, "entre I' Angleterre et la France, ils sont tout préparés à prendre part aux débats, et à jouer le rôle de juge entre les deux plaideurs." Lord Roseberry realized that any delay on the part of Siam would be to her disadvantage, as is seen by one of his telegrams dated July 27, 1893, that "the demands of the French threaten to get worse and worse, if the Siamese continue to resist the conditions as set forth by the ultimatum." For these reasons, Lord Roseberry advised Siam to accept the French terms for the settlement of the dispute.

The French thus got the upper hand in dealing with Siam, and by July 29, 1893, they required the following guarantees from her: 1. The occupation of Chantabun pending her evacuation of the left bank of the Mekong. 2. No stationing of Thai troops in Battambong and Siemrap. 3. The creation of a demilitarized zone within a radius of 25 kilometres of the right bank of the Mekong, starting from the Cambodian frontier. Siam would send police there to maintain peace, and would not have her armed vessels in the Tonlé Sap or Great Lake and the Mekong. 4. The right to establish consulates at Khorat and Nan. On August

5, 1893, the French terms were accepted by the Thai government and the blockade was lifted by the French. Some Thai people believe that the Tsar Nicholas II of Russia, by then a great ally of France, exercised his influence in appealing to her to mitigate her terms out of friendship for King Chulalongkorn of Siam.

Siam was a small Power with a population of seven millions, and her armed forces were poorly equipped. In order to maintain her independence, she yielded to the French, and on October 3, 1893, she signed a treaty with France, the terms of which were as follows: "1. The Siamese Government renounces all the claim on all the territories of the left bank of the Mekong and all the islands in the river. 2. The Siamese Government is forbidden to keep or circulate the landings or armed vessels in the Great Lake, the Mekong and in the tributaries situated in the limits mentioned in no. 3. 3. The Siamese Government will not build a fortified post or a military establishment in the provinces of Battambong and Siem-rap and within a radius of twenty five kilometres of the right bank of the Mekong. 4. In the zones mentioned in no. 3, the police will be exercised according to the usage by the local authorities, having the contingents which are strictly necessary. No regular or irregular armed force will be kept there. 5. The Siamese Government undertakes to open within six months negotiations with the French Government in order to regulate the customs and commercial regime in the territories mentioned in no. 3, and to revise the treaty of 1856. No customs duties will be levied in the zone mentioned in no. 3 until the conclusion of this agreement. The French Government will give reciprocity to the products of the said zone. 6. At the request of the French Government, the Siamese Government undertakes to give all the necessary facilities for the development of the navigation of the Mekong which requires certain works or the establishment of boat relays and wood and coal depots on the right bank. 7. The French citizens and subjects will be able to circulate or trade freely in the territories mentioned in no. 3, if they have a pass, issued by the French authorities. Reciprocity will be given to the inhabitants of the said zones. 8. The French Government reserves for itself the establishment of consuls in any place where it deems proper for the interest of its subjects, especially at Khorat and Nan. 9. The French text will be relied upon in case of difficulties of interpretation. 10. The present treaty will be ratified within four months from the date of the signing."

Prince Dewawongse signed the treaty on behalf of the Thai Government, while M. Le Myre de Vilers signed it in the name of the French Government. On the same day (October 3, 1893), a convention was concluded as an annex to the treaty, containing the clauses as follows: "1. The last military Siamese posts on the left bank of the Mekong must be evacuated within one month as from September 5. 2. All the fortifications of the zone mentioned in no.3 of the present treaty (of to-day's date) must be razed. 3. The authors of crimes of Tung Xieng Kham and Kammoun will be judged by the Siamese authorities. A French representative will be present at the judgment and watch the execution of the sentences. The French Government reserves the right to appraise the punishment, and if it is not sufficient, to ask for a new judgment before a mixed tribunal, the composition of which it will fix. 4. The Siamese Government will have to put at the disposal of the French Minister or French authorities of the frontier all the French, Annamite and Laotian subjects of the left bank and the Cambodians who have been detained by any title whatsoever. It will not put any obstacle to the return to the left bank of the former inhabitants of this region. 5. The Bang Bien of Tung Xieng Kham and his followers as well as the weapons and the French flag, seized by the Thai authorities, will be brought by a delegate of the Ministry of Foreign Affairs to the French Legation. 6. The French Government will continue to occupy Chantabun until the execution of the stipulations of the present convention and especially until the complete evacuation and pacification of the left bank and the zones mentioned in no.3 of the treaty date to-day."

By the treaty and the convention of October 3, 1893, France received 50,000 miles of territory and specific advantages for her subjects in Siam. The French occupied Chantabun as a guarantee, while Siam agreed to demilitarize her eastern frontier. The question of indemnifying the French was not mentioned in the treaty and the convention, but Siam had to pay them an indemnity of two million francs and a guarantee of three million francs for the fulfilment of the above mentioned conditions. These two sums amounted to about 2,580,000 bahts, when one pound sterling was worth 25 French francs or 12.90 bahts.

The treaty of 1893 did not stop the spread of French influence in the Indo-Chinese peninsula, and the French extended almost indiscriminately extraterritorial rights in Siam not only to French subjects, European and Asian, but also to any refugees from French territories and their descendants living in Siam. The French Legation registered almost anyone who presented himself with such claims, requiring no proof of any kind. In 1880, those who registered themselves as French subjects were small in number, that is to say, 29 Frenchmen, 21 Annamites and Indians, and 86 Chinese. As a matter of fact, the Chinese did not belong to the French nation, but the French extended the protection of their Legation to those who were their employees. This was a one-sided interpretation of the treaty to suit the French. The number of French subjects, appearing in a list of the French Legation, increased from 200 in 1893 to 30,000 in 1896. In the city of Bangkok in 1912, the Chinese who registered themselves as French subjects numbered 724, while those who were British subjects were 36 in number.

The French extension of territorial rights to their Asian subjects caused considerable difficulties to the Thai authorities in governing not only the capital but also the provinces. Even the Cambodians who had by the treaty of 1867 been under the Thai courts had their status changed after 1893, as the French registered them as French subjects. So long as the French had designs on the territories, especially Battambong and Siemrap, claimed as Cambodia's lost provinces, nothing could be done to restrict French consular jurisdiction.

The British Government pursued the foreign policy of maintaining Siam as a buffer state. In 1896, Great Britain and France made an agreement concerning their colonial expansion in Africa and the Far East. They adopted the channel or thalweg in the Mekong as the boundary line in the territory sandwiched between Siam and China, that is to say, the Shan States and Laos. In the same year, they signed an agreement concerning Siam, with two main points. 1. The British Government and the French Government would not send their armies into the region between the Mekong and the Tenesserim mountains without the consent of the other party nor would they ask for more privileges and special interests for their nationals than those for nationals of the other party. 2. This undertaking would not stop any action which both parties agreed to take as a necessary measure for the preservation of Thai independence. Siam must not sign an agreement with a third Power in respect of the privileges and special interests which they denied themselves herewith. Siam had no part in the signing of the Anglo-French agreement of 1896. Although it did not guarantee Siam's independence, it would keep both Great Britain and France from violating her sovereignty.

Apparently in following her foreign policy, Great Britain took another step in helping Siam to solve the problem of the Asians as her subjects. In 1899, Siam and Great Britain signed a treaty limiting the right of registration as British subjects. A British subject who was not an Asian could have his children and grand children registered at the British Legation, while an Asian who was a British subject was entitled to the registration of his children only, and his grandchildren would be recognized as Thai subjects.

The next task for Siam to accomplish in this specific matter was to try to come to terms with France. In 1902, the Thai Government and the French Government reached an agreement, whereby the right of registration for French subjects who were Asians would be limited in the same way as that for Asians who were British subjects. The agreement, however, failed to receive approval of the French Legislature and thus it was invalid. In 1904, Siam and France were successful in their negotiations which resulted in the signing of a convention, limiting the right of registration for French subjects. Asians who were permitted to register themselves as French subjects must belong to French protectorates or colonies or must be children of such persons, while French citizens continued to be French subjects in every generation; with regard to the consular jurisdiction, if a defendant was a French subject no matter whether he was a French citizen or an Asian, he was brought to the consular court. There was, however, an exception in the case of a French subject who lived in Chiang Mai, Lamphun, Lampang and Nan, since he went to an international court. Although the advantages accruing from this convention were not of much significance, Siam had to cede to France two territories on the right bank of the Mekong, namely, Paklai opposite Luang Prabang and Bassac (Champasak). Siam got back Chantabun, as the French had evacuated it. In fact, the French should by the treaty of 1893 have returned Chantabun to Siam. Thus the restoration of this town to her should not be regarded as an exchange for the two territories. The preamble of the convention of 1904 did not specify it as such. Besides, after leaving Chantabun, the French occupied Trat pending the implementation of the convention. It should be remembered that in April 8, 1904, France and Great Britain signed a treaty which resulted in the creation of the Entente Cordiale. The treaty, which comprised three conventions, settled their disputes concerning such questions as Egypt, Morocco, the New Hebrides, and Siam. One convention which dealt with Siam confirmed her as buffer state with three zones, namely, the eastern zone as a French sphere of influence, the western zone as a British sphere of influence, and the neutral zone being the Menam or Chao Phya valley. A small point worth mentioning was that it was largely due to the American Foreign Adviser, S.H. Strobel, that Siam determined to make the concessions necessary to liquidate her ancient enmity with France. As a sop to France, the Thai Government employed French legal advisers at Bangkok, and would also allot to the French a share of its public works contracts.

It would not be out of place here to state that in 1905, Denmark and Italy signed conventions after the pattern of the French convention of 1904 concerning the registration of their subjects and the consular jurisdiction, but they did not claim any privilege in return.

Still the ambiguous wording of the 1904 convention caused trouble to Siam. A Boundary Commission under Colonel F. Bernard discovered real difficulties that remained to be solved, and negotiations were resumed. The result was the treaty of 1907, by which Siam ceded Battambong, Srisophon and Siemrap to France. According to Prince Chula Chakra-

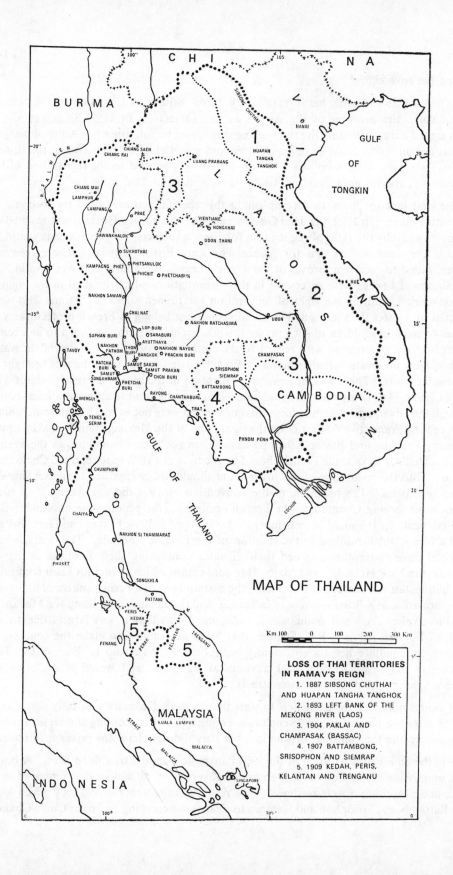

MAP OF THAILAND

**LOSS OF THAI TERRITORIES
IN RAMA V'S REIGN**
1. 1887 SIBSONG CHUTHAI
AND HUAPAN TANGHA TANGHOK
2. 1893 LEFT BANK OF THE
MEKONG RIVER (LAOS)
3. 1904 PAKLAI AND
CHAMPASAK (BASSAC)
4. 1907 BATTAMBONG,
SRISOPHON AND SIEMRAP
5. 1909 KEDAH, PERIS,
KELANTAN AND TRENGANU

bongse's *Lords of Life*, "By this cession, Siam lost the renowned Khmer ruins of Angkor which was probably a good thing for the world in general, as the French were more capable of restoring them through advantages of finance and the intense interest and deep learning of their scholars in oriental studies." By the way, France had by the treaty of 1867 recognized these three provinces as belonging to Siam. On her part in the 1907 treaty, France returned to her Trat and the islands from the south of the Ling promontory to the island of Good. In connection with the extraterritorial rights, the Asians who had registered themselves as French subjects or protégés would be under an international court until all the legal codes were proclaimed and enforced, while those who would register themselves as French subjects or protégés after 1907 were to go to the Thai courts. Both categories of the Asians just mentioned would have equal rights and duties like Thai citizens, but were exempted from military service. The preamble of the 1907 Treaty states that the surrender by France of the extraterritorial rights over her subjects and protégés registered at the consulate after 1907 was made in exchange for the three provinces which were transferred to her, but it would be hard for a Thai to concur with this statement. The said territory was really worth more than the consular jurisdiction. In France, the 1907 treaty was a real diplomatic triumph, to which the press and all shades of party opinion were favourable. It was accepted without debate in the French Chamber of Deputies. In order to show his friendliness to France, Chulalongkorn appointed French jurists to a commission to help with the codification of the Thai laws. This brought to Siam Frenchmen who were to become authorities on the law of the land and to be associated with her juristic progress such as Padoux, Guyon, Lingat and Rivière.

The British policy towards Siam was to maintain her as a buffer state, but Great Britain did not pursue it out of altruism. Since the conclusion of the Burney treaty of 1826, she had been bringing pressure on the four Malay states, Kedah, Perlis, Kelantan, and Trengganu which were under Thai suzerainty. One British governor of Singapore who held office at the end of the nineteenth century went so far to suggest that the British dominion in the Malay peninsula should be extended to the Kra isthmus so as to connect up with Lower Burma, but the British Colonial Office did not favour his opinion. Finally Siam signed a treaty with Great Britain in 1909, whereby she gave up her sovereignty over Kedah, Perlis, Kelantan and Trengganu and the islands off their coasts, which in practice meant their cession to the British - a territory of 15,000 square miles and about one million inhabitants. Great Britain agreed to let the Europeans and the Asians, who had already taken out their registration as British subjects, come under an international court, and after the promulgation and the enforcement of all the Thai legal codes, they would be placed under the jurisdiction of the Thai courts. Those who would register themselves as British subjects in the future, both Europeans and Asians, were to come also under the Thai courts with the stipulations that a European legal adviser would try a case involving a British subject as a defendant and that British subjects would have the same rights and duties as a Thai citizen, but were exempted from military service. In other words Britain surrendered extraterritorial rights not only for British Asian subjects, but Europeans as well, and she was the first European power to do so. Again it cannot be said that the British concession in respect of the extraterritorial rights was made in exchange for the territory transferred to Great Britain, since the Asian subjects who came under the Thai jurisdiction could own land in Siam, in addition to the other rights just mentioned.

In assessing Chulalongkorn's foreign policy, it can be said without contradiction that although he had lost 90,000 square miles of territory to the French and the British, he succeeded in preserving the independence of the country, and he did this in spite of all the threats and pressure that had been brought to bear upon him. If Siam were to be compared to a man and the lost territory to limbs, the King would sacrifice the limbs and keep the heart of the man so as to help him to live on. Thus Siam gained morally by this physical loss, in that she became a more compact and homogeneous country.

To complete the episode of Thai history dealing with the limitation of extraterritorial rights in Siam, it should be stated that in 1913, Denmark signed a convention with Siam, whereby she surrendered consular jurisdiction along the same lines as the British prototype, but she received nothing in return.

Another important task which Chulalongkorn initiated was the revision of the treaties, but he did not live to see it accomplished. The treaties of 1855-1856 which King Mongkut signed with the Western powers greatly impeded the progress of Siam, since they established consular jurisdiction and limited import duties to three per cent which was indeed a very low rate. Moreover, they could not be denounced unilaterally, and their revision was subject to mutual consent. Sir Josiah Crosby stated in his *Siam at the Cross-Roads* that "Although Siam has never ceased to be an independent country, her freedom of action was restricted by the various Treaties which she negotiated with foreign Powers from the year 1855 onwards." At one time, Turkey was encumbered with the system of extraterritoriality, but she could collect import duties to the maximum of eleven per cent.

King Chulalongkorn embarked on a grand programme of modernising the administration along the Western lines. Such a programme required a large annual budget. In order to finance the programme, two alternatives were presented to him, either to borrow the money from Europe or to increase the taxes. The first alternative seemed to him to be out of question at least for the time being, as it would entail political implications, opening a way for the Western powers to seek interference in the internal affairs of the country. The second alternative would cause considerable hardship to the people. The import duties would certainly bring in a much larger revenue to the Thai government, if they could be increased freely instead of being fixed by the treaties with the foreign countries. It was also the desire of King Chulalongkorn to abolish extraterritoriality, since it caused difficulties to the administration of the country.

Chulalongkorn entrusted his general adviser, Dr. Strobel, with the duty of revising the treaties with this objective—to recover full sovereignty for Siam, so that she would enjoy judicial and fiscal autonomy. The adviser himself was convinced that the United States of America would be the first country to negotiate with Siam for the revision of the treaty. He handed a draft of the new treaty to the U.S. Minister at Bangkok, Hamilton King, with a request that it be transmitted to the State Department. Since Siam had difficult questions to solve with France and Great Britain, the U.S. State Department postponed the consideration of the Thai draft. It is sad to say that Dr. Strobel died in harness in 1908, while he was carrying on his negotiations with Great Britain. Though his successor, Mr. Westengaard, who bore the title of nobility as Phya Kalyamaitri, tried hard in this matter; he also failed to have the treaty with the United States of America revised. According to a letter which Prince Dewawongse wrote to Chulalongkorn on August 9, 1910, the U.S. government worried about the land held by the American missionaries. If American nationals were under the jurisdiction of the Thai courts, the land which belonged to the American missionaries might be confiscated, unless the Thai Government guaranteed their ownership of such land. At the same time what caused uneasiness to the Thai Government was that the U.S. Government might not ratify the treaty which was to be revised. This would create a bad precedent which would complicate the negotiations between Siam and the foreign Powers. So the revision of the treaties was stalled temporarily. It can be stated without exaggeration that Chulalongkorn brought vast progress to Siam. In Hall's words, "the fact remains that the real progress that was made possible only through the exercise of his absolute power." His forty two years' reign—the longest in Thai history—ended on October 23, 1910, amidst the unfathomable sorrow of the Thai people who still humbly refer to him as the "Beloved Great." On the anniversary of his demise, which has been declared as a government holiday in deference to his memory, homage in the form of floral tribute is paid to his Equestrian Statue in the Royal Plaza of Bangkok by the old who saw him and the young who have heard about his achievements.

# CHAPTER XII

# BEFORE THE DEMOCRATIC PERIOD

RAMA VI (1910-1925). In furtherance of the policy of modernising Siam along the Western lines as initiated by his enlightened grandfather and systematically implemented by his august father in consonance with the increasing financial strength of the country, Rama VI concerned himself actively with the internal and foreign affairs.

He was born on January 1, 1881, as Prince Vajiravudh, being Chulalongkorn's first son by Queen Saovabhaphongsi. She acted as the Regent during the King's first visit to Europe in 1897. Vajiravudh was educated by private tutors in the Grand Palace before he proceeded to England for further studies at the age of 13. In England, he settled down for a period of nearly three years at a house in Ascot known as "North Lodge," where he undertook a general course of study in English, and showing his early leaning towards literature, even in a foreign language, it is interesting to note that he founded, published and "ran" a weekly journal for juveniles known by the scarcely euphonious but infinitely distinctive title of *The Screech-Owl*. In 1894, Chulalongkorn appointed him as Crown Prince, thus making him the heir-apparent to the Thai throne. On leaving Ascot, Vajira- vudh moved to Frimley Park, near Camberley, where he studied for his military course under an artillery officer by name of Lieutenant-Colonel C.V. Hume, who was deputed by the British Government to assist him in his studies. In due course, he entered the Royal Military College at Sandhurst. He liked the life there, of which he entered into every phase most heartily, and he was very popular with the officers and his fellow cadets; so he went right through the whole course—drilling, entrenching, bridge-building, etc. After passing out of Sandhurst, he was attached to the Royal Durham Light Infantry, under Colonel Wood- land, at the North Camp at Aldershot, where he went through the officers' recruiting course, and therefore obtained a thorough training as a British officer upwards from the beginning right up to the highest point. The Crown Prince who went on manoeuvres with his regiment won wide popularity among his brother-officers and men. At that time, an opportunity cropped up for him to get to know the British Royal Family, for he was called up to re- present Siam at the Diamond Jubilee of Queen Victoria in 1897. From Aldershot, he took up residence at Christchurch College, Oxford, where he took up the study of history in general, together with political economy and geography, and in this course, he had the assistance of a private "coach" by name of Mr. Hassall. The Crown Prince distinguished himself by becoming the author of a work entitled *The War of Polish Succession*, written in English, while he also became a member of the Bullingdon and Cardinal Clubs, both of well-known literary repute, and also of the Cosmopolitan Club, in which members were called upon to regale each other with original papers on a wide variety of subjects, with regard to which he by no means failed in his duty to his fellow-members. On going down from Oxford, he proceeded to pass through the School of Musketry at Hythe, where he not only passed but obtained a special certificate for marksmanship. So the Crown Prince had an excellent academic record which well equipped him for his future kingly responsibilities before he returned home via the United States of America and Japan on his observation tour.

On October 3, 1902, the Crown Prince sailed from Southampton, England, by a German mail steamer which was proceeding to New York. Almost directly after his arrival in New York, he left by the President's special train for Washington, D.C. During his visit to the United States of America, he was accompanied by his beloved younger brother, Prince Phitsanulok. Soon after their arrival in Washington, the Crown Prince and Prince Phitsanulok paid their official call at the White House, where Mr. Hay, State Secretary, awaited them and introduced them to President Theodore Roosevelt, who, owing to a recent operation on one of his legs, was unable to rise to receive his visitors. During the course of the animated conversation which followed, the President expressed his regret that he would not be able, as he had hoped, to accompany the Crown Prince and his brother during their stay in his country.

The President and the Crown Prince discussed various matters together, including that of the fitness of the American cavalry uniform for war-time—a subject on which both of them, owing to their military training, were thoroughly competent to express an opinion, for the then Mr. Roosevelt had, at the outset of the war against Spain in 1898, raised and commanded a mounted corps known as the "Rough-riders." The President then went on to express his earnest desire that relations between their respective countries should enter upon a closer phase, which could only conduce to their mutual benefit.

During his tour of the United States of America, covering a period of nearly two months, the itinerary of the Crown Prince included many big cities and well-renowned sights and a few institutions of higher learning. Besides the Naval College at Annapolis, the Military Academy at West Point, Columbia University and Harvard University, he visited Philadelphia, New York, Boston, Niagara Falls, Pittsburgh, Chicago, St. Louis, Colorado Springs, the Grand Canyon, San Diego in California, San Francisco, Portland in Oregon, and also Victoria on Vancouver Island, where on December 2, 1902, he boarded the Canadian Railway's fine liner, the "Empress of China," en route for Yokohama, Japan.

On his arrival at Yokohama on December 16, 1902, after a voyage prolonged by heavy weather, the Crown Prince was welcomed officially on behalf of the Emperor Meiji or Mutsuhito by Their Imperial Highnesses Prince Komatsu and Prince Fushimi as well as the Master of Ceremonies at the Imperial Court. He was then conducted over the brief space which separates Yokohama from Tokyo to the Shiba Palace which was placed at his disposal during his stay. On December 17, 1902, at 5 o'clock in the afternoon, he paid his state visit to the Emperor, following which he was entertained to dinner in the Grand Palace. at which the Empress was present in person. On the following morning at 11 o'clock, the Emperor returned a state visit to the Crown Prince and conferred on him the Order of the Chrysanthemum. The one-month four of Japan (December 16, 1902 - January 14, 1903), undertaken by the Crown Prince, naturally afforded him a unique opportunity to observe the rapid progress in various fields of activities which that country had been making since the beginning of the Restoration or Meiji era in 1868. It is noteworthy to state that Siam and Japan started to reform themselves at the same time. While the former made rather slow and careful progress, due to many factors such as the aggressive policy of France and Great Britain and the finances of the country, the latter outran her to such an extent that Thai officials were sent out to study how the reform of Japan was being carried out and then Thai students followed suit. For instance, Luang Pisal Silprasart later known as Chao Phya Dharmasakti Montri, Minister of Education, travelled out as the leader of a special mission to inquire into the general system of education in vogue amongst the Japanese.

The Thai royal yacht, "Maha Chakri," which had been sent to Japan to convey the Crown Prince to Bangkok, set sail for Hong Kong where it stopped for coal on January 18, 1903. There the Crown Prince was received by the Governor Sir Henry Blake, G.C.M.G., and the Government House was placed at his disposal during his stay. The reception was a most cordial one. The Crown Prince remained in Hong Kong for three days, during which time he took the opportunity of visiting Canton, prior to sailing on his last stretch for home which he reached on January 29, 1903. Chulalongkorn himself conducted the Crown Prince in a state coach, attended by a large escort of cavalry, to his residence at the Saranromya Palace which had been prepared for his reception on his return.

Chulalongkorn assigned the Crown Prince to work in the army where he rose to be a full general, holding the inspector-general's post as well as being in control of the First Regiment of the Royal Bodyguards. On his second trip to Europe in 1907, the King appointed him as Regent so as to enable him to derive actual practical experience in the administration of the country.

On the demise of his august father, Chulalongkorn, on October 23, 1910, the Crown Prince Vajiravudh ascended the throne as Rama VI. His coronation which took place towards the end of November 1911 was for the first time attended by representatives of the Great Powers such as His Royal Highness Prince Alexander of Teck, representing George V of Great Britain; His Excellency Monsieur P. de Margeri, representing the President of France; Baron C. von Der Goltz, representing the German Emperor; His Imperial Highness Grand Duke Boris Vladimirovitch, representing the Tsar of Russia; His Excellency Chamberlain Count T. de Bolesta Koziehbrodzki, representing the King-Emperor of Austria-Hungary; His Imperial Highness Prince Hiroyasu Fushimi, representing the Emperor of Japan; and His Excellency Mr. Hamilton King, representing the President of the United States of America.

At the beginning of his reign in 1911, Rama VI was probably shaken by the discovery of a plot, hatched by a small party of army and navy officers, civil servants and civilians, with a view to overthrowing the government, but he revealed his magnaminity in dealing with them. They were imprisoned, but none of them suffered capital punishment. Rama VI therefore took quick steps to safeguard his throne and to promote nationalism simultaneously through the creation of the Wild Tigers' Corps and also of the Boy Scouts' Organization in Siam. The Wild Tigers' Corps which was divided into royal and ordinary regiments served him as a kind of territorial army after the British pattern. Generally speaking, the noblemen whom he appointed to be in charge of the royal regiments were his favourites or very close to him, so that he could trust them in performing their duties for him, while those in control of the ordinary regiments were high officials enjoying his confidence. The father of the writer of this book, who attained the highest rank in the Wild Tigers' Corps as a general, was known to the King, as he had the honour of being presented to him in his student days in England.   Although he worked as the Under-Secretary of State for Education, he was on one occasion called by him to serve him for a special assignment.   Being of the same stature and appearance as Rama VI from a distance, though younger in age by about three years, he was to be the King's double, should a serious danger threaten the country.   In the event of his being killed, the King would graciously take care of his family.   Thus in addition to the Army, the Navy and the Police, the Wild Tigers' Corps constituted another line of protection for Rama VI.

Rama VI continued to improve the administration of the country by his re-organization of some ministries.   He combined the Ministry of the Interior and the Ministry of Local Government into one Ministry of the Interior, created the Ministry of Marine and the Ministry of Commerce, revived the Ministry of Privy Seal and changed the name of the Ministry of Public Works into the Ministry of Communications.   The Department of Religious Affairs under the Ministry of Public Instruction was transferred to the Ministry of the Royal Household, so that the Ministry of Public Instruction came to be known as the Ministry of Education.   For provincial administration, the montons or circles were combined to form regions, each region under a Viceroy who shouldered direct responsibility to the King.   The King intended to teach self-government to the people through the construction of a miniature city called "Dusitthani" at Dusit Palace, but this project did not receive wide support and consequently it was dropped towards the end of his reign.   To cope with the increasing needs of the country, a few new Departments were established such as the Royal Air Force Department and the Fisheries Department.   It is of interest to mention that the metric system of weights and measures was adopted on December 17, 1923, long before the Anglo Saxon countries.

In the social uplifting of the people, he created surnames for them in 1913, and what is more, he graciously invented some of them.   The father of the writer of this book felt it a great honour indeed, when the King conferred on him and his elder brother, who was the Governor or Tesa of a monthon or circle, the surname of "Syamananda" on December 26, 1913.   The only means to identify a person before the creation of surnames was to refer to him as a son of Mr. so and so or as belonging to this or that village.   Surnames do certainly help people in their daily contact.   In view of the fact that the majority of the people were prone to seek their fortune by gambling, thus neglecting to pursue their occupations to the best of their ability, Rama VI abolished gambling houses and the "Kaw Khaw" lottery.   A lottery in the Western style was, however, allowed to be drawn at a fair, which was officially organized on a special occasion.   It was largely through his influence that Thai women adopted Western hair styles and one-piece and two-piece skirts in place of short hair en brosse and the panung or waist-cloth with the end pulled between their legs and tucked in at the back.   He was also responsible for the introduction of football and Western dancing into the country as a kind of recreation for the masses.

Education at all levels also engaged Rama VI's attention, and he took active steps to promote it, realizing that if more and more people were educated, they would help in the development of the land better than previously.   In this connection, he proclaimed a new national scheme of education in 1913, whereby a primary or pathom school had a three-year ordinary course of study and a two-year vocational course, while a secondary or matayom school had an eight-year course.   After completing an ordinary course in a primary school, a boy or girl who did not wish to continue schooling at the secondary level

150

could enroll in a vocational course. A Private Schools Act was put on the statute book in 1918 and finally a Primary Education Act of 1921, enforcing compulsory education, was announced, requiring boys and girls from the age of 7 to 14 to attend primary schools free of charge, and if they completed the ordinary course before the age of 14, they were permitted to leave school. Thus Siam became the first country on the mainland of Asia to initiate compulsory education. Regarding university education, which was contemplated in the national scheme of education, as humbly presented to Chulalongkorn in 1898, Rama VI turned the Royal Pages' School into the Civil Service College. The School had been charged with giving a general education with emphasis on training in government administration, while the Civil Service College planned to offer the following courses of study: Agriculture, Commerce, Education, Engineering, Foreign Service, Law, Medicine and Public Administration. On March 26, 1917, the status of the Civil Service College was raised to that of a university; it was named Chulalongkorn University as a memorial to King Chulalongkorn. Thus the first Thai university was born.

Rama VI was equally famous as a lover of art and the theatre and as a writer of prose and poetry, though he was deeply involved in the government of the country as an absolute monarch, acting virtually as Prime Minister in the Cabinet. At first he wrote as a nationalist under the pen name of Asavapahu and Ramchitti. His book entitled *The Jews in the Far East*, for instance, represented his view on the economic conditions of Siam. Later he

KING RAMA VI AWARDING THE SERVICE MEDAL
TO A VOLUNTEER OF THE THAI EXPEDITIONARY FORCE TO EUROPE IN THE FIRST WORLD WAR

switched over to writing for the sake of literature and thus produced such volumes as the *Ramakien* (Ramayana), the royal version of Nala, *Mattanapata* and *Sakuntala*. His literal translation of Shakespeare's plays such as *The Merchant of Venice* and *As You Like It* surely reveals his profound knowledge of both Thai and English. In brief Dr. Wit Siwasariyanon stated in his *Trends and Highlights of Thai Literature* that "King Vajiravudh was a great literary figure with several strings to his bow. Apart from scores of plays, poems and translations of Shakespeare's works, he had to his credit numerous essays, addresses, newspaper articles and polemical tracts. As a prose writer, he was gifted with a clear, direct and forceful style. It was he also who gave an impetus to the development of modern prose fiction in Thailand."

Regarding his private life, Rama VI remained a bachelor until about the last six years of his life. At first he became engaged to Her Highness Princess Vallapadevi, but their wedding never took place. He then married Her Royal Highness Princess Laksmilawan (Pranangthur Laksmilawan), Somdech Pranangchao Intarasakdisachi and Pranangchao Suwattana one after another. Out of Suwattana's wedlock was born Her Royal Highness Princess Petcharat Rajsuda on November 24, 1925, only one day before her august father breathed his last breath on November 25, 1925.

Towards the end of his reign, owing to his excessive generosity and unbounded kindness, coupled with glaring extravagance in his Court, Rama VI became a spendthrift with a result that the annual national budget was unbalanced, as is shown by the following figures in baht:

|  | Revenue | Ordinary expenditure | Special expenditure |
|---|---|---|---|
| B.E. 2466 (1923-1924) | 80,000,000 | 90,216,043 | 18,087,124 |
| B.E. 2467 (1924-1925) | 84,000,000 | 93,125,688 | 15,029,000 |
| B.E. 2468 (1925-1926) | 91,000,000 | 94,825,238 | 9,275,600 |

Apparently he soon realized the importance of a small country like Siam enjoying a balanced national budget, and it was widely known in the Court circle that he contemplated a reduction of the expenditures, but he passed away before any action was taken in this connection.

. King Vajiravudh or Rama VI's greatest accomplishment, which will never go into oblivion, was the successful revision of the treaties with other countries.

On April 1, 1913, the Thai Minister at Washington, Prince Traidosprapandh, called on President Woodrow Wilson to express to him his congratulations on taking the office. The President praised the Thai Government for having helped the American missionaries, and he had met King Rama VI or Vajiravudh when he passed through the U.S.A. on his way home in 1902. The friendly attitude assumed by President Wilson raised hopes of the Thai Government for the revision of the treaty with the U.S. Government, but the negotiations between the two Governments were suspended during the First World War.

When the First World War broke out in August 1914, Rama VI's Government declared itself neutral, which was only natural as far as the Thai people were concerned, having no direct interests in it. But Rama VI was Anglophile, having been educated at the Royal Military College at Sandhurst, and at Oxford University in Great Britain, and he also held the honorary rank of a general in the British army. He sent a large donation to the welfare fund of his old English regiment, the Durham Light Infantry, and he contributed money to charities, organized by the people on the side of the Allies. He resented the so-called atrocities committed by Germany. He wrote pro-Allies articles in the newspapers under different assumed names and translated into Thai both general and technical war articles from English magazines, all of which were favourable to the English cause, thus preparing the people for his momentous decision. On April 6, 1917, the United States of America declared war on the Central Powers and sent a circular appeal to all neutral countries to join in the struggle to support Right against Might. Siam followed suit, and entered the First World War on the side of the Allies on July 22, 1917, in order to uphold the rights and freedom of the small powers. All Germans and Austrians in Siam were quickly arrested and interned, while forty German merchant ships which had taken refuge in the port of Bangkok were seized. The German crews tried to blow up the vessels, but in nearly all cases their attempts were foiled, and the ships were taken intact. The enemy internees were then sent to India to be interned by the British at their request, though they were given good treatment by the Thai authorities. A small, but efficient expeditionary force of 1,200 volunteers, made up of a motor transport corps and air pilots, was despatched to Europe, under the command of Major General Phya Pijaijarnrit (later Phya Devahastin). The men acquitted themselves well; but those aspiring to be pilots were still being trained and acclimatized in the south of France when the war ended in November 1918, and they never saw any action. The Motor Transport Corps operated with the French Army under heavy shell-fire before crossing the Rhine into Germany after the Armistice with other allied forces. During their stay in France, the Thai soldiers became friendly with U.S. troops, which has cemented to this day the Thai friendship with the American people. There were Thai contingents in the victory marches in Paris, London, and Brussels, thus helping to put Siam on the map of the world once more. On their return to Bangkok, they were accorded a hero's reception. They went on a parade and were complimented by the King for their good work.

In 1919, Siam attended the Peace Conference of Versailles as one of the victors, where her delegates made no request for any territory or indemnity as a compensation. The delegates were His Highness Prince Charoonsakdi who was the Thai Minister at Paris, His Serene Highness Prince Traidosprapandh who was the Under-Secretary of State for Foreign Affairs, and Phya Pipatkosa, the Minister at Rome. They stressed the fact that the unequal treaties with the various countries were unfair to Siam, and President Wilson supported this appeal.

Siam followed up this step and opened negotiations for the revision of the treaty with the United States of America. The Thai Minister at Washington, Phya Prabhakorawong, was instructed to take charge of the negotiations. In his report of June 7,1920, to the Thai Foreign Minister, he stated that "the (American) President has shown great interest in our business and I have learnt from trustworthy persons that he has a real intention to conclude this treaty before he leaves the Presidency. If we miss this important opportunity to recover the two fold autonomy for judicial affairs and the export tariff, during the time of President Wilson, I am afraid there will be no hope to get such autonomy when the

President is a Republican."

In the meantime, Siam had abolished extraterritoriality with Germany and Austria-Hungary. In fact, the relations between Siam and Germany in particular had been cordial and German goods had gained a wide market in the country till the First World War. Furthermore there had been no dispute of any kind with either Germany or Austria-Hungary. The Germans had at the same time extended a helping hand to Siam, a noteworthy instance of which was the construction of the northern railways by the German engineers. Some military officers and government officials who had been educated in Germany seemed to have personal sympathy for the Central Powers. When Rama VI made up his mind to join the Allies, however, they rallied to him as one man, as they were well aware of the fact that the vast influence of Great Britain and the United States of America in the Far East was the determining factor for Thai participation in the war. It was believed that the German Government understood the motives of the Thai Government in taking this step. On June 28, 1919, the Treaty of Peace between the Allies and the Associate Powers on one side and Germany on the other side was signed at Versailles. According to Article 135, Section III, Part IV of this Treaty, "Germany recognizes that all Treaties, Conventions, and Agreements between her and Siam and all rights, titles and privileges derived therefrom, including all rights of extraterritorial jurisdiction terminated as from July 22, 1917."

A clause identical with that stated above was contained in the Austrian Peace of St. Germain in Section 110, signed on September 10, 1919, and in the Hungarian Treaty of Trianon, June 4, 1920, Section 94.

By virtue of this provision in the three Treaties, Siam recovered court jurisdiction over German, Austrian and Hungarian subjects. They must go to the ordinary Thai courts in all kinds of cases on the same basis as the Thais themselves. When Germany renewed her relations with Siam after the First World War, she accepted the principle of the equality of states. She did not obtain any special rights or privileges in a provisional economic Agreement and a Treaty of Friendship, Commerce and Navigation which she concluded with Siam in 1921 and 1928 respectively. It should be noted that the 1928 Treaty of Friendship, Commerce and Navigation was an equal one between the two countries.

As one of the Allies in the First World War, Siam signed the Treaty of Versailles, and she became a founder member of the League of Nations which was created in 1919 for the preservation of peace and the promotion of international cooperation. The membership of Siam in the League of Nations at Geneva was again a recognition of her status as being equal to the other civilized countries. However, she did not play a really active role in the League of Nations until the Manchurian Incident broke out in 1931.

The negotiations for the revision of the Treaty with the United States of America were brought to a successful conclusion with Siam making a few concessions concerning the right of evocation of cases for a period of five years after the promulgation and enforcement of all the legal codes as well as the question of land tenure. Thus the U.S. Government recognized indirectly the legal system of Siam as being on par with that of a civilized country. As has already been mentioned, the Thai legal system had been thoroughly modernised in Chulalongkorn's reign. The Ministry of Justice and law courts after the Western pattern were established. Some French and English jurists as well as one eminent Japanese lawyer were employed by the Thai Government as judges and experts in the revision and codification of Thai laws. Thai students were awarded scholarships for futher studies in Law in the West, and most of them went to England.

On December 18, 1920, while Wilson was still the President, Mr. Norman H. Davis, acting Secretary of State of the United States of America, and Phya Prabhakorawong, Envoy Extraordinary and Minister Plenipotentiary of Siam to the United States of America, signed a new treaty at Washington. It was ratified by the American Senate on April 27, 1921, by King Rama VI on April 29, 1921, and by President Harding on May 6, 1921. The treaty was to be in force for a period of ten years as from September 1, 1921, when the exchange of ratifications was effected at Bangkok. It replaced the treaty of 1856 between Siam and the United States of America.

The main points of the treaty and the protocol attached thereto are as follows:

1. "There shall be constant peace and perpetual friendship between the United States of America and the Kingdom of Siam. The citizens or subjects of each of the High Contracting Parties, shall have the liberty to enter, travel, and reside in the territories of the other, to carry on trade, wholesale and retail, to engage in religious, educational and charitable work, to own or lease and occupy houses, manufactories, warehouses and shops, to employ agents to their choice, to lease land for residential and commercial, religious and charitable purposes and for use as cemeteries; and generally to do anything incident to or necessary for trade upon the same terms as native citizens or subjects, submitting themselves to the laws and regulations there established.

2. "The system of jurisdiction heretofore established in Siam for citizens of the United States and the privileges, exemptions and immunities now enjoyed by the citizens of the United States in Siam, as a part of our appurtenant to said system, shall absolutely cease and determine on the date of the exchange of ratifications of the above-mentioned Treaty, and there after all citizens of the United States and persons, corporations, companies and associations entitled to its protection in Siam shall be subject to the jurisdiction of the Siamese Courts.

3. "Until the promulgation and putting into force of all the Siamese Codes, namely, the Penal Code, the Civil and Commercial Codes, the Codes of Procedure and the Laws for Organization of Courts and a period of five years thereafter, but no longer, the United States, through its Diplomatic and Consular officials in Siam, whenever in its discretion it deems it proper to do so in the interest of justice by means of a written requisition addressed to the Judge or Judges of the Court in which such case in pending may evoke any case pending in any Siamese Court, except the Supreme or Dika Court, in which an American citizen or a person, corporation company or association entitled to the protection of the United States is defendant or accused.

"Such cases shall then be transferred to the said Diplomatic or Consular Official for adjudication and the jurisdiction of the Siamese Court over such case shall thereupon cease. Any case so evoked shall be disposed of by the said Diplomatic or Consular Official in accordance with the laws of the United States properly applicable, except that as to all matters coming within the scope of Codes or laws of the Kingdom regularly promulgated and in force, the texts of which have been communicated to the American Legation in Bangkok, the rights and liabilities of the parties shall be determined by the Siamese Law.

"For the purpose of trying such cases and of executing any judgment which may be rendered therein, the jurisdiction of the American Diplomatic and Consular Officials in Siam is continued.

4. "Appeal by citizens of the United States or by persons, corporations, companies and associations entitled to its protection from judgments of Courts of First Instance, in cases to which they may be parties, shall be adjudged by the Court of Appeal at Bangkok.

"An appeal on a question of law shall be made from the Court of Appeal Bangkok to the Supreme or Dika Court.

"A citizen of the United States or a person, corporation, company or association entitled to its protection, who is defendant or accused in any case arising in the provinces may apply for a change of venue and should the Court consider such change desirable, the trial shall take place either at Bangkok or before the Judges in whose Court the case would be tried at Bangkok.

5. "The United States restored to Siam the absolute power in levying taxes and recognized in principle the equal treatment to be accorded to the foreign countries having relations with her; in other words, Siam was free to fix the tariff for exports and imports, but she must not grant special rights to any nation."

According to this treaty, no American could own land in Siam and in the same way no Thai could own land in the United States of America.

The United States of America made a great sacrifice when she agreed to the revision of the treaty. She did this out of altruism and with magnanimity. As Martin asserted in *A History of the Diplomatic Relations Between Siam and the United States of America 1833-1929*, "This friendly deed by the United States changed the whole picture for Siam and made it much easier for Siam in her negotiations with the other countries." It is indeed a true statement. In his *Glad Adventure*, Sayre stated that "Through America led the path to freedom." At the beginning of 1924, Siam concluded a new treaty with Japan. By this treaty, Japan gave up the Consular Court system in Siam in practically the same manner as provided in the American Treaty of 1920. Owing to the most favoured treatment clause theThai-American treaty could not be applied immediately and the treaties between Siam and the other Powers must be similarly revised. Only then Siam would be able to implement the terms of the revised treaties.

Towards the end of Rama VI's reign, Dr. Francis B. Sayre, President Wilson's son-in-law, succeeded Dr. Eldon James as Siam's foreign adviser, and submitted to the King a proposal that a delegation should be sent to Europe, where direct negotiations could be pursued with the various governments so as to expedite the revision of the treaties. Those governments would understand Siam's objective in this matter clearly and thoroughly. On the other hand, the representatives of the western Powers who were stationed in Bangkok seemed to be reluctant to surrender the special rights enjoyed by their nationals, thus delaying the work. Approving of this proposal, Rama VI appointed Sayre as the leader of the delegation with full power to revise the treaties with the European Powers, after the pattern of the American-Thai treaty, and in the execution of this difficult task, he received close cooperation from Prince Traidosprapandh who had succeeded his father, Prince Dewawongse, as Foreign Minister in 1923. Sayre left Bangkok for Europe in September 1924 and accomplished his mission within one year. The King rewarded him with the title of Phya Kalyamaitri, being the second American to be thus ennobled.

Siam had taken the initiative to negotiate with France for the revision of the treaty directly after the First World War. But the French Government did not seem to regard this matter as an urgent one. In January 1919, an official by name of Kahn, representing the French Foreign Office, was sent to contact the Thai authorities at Bangkok for consultations concerning a new treaty. In his letter of December 12, 1919, to the Thai Foreign Minister, Prince Charoonsakdi, the Thai Minister at Paris, felt that France adopted a "wait and see policy" with regard to the whole business, as she would like the other Powers to set an example first and she was particularly interested in the American foreign policy about Siam. However, when M. Pila, the French Minister at Bangkok, visited Paris on official business, he was assigned by the French Ministry of Foreign Affairs to continue consultations with Prince Charoonsakdi with a result that France would agree to the revision of the treaty, if Siam made a pledge on the following proposals. Subsequently Siam carried out these proposals.

1. Siam should set up the Department of Legislative Redaction and appoint the French lawyers who were working in the Division of Legal Codification as legal experts in the new Department. The Thai Government accepted this proposal on the condition that it would not bind itself to engage only French legal experts. The Department of Legislative Redaction was established on October 27, 1924.

2. With regard to the re-organization of the Law School at Bangkok with Frenchmen as its director and professors, the Thai Government set up a committee to administer the School under the direction of a Thai lawyer. A few French lawyers were appointed members of the committee and two French professors were engaged to teach at the School.

3. So long as there was a need for foreign legal advisers, the Thai Government would engage French lawyers in this capacity.

4. The Thai Government would inform the French Legation at Bangkok of a vacancy suitable for a foreigner and would increase the number of scholarships for Thai students to further their studies in France.

5. French should be taught by Frenchmen in Thai educational institutions. As a matter of fact, it was taught in the Faculty of Arts and Science, Chulalongkorn University, and in the Law School. A Frenchman was engaged as a Lecturer in French in the university.

6. The Thai Government appointed Professor Georges Coedès as deputy director of the archaeological service of the Vajiranana National Library.

7. The Thai Government could not comply with a French request for a forest concession at Meta and Melong in the province of Chiang Mai which was already worked by other people. In the hope of getting the treaty revised, a concession at Mechan in the same province was given to the French company instead.

Although the French proposals had been carried out by the Thai Government, the negotiations between Siam and France made no appreciable progress. Dr. Sayre set out to deal with France first about this business and arrived at Paris towards the end of 1924. There he successfully carried out his work. On February 14, 1925, a new Franco-Thai treaty was signed at Paris by M. Edouard Herriot, the French Prime Minister and Foreign Minister, and Prince Charoonsakdi, the Thai Minister at Paris. In attaining success in this matter Dr. Sayre and the other two Thai representatives, Prince Charoonsakdi and M. Charles L'Évêsque, the Counsellor of the Thai Legation at Paris, carried on their negotiations with the French representative, M. Pila, in secrecy. Dr. Sayre wrote in his letter of January 10, 1925, to the Thai Foreign Minister, Prince Traidosprapandh that if the British Foreign Office had known that France was about to conclude a new treaty with Siam, he was afraid that it might have taken steps to prevent her from doing so.

With regard to Great Britain, the Thai delegation to the Peace Conference at Versailles submitted a memorandum of February 22, 1919, to Balfour, the British Foreign Secretary, asking for sympathy for the revision of the treaty. The Thai Minister at London, Phya Buri-nawarat, was then instructed to approach the British Government about the revision of the treaty with Great Britain. In its reply dated November 1, 1919, the British Foreign Office stated that it was willing to consider the revision of the (customs) tariff. However this would take a long time, since consultations had to be held with the Ministries concerned. Regarding the extraterritoriality, Great Britain was not ready to discuss any change, since she gave up more special rights than any other European power in the treaty of 1909. If other countries agreed to revise their treaties with Siam, she would consider a Thai proposal.

After the ratification of the Thai - US treaty of 1920 by the American Senate on April 27, 1921, the Thai Foreign Minister, Prince Dewawongse, telegraphed his instructions to the Thai Minister at London to find ways and means to expedite negotiations for the signing of a new treaty along the same lines as the Thai - U.S. treaty. The British Government was observing the attitude of the French Government towards the Thai proposal about the same matter. However, when it became known that France had agreed to sign a new treaty with Siam, Great Britain changed her policy. In his letter of September 9, 1924, to the new Thai Minister at London, Phya Prabhakorawong, the Thai Foreign Minister, Prince Traidosprapandh, expressed the opinion that the Labour Government, headed by Mr. Ramsay MacDonald, which had just come into power, would be more receptive to the Thai request for judicial and fiscal autonomy than the government of any other party.

Phya Prabhakorawong paid a courtesy call on Sir Austen Chamberlain who had just taken the office of Foreign Secretary in the Conservative Government headed by Mr. Stanley Baldwin. After a review of the Anglo-Thai relations, Chamberlain assured the Thai Minister that he would help in the revision of the treaty. Dr. Sayre met the British Foreign Secretary on February 25, 1925, and they had a frank talk about Siam. The latter said that the U.S.A. granted Siam's wishes in all respects because her trade with that country was on a small scale, while more than eighty per cent of the Thai exports went to the British territories. If Siam was free to raise customs duties, there would be repercussions on the British trade. Great Britain would only consent to a moderate increase in such duties. As regards extraterritoriality, Chamberlain stood by the treaty of 1909. However, if Sayre could get the experts and various chiefs of the sections of the Foreign Office, the Chamber of Commerce, the Department of Overseas Trade, the Colonial Office and the India Office to understand the situation about Siam, he would go along with them. Sayre then talked with the officials concerned and managed to secure their approval of the Thai proposal. But the British Minister at Bangkok, Robert Gregg, wanted to postpone the revision of the treaty until all the Thai legal codes had been enforced. In spite of this objection, the British Government continued negotiations with the Thai representative, while the Thai Government accepted the six points, suggested by the British Minister at Bangkok, as follows :

1. Siam should continue to employ the Europeans as legal advisers until all the legal codes had been enforced.

2. The legal adviser to the Minister of Justice should be an Englishman.

3. The adviser to the Customs Department should be an Englishman.

4. The Thai Government should engage English lawyers who knew the Indian legal codes as lecturers in the Law School.

5. The English law should be applied, if the Thai law did not provide for points arising out of commercial cases.

6. The Thai Government should declare its intention not to raise export duties on teak, tin and rice.

On July 14, 1925, a new treaty was signed in London by Sir Austen Chamberlain and Phya Prabhakorawong and was duly ratified by the British monarch and the Thai King. In the same year, identical treaties were signed with the Netherlands, Spain, Portugal, Denmark, and Sweden, and in 1926 with Italy, the Belgo-Luxemburg Customs Union and Norway.

The contents of the treaties of 1920-1926 could be summarised as follows: 1. Extraterritoriality was abolished in Siam. Foreigners had to go to the Thai Courts. Diplomatic or consular officers had the right of evocation in a case where their national was a defendant for the sake of justice. However the case could not be evoked, after it had reached the Supreme or Dika Court. Such a right would continue for a period of five years after the promulgation and enforcement of all the legal codes. 2. Siam recovered freedom to fix customs duties, subject to a few restrictions. For example, the Treaty of Commerce and Navigation which was concluded with Great Britain in 1925 stated that for period of ten years as from henceforth, Siam could impose a maximum of five percent import duties on raw cotton thread, cotton thread, cloth, other cotton piece goods, iron, steel, and iron and steel products as well as machinery and spare parts. This was probably intended to protect British goods in the Thai market.

Having recovered the greater part of judicial and fiscal autonomy, Siam pursued the foreign policy with a view to promoting international cooperation by peaceful means. The Franco-Thai treaty of 1925 stated that if the two countries could not settle their dispute through the diplomatic channels, they would submit it to arbitration or the Permanent Court of International Justice for a decision. In 1925, Siam signed a convention of arbitration with Great Britain, while in 1928 she concluded with the Netherlands, a treaty for the settlement of legal disputes and conciliation. For the purpose of extending her diplomatic relations, she made a treaty of amity and commerce with Switzerland in 1931. She participated actively in the work of the League of Nations, especially in the social and humanitarian fields.

PRAJADHIPOK OR RAMA VII (1925-1935). He was one of Rama VI's younger brothers. Being the 76th child of Chulalongkorn and the fourth in the direct line of succession, he did not expect to occupy the throne. However, due to the untimely death of his elder brothers, namely, Prince Phitsanulok, Prince Nakhon Ratchasima and Prince Phetchabun the Crown devolved upon him and he was immediately confronted with the most urgent problem of balancing the national budget. Prajadhipok was born in Bangkok on

November 8, 1893. Having studied Thai and English for some years in Siam, he proceeded to England where as Prince Sukhothai, he entered the world-famous Eton College at Windsor for his secondary education and then took a course in military science. On his return to Siam in Rama VI's reign, he joined the Army for sometime. He interrupted his army career in order to undertake further military studies at the Ecole Supérieure de Guerre in France. Before his accession to the throne, he held the post of the commander of the second Army Division and his princely rank was raised to that of a Krom Luang known as Krom Luang Sukhothai Tammaraja.

To assist him in the government of the realm, Prajadhipok appointed as his advisory body the Supreme Council of State which comprised three uncles . . . . Prince Bhanubhandhu Wongworadej, Prince Narisranuwattiwong and Prince Damrongrajanubhab, and two half-brothers. . Prince Nakhorn Sawan and Prince Chantaburi. It was generally agreed that they were suitable for membership of the Supreme Council of State, since they possesed first-rate administrative experience, having held or holding cabinet posts. Nevertheless a murmur arose that a commoner of the Chao Phya rank should serve on this Council, since he would have a chance to keep it in touch with the people. In his *Private Short Diary*, Luang Sukhum Naipradit, the late Secretary-General of the Civil Service Commission, wrote that "Politically speaking, King Prajadhipok was weak by nature, fearing to hurt the feelings of his elder half-brothers and uncles, and since he possessed little political experience, due to his frequent absence from Siam, or even if he remained in the country, he did not occupy a very important post, he therefore appointed the Supreme Council of State which exercised power over the Cabinet. The Supreme Council of State consisted of five princes of the high rank. In this connection, there had been a lot of talk, suggesting that a commoner should be included in the Supreme Council of State so as to win the public sympathy. The government officials felt that this new policy favoured princes, being contrary to Rama VI's policy which favoured not only princes but also common people." As the Privy Council had not been functioning as expected since its inception in 1874, Prajadhipok reconstituted it by appointing a new set of members, including princes and high government officials both on active service and in retirement, on the ground of their enjoyment of his confidence and also of their past achievements. Acting as another advisory body of the King for the consideration of government schemes and the submission of opinions and proposals for the benefit of the people, the Privy Council met for the first time on November 30, 1927, when it proceeded to elect Prince Bidyalongkorn, who was well-known as a writer under the pen-name of N.M.S. to the public, as its president, but later events show that it did not play the same important role as the Supreme Council of State in the government of the country.

Credit should be humbly tendered to Prajadhipok who proved himself to be a conscientious and thrifty monarch. At the advice of the Financial Adviser, Sir Edward Cook, he made praiseworthy efforts to put the finance of the Kingdom in good shape. Obviously retrenchment was a prime remedy for the balancing of the national budget, since Prajadhipok was unwilling to borrow from a foreign power which would probably open a loop-hole for it to interfere in the internal affairs, nor did he wish to increase the taxes, which would certainly cause untold suffering to the people. He therefore began the retrenchment with himself through the reduction of his civil list of nine million bahts to six million bahts per annum. Then the Ministry of Privy Seal was abolished and combined with the Royal Secretariat-General, while the Ministry of Commerce was merged in the Ministry of Communications to form the Ministry of Commerce and Communications in order to save the national expenditure. With the same purpose in view for the provincial administration, the vice-regal regions were done away with and the number of the montons or circles was reduced from 18 to 14. The retrenchment of many hundreds of government officials was effected, resulting in the improvement of the financial situation of the realm.

It is gratifying to note that in spite of the retrenchment just mentioned, Prajadhipok still realized the importance of education. The awarding of scholarships to outstanding students for foreign education was suspended at the end of Rama VI' reign, due to the financial stringency of the Government, and at royal command, it was resumed in due course. The writer of this book won one such scholarship for further studies in England. Since the collection of the National Education Contribution from the people for the use of public schools had proved to be an onerous burden for them, the King abolished this tax and made an allocation of three million bahts from the national budget instead in 1930. In the meantime, he had paid a visit to Chiang Mai in January 1927, where he was presented with a white elephant. He then proceeded on a tour of Java in 1929. One year later, he paid a state visit to French Indo-China in order to strengthen the cordial relations between Siam and the French Union. In 1931, he made a trip to the United States of America principally for an eye operation via French Indo-China, Hong Kong, Shanghai, Japan and Canada.

Nevertheless the retrenchment did not produce lasting results; it merely gave temporary relief to the Government, as far as the financial situation was concerned. The world economic depression which started in 1929 soon hit Siam badly, as her chief exports such as rice could not be sold abroad in the same amount and at the same price as in the previous years, thus reducing the national income considerably. The chief markets of Thai rice were the British territories such as Malaya, Singapore and Hong Kong. In 1931, Great Britain abandoned the gold standard with a result that the value of the pound sterling went down by about one-third, but Siam did not follow her immediately in this matter, though the baht was linked to the pound. The baht therefore became dearer and the rate of exchange was eight bahts to one pound instead of eleven bahts, thus affecting the easy sale of rice. Realizing her mistake about the maintenance of the value of the baht, Siam went off the gold standard in May 1932 but it was too late to correct the trade balance for rice temporarily. Consequently the expenditure was in excess of the revenue in the national budget, and retrenchment of government officials was once more resorted to as from April 1, 1932. The montons or circles were reduced from 14 to 10 in number, while the provinces (Changwat) were whittled down from 79 to 70. The Ministry of Marine was amalgamated with the Ministry of War to form the Ministry of Defence. This Ministry objected more strenuously than any other ministry when this later reduction in salaries and personnel became known. On February 5, 1932, Prajadhipok explained the reductions to the officers at the Ministry of Defence. One important paragraph of his explanation is as follows :

"I feel that I am born to a time of curtailment and enforced economies. I have imposed one reduction in salaries already and now must impose a second. And I am not sure of the future. It seems to be my fate that this burden should fall upon me. I have tried in every way to avoid further curtailment, but without success. It makes me feel more heavy-hearted than it did on the previous occasion. Formerly there were more employees than were needed so that it was proper to dismiss some, and at that time, outside employment could be found for those dismissed. I accordingly was not unduly distressed when it became necessary to dismiss employees and to decrease salaries. But this second reduction will mean a reduction in the amount of work done. I know that the armed forces, in particular, are not fully staffed. This present cut will tend to destroy their efficiency. But every ministry is in the same condition."

The national budget of B.E. 2475 (1932-1933) was balanced with the revenue of 74,846,000 bahts and the expenditure of 74,455,160 bahts, but the retrenched officials became disgruntled when they failed to find new employment, and thus they constituted good material for revolutionary propaganda. To add more oil to the fire, a new salary tax, had, in the meantime, been imposed, striking at the government officials more than at any other group. A party of army and navy officials, civil servants and civilians therefore conspired to bring about a change of the regime. According to the Under-Secretary of State for the Interior, Phya Rajanukul, who was the father of the writer of this book, the police knew the names of the conspirators and reported them to the Minister of the Interior, Field-Marshal Prince Nakhon Sawan. Had he ordered their arrest, there might have been no revolution in Siam. Actually he hesitated to do so, since he knew them personally, believing that they would not turn traitors against him. But he put his trust in the wrong persons and so a revolution broke out on June 24, 1932, resulting in a change of the regime from an absolute monarchy to a constitutional government.

# CHAPTER XIII

# DEMOCRACY IN THAILAND

The year 1932 should be definitely regarded as an important milestone in the history of Thailand, deserving the same general attention as the invention of the Thai alphabet by Ramkamhaeng the Great in 1283, the recovery of national independence by Naresuan the Great in 1584, the foundation of Bangkok as the Thai capital in 1782, the signing of the Bowring Treaty in 1855, the reorganization of the government by the establishment of twelve ministries in 1892, the Incident of 1893 between Siam and France, the abolition of Thai slavery in 1905, the declaration of war by Siam against the Central Powers in 1917 and the conclusion of a Treaty between Siam and the United States of America in 1920. At five o'clock on the morning of June 24, 1932, the revolution broke out in Bangkok, ushering in a new era of constitutional government and terminating an absolute monarchy which had prevailed in Siam from time immemorial. It was brought about by the People's Party, the leading members of which were educated in Europe. Of the fifteen members of the first Executive Committee of the Party exercising control over the cabinet ministers under the democratic regime, thirteen received their education in France, Germany, Great Britain, Switzerland and Denmark. For instance, Phya Manopakornnitithada (1884-1948), the first Prime Minister, was an English barrister-at-law; Colonel Phya Bahol Polpayuhasena (1888-1947), who later became the second Prime Minister with the rank of a full general, was graduated from a military college in Germany; Major Luang Pibulsonggram (1897-1964), who was the third Prime Minister and a Field-Marshal, studied at the Artillery School at Fontainebleau, France; Luang Pradit Manudharm or Dr. Pridi Panomyong (1900-), who received his Docteur-en-Droit from the University of Paris, became the Regent for about two years and the seventh Prime Minister; Lieutenant-Commander Luang Sindhusonggram-chai, who finished his naval studies in Denmark, reached the rank of a full admiral as commander-in-chief of the navy, and Luang Dejsahakorn or Mom Luang Dej Snidvongse, who was awarded a doctorate in Economics by a Swiss University, was the President of the Privy Council. Among other prominent members of the People's Party, two names should not be forgotten. Mr. Khuang Abhaiwong (Luang Kovit Abhaiwong) (1902-1968), who pursued his Engineering studies at the École Centrale de Lyon in France, became the fourth Prime Minister, while Mr. Tawee Bunyaket (1904-1971), who received his general education in England and studied Agriculture in France, was the fifth Prime Minister. According to *Public Administration in Siam* by W.D. Reeve, "many of the promoters of the revolution were undoubtedly genuine patriots who, convinced of the advantages of democracy, felt the time had come for a change in the system. Others were prompted by motives less disinterested; personal gain and personal advancement undoubtedly secured the co-operation of many in the Defence Forces, without whose help it would, of course, have been impossible for the civilians to enforce their demands on the King and the Ministers." Prajadhipok himself had shown an inclination for a constitution, as he had given an interview along this line to the press during his visit to the United States of America. Moreover, he requested Phya Kalya Maitri (Dr. Francis B. Sayre) to propose a constitution, and then he commanded the Under-Secretary of State for Foreign Affairs, Phya Srivisarnvacha, and the Adviser for Foreign Affairs, Mr. Raymond B. Stevens, to draft a tentative constitution, but at the advice of most members of the Supreme Council of State, he did not apparently proceed any further. In the opinion of the Supreme Council of State, the majority of the people were not sufficiently educated for the smooth working of the democratic system of government, and moreover, they did not make any effort to organize a movement for it. Many events after 1932 have apparently corroborated this opinion.

In his lectures on *My Life*, Mr. Khuang related how he took part in the revolution on the night when it broke out. As an official of the Department of Post and Telegraph, he led a few other promoters of the revolution to the Wat Lieb Exchange near the Memorial Bridge, where they forced their way in and cut all the telephone lines, thus completely paralysing the telephone communication of Bangkok. When he returned home early in the morning on that day, he was so nervous about his action that he could not eat his breakfast, brought in by his wife. He was really wondering about the outcome of the revolution. Should it fail, he would be arrested and beheaded. Luckily for him, the revolution proved to be a success and he was appointed a member of the National Assembly in accordance with the terms of the provisional constitution of June 27, 1932.

The People's Party held as hostages in the Anantasamakom Hall on the revolution day about forty princes and senior military officers such as Field Marshal Prince Nakhon-Sawan, Minister of the Interior, who acted as the Regent during Prajadhipok's absence in the United States of America; Lieutenant-General Phya Sriharajdejojai, Chief of the Army General Staff; Police Lieutenant-General Phya Atikornprakas, Chief of Police; Lieutenant General Phya Chaloemakas, Chief of the Air Force; Major-General Pijaisonggram, Commander of the first army corps; and His Serene Highness Prince Wongnirachorn Devakul, Chief of Secret Police. The military committee in defence of the capital, consisting of Colonel Phya Bahol Polpayuhasena, Colonel Phya Songsuradej and Colonel Phya Riddhi-Aganey, sent the following ultimatum to the King who resided at his summer palace "Klai-kangvol," Hua-Hin, a seaside resort on the west coast of the Gulf of Thailand about 140 miles or 228 kilometres from Bangkok:- "The People's Party consisting of civil and military officials have now taken over the administration of the country and have taken members of the Royal Family such as H.R.H.Prince Nakhon Sawan as hostages. If members of the People's Party have received any injuries, the Princes held in pawn will suffer in consequence. The People's Party have no desire to make a seizure of the Royal possessions in any way. Their principal aim is to have a constitutional monarchy. We therefore invite Your Majesty to return to the Capital to reign again as king under the constitutional monarchy as established by the People's Party. If Your Majesty refuses to accept the offer or refrains from replying within one hour after the receipt of this message, the People's Party will proclaim the constitutional monarchical government by appointing another Prince whom they consider to be efficient to act as King."

Prajadhipok accepted the fait accompli in his reply of June 25 to the ultimatum as follows:-

"I have received the letter in which you invite me to return to Bangkok as a constitutional monarch. For the sake of peace; and in order to save useless bloodshed; to avoid confusion and loss to the country; and, more, because I have already considered making this change myself, I am willing to co-operate in the establishment of a constitution under which I am willing to serve.

"Furthermore, there is a possibility that, if I decline to continue in my office as king, the foreign powers will not recognize the new government. This might entail considerable difficulty for the government.

"Physically I am not strong. I have no children to succeed me. My life expectancy is not long, at least if I continue in this office. I have no desire for position or for personal aggrandisement. My ability to advance the progress of the race alone constrains me.

"Accept this sincere expression of my feelings."

Prajadhipok returned to Bangkok with his entourage from Hua-Hin on June 25, 1932, and two days later on June 27, 1932, he granted a provisional constitution, establishing the National Assembly of 70 appointed members and vesting the government of the country in the Executive Committee of the People's Party, under the chairmanship of Phya Manopakornnitithada, former Chief Judge of the Court of Appeal. This Committee proceeded to declare six principles as its policy and appointed a committee to draft a permanent constitution.

The six principles were as follows: 1. Independence in all respects. 2. Peace and security. 3. Promotion of people's happiness through a national economic plan. 4. Equality for all. 5. Freedom and liberty, not in conflict with the first four principles. 6. Education for all.

Thus the revolution passed off without bloodshed, thanks to the wise and far-sighted action of Prajadhipok, and the general situation remained calm and peaceful, though all the ministers, under-secretaries of state and most of the departmental chiefs were retired with a pension from the government service. The drafting of the permanent constitution proceeded smoothly. On December 10, 1932, King Prajadhipok promulgated a permanent constitution, the main features of which were as follows:

1. The King was the Chief of State and enjoyed certain prerogatives. He was the head of the armed forces and the upholder of religion. He could issue royal decrees, proclaim martial law, declare war, make peace, conclude treaties with foreign states, and was vested with the right to grant pardons. He could convoke and prorogue regular sessions of the National Assembly, and he also had the right to dissolve it.

2. The King appointed the President of the Council of Ministers or the Prime Minister on the recommendation of the National Assembly. The Prime Minister then formed his Cabinet.

3. There were two categories of members of the National Assembly, namely, first and secondary category members. First category members were elected by tambon (commune) representatives who were in turn elected by both men and women. Thus universal suffrage was given to Thai people far in advance of the Japanese by 15 years. Japan was the first country to adopt a constitutional government in Asia, but she did not grant suffrage to women until 1947.

Second category members were appointed by Royal Command on the recommendation of the Cabinet. The tenure of their office was limited to ten years, at the end of which it would be abolished, if more than half of the Thai people were literate.

Members of the Royal Family from the rank of the Mom Chao (His Serene Highness) were barred from politics.

4. Besides enjoying equality before the law, every citizen was guaranteed freedom of religion and full liberty of his person, abode, property, speech, writing, publication, education, public meeting, association or vocation.

A royal pardon was granted to those who took part in the revolution.

Phya Manopakornnitithada was appointed first Prime Minister whose unenviable task was to sail the Thai ship of state through the seas of six principles, as enunciated by the People's Party. On April 1, 1933, he ordered the prorogation of the National Assembly and suspension of certain articles of the permanent constitution on the ground that the Cabinet could not agree on a national economic policy, as submitted by Luang Pradit Manudharm. It smacked of communist tendencies. Luang Pradit Manudharm was then relieved of his cabinet post and quietly left for France for a few months' sojourn. Phya Manopakornnitithada's action caused much dissatisfaction to most members of the People's Party who claimed that it belittled the sanctity of the constitution and constituted a threat to the national security. They therefore joined forces together under the leadership of Colonel Phya Bahol Polpayuhasena with the following assistants, namely, Lieutenant-Colonel Luang Pibulsonggram in charge of the army, Lieutenant-Commander Luang Supachalasai in charge of the navy, and Luang Naruebesmanit in charge of the civilians. They plotted a coup d' état and successfully carried it out on June 20, 1933, forcing the government of Phya Manopakornnitithada to resign. He went into self-exile at Penang where he lived until the end of his life. The National Assembly was then reopened and Colonel Phya Bahol Polpayuhasena became the Prime Minister.

A strong reaction against the constitutional government of the new Prime Minister resulted in a revolt which was led by General Prince Bovoradej, former Minister of Defence, and some retired high army officers. Fighting broke out in the area around Bangkhen, Laksi and Donmuang on October 11, 1933, and ended on the 24th of the same month with the government army under Colonel Luang Pibulsonggram on the winning side. A special tribunal was set up to try those who were involved in the revolt and punishment was meted out to them according to the seriousness of their crimes. This sad event, involving Thai soldiers fighting against one another, however, did not delay the general election in accordance with the terms of the permanent constitution. Seventy-eight members of the first category were elected to sit in the National Assembly, while an equal number of members of the second category was appointed by the King on the recommendation of the Cabinet. At its first meeting on December 10, 1933, the National Assembly proceeded to elect Chao Phya Dharmasakmontri, former Minister of Education, as its first president.

Apparently King Prajadhipok did not feel happy about the political situation prevailing at that time, so he decided to leave for Europe on the pretext that he needed a proper treatment for his eye trouble. During his stay abroad, he came into conflict with the Government of Phya Bahol Polpayuhasena on many matters, such as the inheritance bill and the bill for the amendment of the criminal law. A committee, consisting of Chao Phya Sritammatibet, President of the National Assembly, Luang Thamrongnavasvasti, Secretary General of the Cabinet, and Mr. Direk Jayanam, Secretary to the Ministry of Foreign Affairs, was despatched to London in order to invite the King to return to Bangkok, but its efforts were in vain. Since the Government could not meet all his wishes, he abdicated on March 2, 1935, and he continued to live in England, where he died at the age of 48 on May 30, 1941.

As Prajadhipok did not designate a successor, the National Assembly proceeded with Article 9 of the constitution, invoking the Law of Succession of 1924 as laid down by King Vajiravudh, and proclaimed the legal heir, Prince Ananda Mahidol, as the eighth king of the Chakri Dynasty. The new king was a boy of ten, being the elder son of His Royal Highness Prince Mahidol of Songkhla, and at his accession to the throne, he was living with his mother, brother and sister at Lausanne, Switzerland.

The genealogy of the Royal House of Chakri is as follows:-

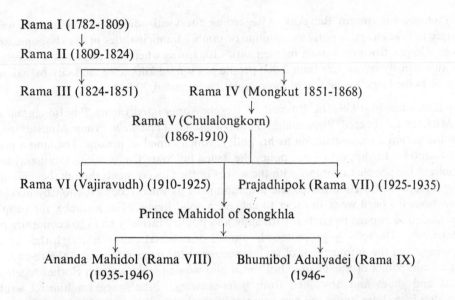

Rama I (1782-1809)
↓
Rama II (1809-1824)

Rama III (1824-1851)          Rama IV (Mongkut 1851-1868)
↓
Rama V (Chulalongkorn)
(1868-1910)

Rama VI (Vajiravudh) (1910-1925)     Prajadhipok (Rama VII) (1925-1935)

Prince Mahidol of Songkhla
↓

Ananda Mahidol (Rama VIII)      Bhumibol Adulyadej (Rama IX)
(1935-1946)                      (1946-      )

Since Ananda Mahidol was a minor and continued his study in Switzerland, the National Assembly appointed a Council of Regency to act on his behalf. The first Council of Regency comprised Colonel His Royal Highness Prince Anuvatchaturonta, Lieutenant-Commander His Highness Prince Adityatipapha, and Chao Phya Yomarat, former Minister of the Interior. In the meantime, Luang Pradit Manudharm had returned to Bangkok, where he was whitewashed of communist ideology by a committee consisting of Prince Wanwaithyakorn, Adviser to the Cabinet, Phya Srisangkorn, Chief Judge of the Supreme Court, and Sir Robert Holland, Adviser to the Ministry of Justice. Soon afterwards Luang Pradit Manudharm was appointed Minister of Foreign Affairs, entrusted with the principal duty of revising the treaties with foreign countries. In spite of the attacks of two members of the National Assembly concerning the national budget and the sale of some land belonging to the Privy Purse Department, Colonel Phya Bahol Polpayuhasena managed to bring his government to a successful conclusion in accordance with the constitution.

One noteworthy result of the revolution was the acceleration of the extension of education, since it was the policy of the government to make all the people literate in the shortest possible time. Two national schemes of education were proclaimed in 1932 and 1936 respectively—the first one extending primary education to four years (Prathom 1-4), and the second one putting the stress on vocational education and transferring the last two classes of the secondary school (Matayom 7-8) to pre-university schools as instituted by the universities and the military and the naval academies. At the same time, the general administration of the Kingdom was streamlined, as it was divided into the central administration, the provincial administration and the local administration. For the central administration, the Ministry of Commerce and Communications was split up into the Ministry of Communications and the Ministry of Economic Affairs. The Publicity Bureau which later became the Department of Public Relations was established, and among its duties was the dissemination of correct information to the public. By the abolition of all the circles or montons, the provincial administration permitted the 70 provinces or changwats to deal directly with the

Ministry of the Interior in Bangkok. Regarding the local administration, people were encouraged to take an active part in commune or tambol municipalities in thickly-populated groups of villages, town or muang municipalities for towns where the population exceeded 5,000 with a density of not less than 2,000 people per square kilometre, and city or nakorn municipalities for large towns where the population exceeded 30,000.

On December 16, 1938, the Council of Regency appointed Luang Pibulsonggram as Prime Minister to succeed Phya Bahol Polpayuhasena. The new Prime Minister proclaimed the national reconstruction as his policy, which aimed at making Thailand a progressive country. In support of this policy, he issued ten State Conventions (Rathaniyom) which obliged the people to comply with the wishes of the Government, though they did not have the force of law. He initiated the programme of national reconstruction by making public requests for hard work in order to achieve a good living. For instance, the people were persuaded to engage in kitchen gardening and poultry farming so as to economize on living expenses. He actively promoted the spread of national culture through the use of Thai language and the enforcement of such measures as the dress reform and the re-adjustment of certain habits of the Thais. Both men and women wore western clothes together with hats and shoes and abstained from betel-chewing. Pibulsonggram himself wrote articles along these lines under the pen-name of "Samakkhijai" in order to give an impetus to the campaign of national reconstruction. He turned over a new leaf for the Thai new year by fixing January 1, B.E. 2483 as January 1, B.E. 2484 (1941). So the Thai new year started on January 1, instead of April 1, thus in keeping with the universal practice.

In the economic field, the Government sponsored an eighteen year road programme for connecting towns throughout the kingdom. A remark should be made here that no provision was made for roads leading out of Bangkok before the revolution of 1932. Only the railways and the waterways served as the means of communication for those who wished to travel to the provinces and vice versa. In agriculture, the Department of Agriculture was instituted in order to take care of and develop the rice cultivation and the growing of cotton, Virginia tobacco, sugar-cane, ramie and soya-bean. The co-operative movement was expanded in order to help farmers in their pursuits. Thai people were encouraged to engage in trade and banking which had been in the hands of foreign merchants. In industry, a paper factory and a sugar factory were erected at Kanchanaburi and Lampang with a view to spreading work among people in the provinces, while a textile factory was under the management of the Army. The Ministry of Finance bought the British-American Tobacco Company and turned it into the Thai Tobacco Monopoly. In order to co-ordinate or control the work of the factories, the Government established the Ministry of Industry in 1942. With the creation of the Youth Movement and the Air Force in 1936 and 1937 respectively and the purchase of arms and ammunition, tanks, warships and airplanes, the armed forces of the Kingdom were greatly developed and strengthened.

The Government exercised praiseworthy care in maintaining the same exchange value of the baht (11 bahts £1 sterling), in spite of the increased amount of bank-notes in circulation, as is shown by the following figures:

| | |
|---|---|
| March 31, 1932 | 113,371,690 bahts |
| March 31, 1939 | 150,032,498 bahts |
| December 31, 1940 | 234,775,722 bahts |

There was, however, one difficulty in increasing the national revenue. So long as the treaties which Thailand had signed with the foreign countries in the nineteenth century were not completely revised, she enjoyed no freedom in juridical and fiscal matters. The Government of Thailand after the revolution of 1932 was nationalistic in its outlook and accepted as its platform the six-point statement of the People's Party in its original announcement. The first point of principle of the Government policy was the firm maintenance of national independence in politics, in the law courts, in the economic field, etc. In the implementation of this policy, full sovereignty must be recovered in all respects through the complete revision of the treaties. According to the treaties of 1920-1926, the foreign Powers still reserved the right of evocation of cases from all the Thai courts except the Supreme or Dika Court for a period of five years after the promulgation and enforcement of all the legal codes. Restrictions were imposed on the import duties of such goods as cotton, cotton products, iron, iron products, motor-cars, machinery, hats, condensed milk and spirits for a period of ten years which would end in 1936. Moreover, Thailand was unilaterally bound in the matter of the reimbursement of the tax on gunny bags, the collection of customs duties within a radius of twenty five kilometres from the right bank of the Mekong river, the possession of immovable property and the nationality of certain categories of people born in Thailand. Lastly Thailand could not set up monopolies nor could she put in force a military requisition.

The Thai Government ordered the Department of Legislative Redaction, later known as the Judicial Committee, to expedite the drafting of all the legal codes. To the entire satisfaction of all concerned, this was accomplished within three years after the inauguration of the democratic regime. The Civil and Commercial Codes Books V and VI, the Civil Procedure Code, the Criminal Procedure Code and the Law on the constitution of the courts had been issued and enforced by 1935, thus filling the list of all the legal codes of Thailand, and the right of evocation of cases would consequently come to an end in 1940.

In 1936, Luang Praditmanudharm was the Foreign Minister and Prince Wan Waithyakorn was the Thai Adviser to the Ministry for Foreign Affairs. They cooperated very closely in negotiating a new set of treaties, so that Thailand should attain full freedom and equality in her relations with the foreign Powers. Instead of revising the existing treaties, as was the procedure adopted in Rama VI's reign, the Government under the democratic régime denounced them and requested the foreign Powers concerned to sign identical treaties on the basis of equality, reciprocity, justice and mutual interests. The draft of such a treaty was copied from the Treaty of 1923 between the United States of America and Turkey, the Treaty of 1924 between the United States of America and Finland, the Treaty of 1924 between Denmark and Persia, and other similar treaties, and it was then modified to suit the Thai wishes.

Thailand opened negotiations for a new treaty with the United States of America first, since she had kindly set a good example in signing the treaty of 1920. This treaty had reached its ten years limit before the treaties with the other Powers, and Thailand hoped to secure her full cooperation in this matter again. On Novermber 5, 1936, the Thai Minister at Washington, Phya Apibarnrajmaitri, sent to the U.S. State Secretary, Cordell Hull, a letter denouncing the treaty of 1920. The Thai Government submitted the draft of a new treaty to the U.S. Government for consideration, and Dr. Sayre, who was closely connected with the Roosevelt Administration, again helped Thailand. He reported the results of the

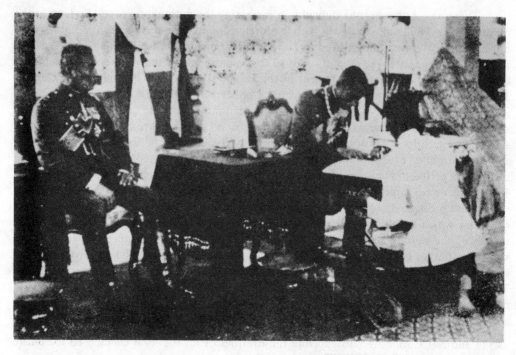

IN THE NAME OF KING ANANDA MAHIDOL,
H.R.H. PRINCE ADITYATIPAPAH, PRESIDENT OF THE COUNCIL OF REGENCY,
ANOINTING THE NEW SET OF TREATIES WITH FOREIGN COUNTRIES,
GIVING FULL SOVEREIGNTY TO THAILAND
JUNE 24, 1939

consideration of the draft treaty by the U.S. Government to the Thai Government. Soon after that, the Thai Government pursued negotiations with the other countries for a similar purpose.

The United States of America granted the Thai request to terminate the right of evocation before it reached the time limit of five years. Great Britain followed suit with one condition. Thailand must promulgate an Act on the Conflict of Laws within twelve months after an exchange of notes following the signing of a new treaty. With regard to France, however, there was some delay in concluding a new treaty, due to the fact that the French Government had expressed anxiety about the frontier between French Indo-China and Thailand. The colonial party at Paris urged the French Government to demand concessions from Thailand. In Bangkok, the Frenchmen who were the legal advisers and professors of Law and French language tried to prolong the negotiations for their self-interests. The Thai Government, however, succeeded in solving all the problems arising out of the negotiations. So in 1937 Thailand signed a Treaty of Friendship and Commerce with Switzerland, a Treaty of Friendship, Commerce and Navigation with the Belgo-Luxemburg Economic Union and a Convention on residence with Belgium. She also concluded in the same year identical Treaties of Friendship, Commerce and Navigation with Denmark, Sweden, the United States of America, Norway, Great Britain, Italy, France, Japan, Germany, and the Netherlands, and in 1938 with Portugal. With France she made a commercial and customs agreement dealing with French Indo-China, in addition to the treaty.

Through these equal treaties, Thailand recovered full sovereignty in all matters affecting the country, and they were celebrated on a grand scale on June 24, 1939, being at that time fixed as the National Day. Thus the Thai Government was free to impose customs duties on imports and exports as it thought fit. It could make a military requisition and establish monopolies. It had the power to keep those who were born in the country as Thai nationals and to reserve land for Thai citizens, while the Thai courts had jurisdiction over foreigners. The treaties were subject to revision and denunciation after they had been in force for five years.

With the recovery of juridical and fiscal autonomy, the Government of Major-General Luang Pibulsonggram went ahead with the reform of the system of taxation. Such outdated taxes as the capitation tax and the garden tax were abolished and a revenue code was announced for the collection of both direct and indirect taxes such as the income tax, the business tax and the internal tax on beer and spirits with a result that the annual national revenue was considerably augmented.

In the field of international relations, the Thai Government, headed by Phya Manopakornnithitada, took a significant step in the Manchurian Incident. In February 1933, the Lytton report was considered by the Assembly of the League of Nations. According to its recommendations, Japan should withdraw her troops from Manchuria, and the member States of the League should not recognize Manchukuo as a new State, since its government was under the Japanese influence. The Assembly unanimously accepted the report with forty two members in favour, but Thailand and Poland abstained from voting on it. Phya Srivisarnvacha, the Foreign Minister, related how he had to make a quick decision about this matter. He received at 12 o'clock a cablegram from the Thai delegates to the League of Nations at Geneva, with a request for a reply at 14 o' clock on the same day, while he was about to lunch with the Prime Minister, Phya Manopakornnithitada. The two ministers consulted together, and in view of the fact that there was no time to call a Cabinet meeting, they agreed to send a reply for abstention to the Thai delegates. This may be accounted for by the fact that Thailand pursued her foreign policy with a view to maintaining friendly relations with the foreign Powers and in doing so it became necessary to develop a good understanding already existing between them and to promote mutual confidence to a higher degree. This policy was enunciated by the Government of Phya Manopakornnithitada on December 10, 1932, and was duly approved by the National Assembly. Apart from Japan and China, Thailand was at that time the only independent country in the Far East and some leading personalities of the new regime looked to Japan as a worthy model for bringing quick progress to it. The Thai army and navy were small and did not really count in a great war. Had she voted for the Lytton report, she would certainly have antagonized Japan to no purpose, since she could not expect protection from the Great Powers against a hostile act from the Japanese. Great Britain and France were the only Great Powers in the League of Nations who could perhaps take an effective action to halt a Japanese aggression in Manchuria, but their self interest kept them from taking such a step. Later events proved that Thailand adopted the right policy in the Sino-Japanese dispute. Failing to obtain real assistance from the League of Nations and Great Britain and France, China under Chiang Kai-Shek made the Tangku truce with Japan in 1933. Meanwhile Japan had expressed her gratitude to Thailand for having taken a neutral stand in the Manchurian Incident, and this strengthened the bonds of amity between the two countries.

At the outbreak of war in Europe on September 3, 1939, Thailand declared her neutrality so as to be in conformity with the wishes of her people. There was, however, great anxiety in the country as it was widely believed that sooner or later Japan would join the Axis Powers, Hitler's Germany and Mussolini's Italy, which would bring war to the doorsteps of Thailand. By the way, this belief was afterwards corroborated by the formation of the Rome-Berlin-Tokyo Axis. In order to safeguard herself against a possible aggression from outside, Thailand and Japan concluded a treaty, whereby they would develop an alliance and respect one another's territorial integrity. On June 12, 1940, Thailand signed non-aggression pacts with Britain and France.

The loss of a large territory to France and the French blockade of the Chao Phya river in 1893 remained firmly implanted in the mind of the Thai people who recalled those events with bitterness and sometimes with resentment. Being desirous of removing such feelings with France, the Thai Government under Pibulsonggram handed in September 1940 a note to the Vichy French Government asking for a slight modification of the boundary line along the Mekong river between Thailand and French Indo-China so as to be in consonance with the natural conditions of the area and justice. By this request, Thailand meant the transfer to her sovereignty of a territory opposite Luang Prabang and another one opposite Pakse, that is, Champasak or Bassac, and the fixing of the thalweg or deep channel in the Mekong as the boundary line. The French Government refused to consider most of the points contained in the Thai note. Frontier incidents broke out on November 28, 1940; the Thai soldiers advanced into the border area of Battambong and Srisophon along the Cambodian frontier and also into Champasak. A small scale bombing of the military installations near the Thai-Indo-Chinese frontier was carried out, and a blackout was enforced in Bangkok for a few nights in anticipation of an aerial attack, but luckily no hostile plane appeared in the calm sky over the capital. The fighting was ended with Japanese mediation on January 28, 1941. Since July 1937, Japan had been struggling with China in the war known to the Japanese as the China Incident and had occupied the greater part of China Proper including all the sea-ports, thus forcing Chiang Kai-Shek to move farther inland and set up his capital at Chungking in Szechuan. By 1941, she had embarked on an expansionist policy towards South-East Asia. Such was the reason which had led her to offer herself as mediator, so that she could intervene in French Indo-China-another step in her march towards Singapore. In order to resist the Japanese southward expansion which was threatening their territories, the United States of America, Great Britain and the Dutch East Indies had joined China in forming a A.B.C.D. bloc. With regard to the dispute for the return of the territories, Thailand and France had sent their delegates to a conference in Tokyo which was held under the auspices of Japan, and on May 9, 1941, they signed a peace convention, whereby Thailand recovered the two territories already mentioned plus Battambong, Srisophon and part of Siemrap which were to be demilitarized. But the demilitarization of the 25 kilometres zone on both banks of the Mekong was abolished. After the conclusion of the Tokyo Convention, Thailand and Japan signed a protocol, whereby they would make efforts to maintain peace in East Asia, develop friendly relations as good neighbours and promote the economic ties between them.

There was in Thailand great rejoicing at the retrocession of the former territories from France, which were then split up into four provinces, namely, Battambong, Pibulsonggram, Nakorn Champasak and Lanchang. In the name of His Majesty King Ananda Mahidol, the Council of Regency, headed by His Royal Highness Prince Aditya, promoted Major General Luang Pibulsonggram, who was the Prime Minister and Supreme Commander of the armed forces, to be a field-marshal, an admiral of the fleet and a marshal of the air, later known as Marshal Pibul for the sake of brevity. The delimitation of the new boundaries between Thailand and French Indo-China was carried out according to the terms of the Tokyo Convention and was completed on July 11, 1942. By that time the Second World War had engulfed South-East Asia.

On December 8, 1941, Japan started the war of Greater East Asia by an attack on Pearl Harbor on the island of Oahu in Hawaii, bombing the Philippines and Singapore, and landing troops a Kota Bahru in North Malaya. In Thailand, it had been expected for some time that Japan would strike a blow against Great Britain and the United States of America, as her army had entered Cochin China (South Vietnam) in July 1941. On December 7, 1941, at 10.30 p.m.the Japanese Ambassador at Bangkok, Tsubokami, demanded free passage through Thailand for the Japanese troops on their march against the British territories. The Thai soldiers at Prachuap Khiri Khan, Nakhon Si Thammarat and Songkhla put up a heroic resistance against the Japanese who had landed on the beaches. At the receipt of Winston Churchill's reply advising Thailand to defend herself, Marshal Pibul's Government accepted the Japanese demand for free passage and ordered, on December 8, all resistance to the Japanese to cease at once. Direk Jayanam, who was the Foreign Minister, noted in his two volumes on *Thailand and the Second World War* that "Finally the Prime Minister asserts that it is no use trying to resist the Japanese, since we have no forces." Japan made a pledge that she would respect the sovereignty and independence of Thailand. Fifield's book on *The Diplomacy of South-East Asia* states that "Thailand, of course, would have preferred neutrality. but faced with overwhelming Japanese power, she bent like a reed." On December 21, 1941, Thailand and Japan signed an alliance with a secret protocol wherein Tokyo agreed to help Bangkok get back territories lost to Britain, and Thailand undertook to assist Japan in her war against the United States of America and the United Kingdom. In January 1942, British planes began to raid Bangkok and other towns and were soon joined by American planes. By that time, the war of Greater East Asia or the Pacific War had merged with the European War as the Second World War. On January 25, 1942, Thailand made a declaration of war against Great Britain and the United States of America.

The Thai Minister at Washington, M.R.Seni Pramoj, refused to obey orders from Marshal Pibul and set about forming a Free Thai Movement in the U.S.A. Most of the Thai students in Great Britain who did not seek repatriation joined the Movement for the liberation of their fatherland under the leadership of H.S.H. Prince Supasvat Svasdivat. The majority of the Thai people condemned the Japanese occupation of their country, while the rest either showed indifference to them or cooperated with them for the sake of material benefits. In fairness to the Japanese, one could say that they hardly interfered with the daily life of the Thai people. However, as economic conditions deteriorated through the effects of the war, they became more and more disliked. For example, inflation pinched the Thai people very badly throughout the length and breadth of the country. The Japanese transfer of the four Malay States taken by Great Britain in 1909-Kedah, Perlis, Kelantan and Trengganu-and the two Shan States of Kengtung and Mongpan to Thailand in 1943 failed to arouse a popular response among them. About the same time, Dr. Pridi Panomyong, who was a Regent, organized an underground resistance movement against the Japanese inside the country, which was soon able to contact the Free Thai Movement abroad. The two Movements, which gained sympathy and support of the Allies, helped in mitigating the harsh demand imposed on Thailand when the war ended on August 15,1945, recognized as the VJ day. The good treatment given to the prisoners of war by Thailand was generally commended.

A basic difference developed, however, between the British and the Americans on how to interpret the actions of the Pibul's government and how to deal with the "Free Thai" movement led by Seni Pramoj, the Thai Minister to the United States. The British compared the respective positions of Denmark in Europe with reference to the Nazi occupation and of Thailand in Asia with reference to the Japanese. They observed that Thailand took the occasion to declare war and to make territorial gains. As a consequence of Thailand's declaration of war, Great Britain took the position that it would have to be legally terminated by the two powers. On the other hand, the United States ignored the declaration by the Pibul regime and recognized the Free Thai Movement.

Towards the end of July 1944, the Government of Marshal Pibul was toppled by the National Assembly, due to a defeat on the bills to set up Phetchabun as another capital and to build a Buddhist city covering an area of about 6,000 rais or 2,400 acres at Saraburi. During his first premiership (1938-1944), due to the outbreak of the War of Greater East Asia, the teaching at all levels of education, from universities down to primary schools, was disorganized, so at the order of the Ministry of Education, students who had 60% attendance in the academic year 1941 were given a pass. More than one year later Bangkok was completely inundated in a big flood which forced all the universities and schools to close from October 2, to November 15, 1942. In view of the intensified bombing of Bangkok by enemy towards the end of the war, students were evacuated to schools outside the metropolitan area where all universities and schools remained closed from June 1944 to November 1945. The President of the Council of Regency, Prince Adityatipapha, did not endorse the appointment of Mr. Khuang Abhaiwongse as Prime Minister to succeed Marshal Pibul and submitted his resignation which was accepted by the National Assembly, as he did not feel like incurring the displeasure of the Pibul party. Dr. Pridi Panomyong, who had become a member of the Council of Regency in 1942, therefore emerged as the sole Regent of King Ananda Mahidol who was still pursuing his studies in Switzerland. The Regent and the new Prime Minister were secretly sympathetic to the Allies who were winning on all the fronts. Thus the surrender of Japan in the war saw a pro-Allies government in power in Bangkok, seeking ways and means to alleviate the fate of Thailand.

On the assumption of his Premiership in August 1944, Khuang Abhaiwongse made a statement of his Government's policy to the National Assembly in which he declared that he would show sympathy to the people in the administration of the country. With this aim in view, he would make attempts to prevent the Japanese troops who were stationed in Thailand from encroaching upon the rights of the people to an unreasonable limit. Having abolished the simplified writing of Thai language and the dress reform which had been enforced by Marshal Pibul, he reverted to the old styles in these matters. The titles of no-bility which had been done away with in 1942 were revived and returned to those who would accept them of their own free will. What particularly pleased all segments of the people was that he released all the political prisoners who had been in gaol from 1933, and, to add joy to happiness of all concerned, the ranks and titles of nobility were later returned to them, if they held them previously.

Immediately after the VJ day, on August 16, 1945, the Regent of Thailand, Pridi Panomyong, issued a proclamation, approved the same day by the National Assembly, repudiating the declaration of war on the United States and Great Britain. In the proclama-tion, it was stated that Thailand had no desire for the territories in Burma and Malaya which Japan entrusted to her and was ready to arrange for their delivery as soon as Great Britain was ready to take delivery thereof. Thanks to his diplomacy and farsightedness, James Byrnes, who was then the American Secretary of State, declared that the U.S.govern-ment considered the Thai declaration of war null and void. Consequently a peace treaty between the two States was not necessary. "Exerting a moderating influence on Great Bri-tain in her peace negotiations with Thailand, the United States joined its European friend in re-establishing diplomatic relations with the Bangkok government on January 5, 1946." On January 24, the United States announced that as a result of conversations with the Thai government, "it has been recognized that the treaties and other international agreements in force between the United States and Siam prior to the outbreak of war in the Far East con-tinue in full force and effect." Thus Thailand was cleared of the war guilt, as far as the United States was concerned, showing how adept at diplomacy she was. According to Hall's *A History of South-East Asia*, "As diplomatists the Thais have never been sur-passed."

In the meantime, the Thai National Assembly on September 1,1945, had given appro-val to the statement of policy of the Government, headed by Tawee Bunyaket, because Khuang Abhaiwongse had resigned from office on the ground that he had fulfilled his duties as a wartime Prime Minister. Dealing with the foreign policy, the Government would co-operate and promote friendly relations to the fullest extent with the United Nations in every respect, and was also prepared to join the United Nations in building up the stability of the world on the basis of the ideals which had been laid down by the United Nations at San Francisco. It made a pledge that it would try its best to give the most beneficial results and cause the least repercussions to Thailand. On September 19, 1945, the new Government under the premiership of M.R. Seni Pramoj, sought and received endorsement of the Nation-al Assembly for its statement of policy which, in the field of foreign affairs, repeated the pledge of the previous Government. M.R. Seni Pramoj (1905-    ) was a brilliant student in England. Having finished his legal studies with a Bachelor of Arts degree with second class honours at Oxford, he passed the Bar Final Examination with still better results, being placed at the head of the First Class and was awarded the Bar Studentship and the Lord Justice Holker Senior Scholarship of Grey's Inn. He did very well again in the Thai Bar Final Examination and thus he became both an English barrister-at-law and a Thai barrister-at-law. He was a judge of the Court of Appeal before his appointment as Thai Minister to Washington.

Before the resumption of the diplomatic relations, negotiations between the U.K. plenipotentiary, M.E. Dening, and the plenipotentiary of the Government of India, M.S.

Aney, on one side and the Thai plenipotentiaries, Prince Wiwatanachai Chaiyant, Lieutenant-General Phya Apai Songgram, and Dr. Serm Vinicchayakul on the other side, had led to the signing at Singapore, on January 1, 1946, of a "Formal Agreement for the Termination of the State of War between Siam and Great Britain and India." The Thai peace settlement included an agreement between Australia and Thailand, signed on April 3, 1946, to end the state of war between them, an agreement between France and Thailand, signed on November 17, 1946, regulating their relations and notes exchanged between the Netherlands and Thailand, January 30, 1947, on diplomatic relations.

The twenty-four articles of the Formal agreement between Thailand and Great Britain and India could be summarised under the following headings:

1. The restoration of the territories and property to Great Britain. Thai acquisition of territory in Burma and Malaya, for example, was declared null and void and compensation would be made for losses incurred as a consequence of the Thai occupation.

2. The supply of rice. Thailand would make available to Great Britain a maximum of one and a half million tons of rice free of charge.

3. The Kra Canal. Thailand would not cut a canal linking the Gulf of Siam with the Indian Ocean without the prior concurrence of the Government of the United Kingdom.

4. Thailand and the United Nations Organization. The Thai application for membership in the United Nations would be supported by Great Britain and India.

5. Compensation would be paid by Thailand for the various properties seized from the British during the war.

6. New treaties. New treaties of commerce and navigation would be negotiated with Great Britain and India at a consular convention with Great Britain only.

The "Final Peace Agreement" between Thailand and Australia was similar to the Formal Agreement with some exceptions.

With a strong desire for membership of the United Nations Organization, Thailand returned to France by the agreement of November 17, 1946, the territories which she had obtained through the Japanese mediation on May 9, 1941. France agreed not to veto the Thai application to be a UN member, and she then resumed diplomatic relations with Thailand. There still remained at that time two other Great Powers, Nationalist China and Soviet Russia, with whose wishes Thailand must comply before she would be admitted into the UN. On January 23, 1946, she signed a Treaty of Amity with the Republic of China, and it was ratified on May 28, 1946. An exchange of notes was made between the Thai Minister and the Russian Minister at Stockholm in December 1946, thus reviving the diplomatic relations which existed between Thailand and Russia before the end of the Romanov dynasty in 1917.

Special attention should be paid to the Treaty of 1946 between Thailand and Nationalist China, being the first one between them. Thailand had been in constant intercourse with China since the Sukhothai days, but she had concluded no treaty with her on the ground that she concentrated on trading with her and welcomed the assimilation of Chinese immigrants to be Thai citizens. Any approach or move by China since the change of régime in 1911 had been politely brushed aside by Thailand. During the Second World War, China became a Great Power through which the members of the Free Thai Movement operated in their contact with the Resistance Movement at home. Necessity therefore arose for Thailand to cultivate friendly relations with China in accordance with general diplomatic practice. The Treaty of 1946 resulted in the exchange of envoys at the ambassadorial level.

Thailand had found herself in a dilemma at the end of the Second World War; she was neither a defeated or a liberated country. Thanks to the skill and experience of her diplomats, she succeeded in preserving her status ante bellum. The treaties of 1937-1938 were put back in force. She was admitted as the fifty-fifth member of the United Nations Organization in December 1946, and then joined the UN Specialized Agencies such as UNESCO, WHO, FAO, and ICAO. She has been participating actively in the UN activities up till now. She responded at once to the UN appeal for troops to fight in the Korean war in 1950.

The diplomatic activities of Thailand have increased enormously since her neighbours in South-East Asia achieved their independence, namely the Philippines in 1946, Burma in 1948, Indonesia in 1949, Cambodia, Vietnam and Laos in 1954, and Malaysia in 1957. Since 1946, practically every Thai Government which assumed office has emphasized in its statement of policy the importance of promoting the friendly relations with the neighbouring countries. Thailand signed a treaty of amity or friendship with each of the following countries, namely, the Philippines on June 14, 1949, Indonesia on March, 3, 1954, and Burma on October 15, 1956. These treaties are equal ones, as may be seen from the main points of the treaty of friendship between Thailand and Burma. "1. The two States shall maintain perpetual peace and friendship and shall ever strive to strengthen and develop the friendly relations existing between the people of the two countries. 2. The nationals of each of the High Contracting Parties shall be permitted to enjoy, on condition of reciprocity, the right to travel, to reside, to carry on all kinds of profession and occupations, to engage in industries and trade and, to acquire, inherit, possess, lease, occupy and dispose of any kind of movable or immovable property, throughout the territories of the other, under the same conditions as the nationals of any third country, subject always to the Constitution, laws and regulations promulgated, or which may hereafter be promulgated, by the other. They shall enjoy, in matters of procedure, the same treatment as is accorded to the nationals of the other, with respect to the protection and security of their persons and property and in regard to all judicial, administrative and other legal proceedings. 3. This Treaty shall continue in force for five years from the date of its coming into force and shall thereafter remain in force. Provided that after the termination of the said period five years, either party may give to the other party a notice of not less than six months intimating its intention to terminate this Treaty and on the expiry of the period of such notice this treaty shall cease to be in force."

Thailand recognized India and Pakistan as separate States when they attained independence on August 15, 1947. She accorded the same treatment to Ceylon soon after her first independence day, February 4, 1948. For the regulations of the diplomatic relations, Thailand and India exchanged notes on December 31, 1948, which recognized the Treaty which the former had concluded with Great Britain as applying to the latter, thus eliminating the necessity for a new treaty. With Japan, diplomatic relations were resumed after the Treaty of San Francisco in 1951.

The internal politics of Thailand has to a certain extent been bound up with her foreign policy up to the present day. M.R. Seni Pramoj, who was the Prime Minister after the war, left office following the General Election, but continued as Minister of Education in the Government headed by Khuang Abhaiwongse in February 1946. With the support of the Sahacheep party and other parties, Pridi Panomyong succeeded Khuang Abhaiwongse who had been defeated in the National Assembly towards the end of March, because of his refusal to accept a bill for the reduction of public expenses. During that time, Marshal Pibul and a few of his friends and collaborators such as General Mangkorn Promyothi, General Charoon Seriruangrid, and Lieutenant-General Prayoon Pamonmontri, who had been arrested and charged as war criminals for their parts in bringing Thailand into the war on the side of Japan, were released, since the special court upheld that the law on war crimes, which was passed after the war, was not retroactive. King Ananda Mahidol who had been living with his mother, sister and brother in Switzerland throughout the war years returned to Thailand at the age of twenty and immediately won the hearts of the people of all classes. On May 10, 1946, a new constitution, providing for a two-chamber Assembly, was proclaimed.

To the great astonishment and deep sorrow of the whole Thai nation, King Ananda Mahidol, who was about to leave for Switzerland to complete his studies, was found shot dead in bed in the Grand Palace on the morning of June 9,1946. The National Assembly proclaimed his only brother, Prince Bhumibol Adulyadej as the new sovereign on that night. Upon the departure of King Bhumibol for Switzerland, where he resumed his studies, his uncle, Prince Rangsit of Jainat, was appointed Regent. In August 1946, Rear Admiral Thawal Dhamrongnawaswasti relieved Pridi Panomyong of his onerous duties so as to enable him to proceed on a world tour as an Elder Statesman. The new Prime Minister was born in 1901. As a result of his success in the Thai Bar Final Examination, he became a barrister-at-law and joined the Navy. As one of the promoters of the revolution of 1932, he won quick promotions. He was appointed as Secretary-General of the Cabinet, the Minister of the Interior and the Minister of Justice in succession. He was well-known as a brilliant speaker. The mystery surrounding the death of King Ananda Mahidol remained unsolved, in spite of the fact that a public investigation had been made about it. The economic conditions deteriorated, forcing the cost of living to rise and the people suffered from it. Scarcity of rice arose, due to excessive smuggling of this staple product for export. There was a great demand for it in Singapore, Malaya, Hong Kong, China and India. The price of rice, sold under the government to government basis, was much below the black market one. These were the causes which led to the bloodless coup d' état of November 8, 1947. The leaders of the coup were Lieutenant-General Phin Chunhawan (Field Marshal), Group Captain Kach Kachsonggram (Lieutenant-General), Colonel Sarit Thanarat, then commander of the first regiment at Bangkok, (Field Marshal), and Colonel Phao Sriyanon (General). It is interesting to note that most of these officers had not participated in the 1932 revolution. They proclaimed a new provisional constitution on November 9, 1947-providing for a bicameral system. At the invitation of the coup leaders, Khuang Abhaiwongse assumed the premiership for the third time, and with their support, Marshal Pibul became the commander-in-chief of the army. Pridi Panomyong and Thawal Dhamrongnawaswasti had already fled from the country, but the latter returned about one year later.

Events indicated that all the rice clauses of the Formal Agreement could not be carried out. The Thai Government did not own rice and consequently could not supply it free to Great Britain. Again the United States Government came to the help of Thailand on this matter. By a revised agreement of May 1946 providing for Anglo-American-Thai participation for the supply of rice, Great Britain paid £ 12. 14s. per ton of rice and by the end of 1946, she increased its price to £ 24 a ton, still below the black market one. In trying to implement the Formal Agreement to the best of her ability, Thailand bought for £ 1½ million the part of the Thai-Burmese railroad or "death railway" in this territory in October 1946. As a result of further negotiations, she agreed in January 1951, to pay Great Britain, Australia, and India a lump sum of £ 5,224,220 for the settlement of the outstanding Commonwealth war claims. On January 14,1954, an exchange of notes terminated the Formal Agreement of January 1, 1946, as regards Great Britain and Thailand. It was carried out by the Government of Marshal Pibul.

On April 6, 1948, Premier Khuang Abhaiwongse was forced by the Army to resign on the ground that he had failed to bring down the high cost of living, and Marshal Pibul succeeded him, thus returning to politics with full power. However, Pibul's Government was not safe from serious troubles. Two attempted coups d'état by parts of the Navy (February 26, 1949 and June 29, 1951) ended in failure, having been suppressed by the Army and the Police with the co-operation of the Air Force. The abortive coup d'état of June 1951 was sometimes known as the "Manhattan" revolt. "Manhattan" was the name of a dredger which the United States Government transferred in an official ceremony to Marshal Pibul under the Military Assistance Programme. During the ceremony which was held at the Rajaworadit Landing in front of the Grand Palace and within the Navy headquarters, the Navy rose against him. He was arrested and guarded on board H.M.S. Si Ayutthaya. Fighting broke out and ended in three days. Marshal Pibul was safe and free.

To replace the provisional constitution of November 9, 1947, a constitution — the third so-called permanent constitution — was promulgated on March 23, 1949. It provided for a nominated Senate and an elected House of Representatives, but lasted only two years eight months and six days. It was annulled by a coup d'état, which was engineered by the military group forming the Government on November 29, 1951. As no forces were used, it became known as the silent coup. According to a Government communique, the aim of the coup was to eliminate the ministers who held communist ideas from the Cabinet and the National Assembly. The permanent Constitution of December 10, 1932, with one chamber Assembly of nominated and elected deputies in two equal halves, was brought back, and another trial period of ten years for political freedom was proclaimed. Marshal Pibul continued to be the Prime Minister, with Marshal Phin as Deputy Prime Minister, General Sarit as Deputy Minister of Defence and Army Commander-in-Chief and Police-General Phao as Deputy Minister of the Interior and Police Chief. The two Generals were gaining much influence and were said to be rivals. Prince Wan Waithayakorn became Foreign Minister, thus relinquishing the post of Thai Ambassador at Washington.

Since the assumption of his second premiership, Marshal Pibul had apparently been trying his best to right the wrong done to the United States of America and Great Britain by promoting close friendship with them, particularly with the United States, and extending prompt co-operation to the United Nations Organization when fighting broke out in Korea on June 25, 1950. Thailand was among the first which sent troops to join the UN army in the Korean War. As the communist influence was spreading on an extensive scale in South-

East Asia, Thailand leaned more and more on the Western bloc, especially the United States. On September 19, 1950, an Economic and Technical Cooperation Agreement was signed between Thailand and the United States, and on October 17, 1950, a military assistance agreement followed. On September 8, 1954, Australia, France, New Zealand, Pakistan, the Philippines, Thailand, the United Kingdom and the United States of America signed the Southeast Asia Collective Defense Treaty or the Manila Pact to halt and combat communist aggression. Thus the SEATO came into being with its headquarters in Bangkok.

With the lapse of time, Marshal Pibul gradually lost popularity with the armed forces, particularly the army which was headed by Field Marshal Sarit Thanarat. In 1955, he went on a world tour, and after his return to Bangkok, he became more liberal in his outlook on politics than before, and this apparently led him to commit political blunders by permitting the founding of an unlimited number of political parties and the organization of free meetings in the "Hyde Park" style, and also by conniving at his Serimanangkasila party, tampering with the general election which was held towards the end of February 1957. There were at one time more than twenty parties, some of which were permeated by communist influences, while the "Hyde Park" meetings were swayed by leftist tendencies. A public procession went to the Government House in protest against the recent general election. The general situation of the country deteriorated rapidly and therefore the Military Party, led by Sarit Thanarat, took the matter in its own hands. On September 16, 1957, the Military Party seized the power and ousted Marshal Pibul and Police General Phao Sriyanonda. Marshal Pibul fled the country for Cambodia and Japan, where he took up residence in Tokyo till his death in 1964, while Police General Phao Sriyanonda was forced to leave in a hurry for Switzerland, where he died a few years later. At the request of the Military Party, Mr. Pote Sarasin, who had just filled the post of SEATO Secretary-General, formed a caretaker government. He was born in March 1907, and as a boy, he entered Will Abraham College in the United States of America. He studied Law in Bangkok and London and thus became a Thai barrister-at-law as well as an English barrister-at-law. In 1948, he joined the Government of Marshal Pibul as the Deputy Foreign Minister and about one year later, he was appointed Foreign Minister to handle the foreign affairs of Thailand after the Second World War. After leaving the Ministry of Foreign Affairs for some time, he re-joined the government service as Thai Ambassador to Washington for a period of five years (1952-1957). Marshal Pibul produced remarkable achievements in all the fields of activities for Thailand during his ten-year tenure of office as head of the Government. To state all of them would require a long account. Suffice it to mention a few of them here. With regard to the mystery concerning the death of King Ananda Mahidol the Supreme Court gave a judgment in 1954, sentencing three palace officials Jit Singhaseni, Boosya Pattamsarin and Chaleo Patumros to death. A new national scheme of education was proclaimed in 1951, officially providing for both government and private schools to conduct pre-university classes. In May 1957, the Government of Marshal Pibul sponsored the celebration of the 25th century of the Buddhist era on a grand scale. In the economic field, not only was the annual national budget fixed as a balanced one, but it also continued to be increased from 1,666,094,600 bahts in 1948 to 3,055,000,000 bahts in 1956. The value of the baht in relation to foreign currencies was stabilized at about 21 bahts to one U.S. dollar and about 58 bahts to one pound sterling, thus constituting a boon to business transactions. The Government of Marshal Pibul invited the International Bank to send a general survey mission. Its purpose was "to help the Government plan its contribution to the economic and social development of the country during the next several years, and to advise on the forms of organisation which are likely to be most effective in fostering these developments" (I.B.R.D. 1959:Vii). The Mission spent a whole year on collecting data for its report in Thailand from July 1957 to June 1958. The recommendations of the Mission were submitted to the Government of General Thanom Kittikachorn, who was reportedly under the influence of Field Marshal Sarit Thanarat.

In January 1958, after a general election, General Thanom Kittikachorn became the Prime Minister for the first time. He was born on August 11, 1911. After passing out of the Royal Military College in Bangkok, he was assigned to various army units. As a lecturer in military science at the Royal Military College, he brought his cadets to join Field Marshal Phin Chunhawan and Field Marshal Sarit Thanarat in the coup d'état of November 8, 1947, after which he was promoted to the posts of the commander of the eleventh regiment, the first division, and the first army corps one after another. He held the portfolio of Defence in the Cabinet of Pote Sarasin.

During the first premiership of General Thanom Kittikachorn, the political parties were still numerous, including the "Chart Sangkom" or "National Social" party which was founded by Field Marshal Sarit Thanarat. Some members of the parties supporting the Government were so grasping in their requests for funds that they proved to be intolerable. General Thanom Kittikachorn was thus confronted with an urgent problem as to how to control them. Finding no effective remedy for it, Sarit Thanarat decided on a revolution which he successfully carried out immediately after the resignation of the Government of Thanom Kittikachorn on October 20, 1958. According to *L'Evolution de la Thaïlande Contemporaine* by Fistié, "L' armée finit donc par l' emporter après avoir éliminé et s'être subordonné ses rivales moins favorisées ou moins bien pourvues: L'administration civile en 1947, la marine en 1951 et la police en 1957. Après quoi, èn 1958, elle finit par abolir purement et simplement un régime représentatif donc le caractère illusoire n'échappait à personne." In his capacity of leader of the Revolutionary Party, Field Marshal Sarit Thanarat declared Martial Law and ruled by orders of the Party which altogether numbered 57 and had the force of law. The Order of the Revolutionary Party number 3 abolished the constitution and all the political parties. Subsequently, on January 28, 1959, the Revolutionary Party proclaimed the Interim Constitution, creating the Constituent Assembly or the National Assembly which then proceeded to nominate Sarit Thanarat as Prime Minister.

Sarit Thanarat was born in Bangkok on June 16, 1908. He was educated at the Royal Military College from which he passed out at the age of 21. He was posted to various infantry regiments in the capital and the provinces before he commanded the Regiment of the Royal Bodyguards (First infantry regiment) in January 1946. He had kept aloof from politics until he was persuaded by Field Marshal Phin Chunhawan and Lieutenant-General Kach Kachsonggram to join them in the coup d'état of November 8, 1947. He was then promoted to be the commander of the First army division, and after relinquishing his army corps, he was appointed commander-in-chief of the army and he attained the rank of a field marshal at the age of 48. He resigned from the portfolio of Defence only four days before the outbreak of the coup d'état of September 16, 1957. He was a capable leader who made quick and bold decisions in all matters.

The Government of Sarit Thanarat declared the national development as the main plank of its policy and announced, in 1961, the First National Economic Development Plan (1961-1966), commonly known as the "First Six Year Plan." During the past few years before the Plan, the national income had been increasing at a rate of about 5 per cent per annum, permitting an annual rise of only about 2 per cent in per capita income. Since the launching of the First Plan, the structure of the Thai economy has changed considerably for the better. The gross national product increased from 55,717 million bahts in 1960 to 81,274 million bahts in 1965 and reportedly rose to about 96,802 million bahts in 1966. This represented a total increase of 44 per cent against the planned target of 38 per cent. The annual average rate of growth of 7.2 per cent, achieved during the Plan period, surpassed the 6 per cent growth rate target of the Plan and was substantially higher than the 5 per cent growth rate of the past decade.

In his article entitled *A Summary of the Second Five-Year Economic and Social Development Plan (1967-1971)*, the late Secretary-General of the National Economic Development Council, Mr.Prayad Buranasiri, estimated that barring unforeseen circumstances the national growth rate would rise to 8.5 per cent per annum and the average per capita income per annum in 1971 would be approximately 3,900 bahts in comparison with 2,925 bahts in 1966.

Besides the First Six Year Plan, all the other activities of the Government were greatly developed and the Government created the National Economic Development Council, the National Research Council and the National Education Council. With the approval of the National Education Council, the Government proclaimed the National Education Scheme on October 20, 1960, to replace that of 1951. Besides fixing 7 years for the primary school, the National Education Scheme extended a period of compulsory education from 4 to 7 years and promoted the establishment of universities and more colleges and schools in the provinces so as to stem students from flocking to Bangkok for their education. The Board of Investment was set up, offering many privileges to foreign capitalists to invest their money in opening industrial plants in Thailand. At the same time Sarit Thanarat took decisive measures against communist leaders. If they were found to be pursuing their nefarious propaganda, they were executed, such as Messrs. Supachai Srisati and Kong Chindawong.

Sarit Thanarat did not live to witness the full implementation of the First Six Year Plan and the proclamation of a new constitution, as he died on December 8, 1963. A committee of inquiry which was set up by the Government discovered that he had misappropriated state funds to the amount of more than 600 million bahts. Almost all the funds have been found and duly returned to the Thai Treasury. His Majesty King Bhumibol Adulyadej appointed Field Marshal Thanom Kittikachorn, who had served Field Marshal Sarit Thanarat as one of the two Deputy Prime Ministers, as the new Prime Minister. In his statement of policy to the National Assembly on December 19, 1963, Prime Minister Thanom Kittikachorn confirmed that he would pursue the same policy of the previous Government.

After five years of drafting, a new constitution was presented to the King who thereupon signed and proclaimed it on June 20, 1968. According to this constitution, the Parliament consisted of the Senate and the House of Representatives. The Prime Minister was responsible to the Parliament for the administration of the country, but members of Parliament were barred from membership of the Cabinet. After the passing of a law, permitting the formation of political parties, the general election was held on February 10, 1969. As the leader of the United Thai People's Party who secured the majority of votes, Field Marshal Thanom Kittikachorn became Prime Minister for the third time on March 7, 1969.

In his statement of policy to the Members of Parliament, Field Marshal Thanom Kittikachorn emphasized the great importance of national stability and economic and social development for the continued progress and prosperity of Thailand. The Third Economic and Social Development Plan (1972-1976) was proclaimed and implemented.

The constitutional system of government, however, did not work out smoothly as had been expected. In the House of Representatives were found three large groups of members, namely, the United Thai People's Party, the Independents, and the Democratic Party which was in opposition, each numbering 76, 71, and 57 respectively. Should the Democrats and the Independents join together, they would very likely constitute a formidable obstacle to the Government of Field Marshal Thanom Kittikachorn in legislative matters. Incidentally the Government managed to win over the Independents to its side. It was common knowledge that some members supporting the Government put forward their requests for excessive favours which could not be complied with. They did not seem to co-operate energetically with the Government for the normal administration of the country. At the same time the situation both inside the country and in the neighbouring countries caused greater concern to the Government than previously. Some terrorists in the north, the north-east and the south who received clandestine support in money and weapons from abroad increased their efforts to attack the police and soldiers openly.

The situation, just described, became so intolerable that Field Marshal Thanom Kittikachorn made a bold decision to take over control of the Kingdom on November 17, 1971. The Constitution was abrogated. Parliament was dissolved. The Cabinet was disbanded. Martial law was proclaimed.

The leader of the Revolutionary Party, Field Marshal Thanom Kittikachorn, accompanied by General Prabhas Charusthira, Mr. Pote Sarasin, Police General Prasert Ruchirawongse and Air Chief Marshal Dawee Chullasapya, had an audience with the King at Chitralada Palace where he reported to Him on the necessity for the Revolutionary Party to take action. He expressed hope that the work of the Revolutionary Party would bring progress and safety to the nation. He asked the Revolutionary Party to work with unity and success for the sake of the nation.

The Revolutionary Party gave the following reasons for seizing control of the Kingdom:

1. "It has given consideration to the dangers threatening national security and the Throne, dangers which are intensifying, aimed at changing the system of government from constitutional monarchy to an undemocratic form, as can be seen from the incitement of terrorists to cause trouble in various parts of Thailand.

"If the situation is not dealt with firmly, it will endanger the country, the Throne and the people.

2. "Since the promulgation of the Constitution of B.E. 2511 (1968) and after general elections some groups of people have abused their constitutional rights and caused incitement and destruction and used their influence within and outside Parliament to disrupt the work of the Government, raising difficulties and causing delays, all for personal gain.

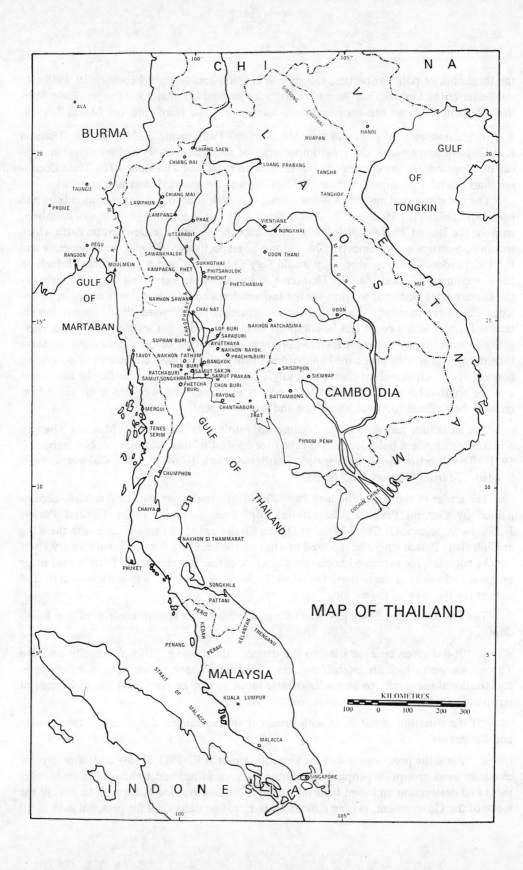

MAP OF THAILAND

KILOMETRES
100    0    100    200    300

ORDINATION OF KING BHUMIBOL ADULYADEJ AS A BUDDHIST MONK
OCTOBER 22, 1956

"Instead of co-operating to solve problems and forestall the threats, certain groups took the opportunity to create disruption, obstruct and prevent the Government from solving the problems easily.

They incited the public and various institutions to oppose and resist the Government, students to demonstrate and labourers to strike.

"These actions impeded the work of the Government. The Government tried in every way to be just to everyone, including the Legislative and Executive branches. Solving the urgent problems by constitutional means would not be adequate.

"It is necessary to take over power for the decisive and timely actions.

"No matter how bad the outside situation, it would be easy to solve if there is internal peace and order. If there is confusion, divisiveness and dissension inside the country, it would be infinitely more difficult to solve both internal and external situations."

Field Marshal Thanom Kittikachorn continued to be the leader of the Revolutionary Party or Chairman of the National Executive Council until a new interim constitution was promulgated on December 15, 1972. The Revolution of November 17, 1971, then came to an end. The Legislative Assembly, created by the interim constitution, entrusted him with the task of forming a new cabinet. He thus became Prime Minister for the fourth time.

The public opinion prevailing at that time was that he was carrying out his duties to the best of his ability for the benefit of Thailand, but a few months later, he was faced with an increasing demand for a permanent constitution. It is true that he had already appointed a committee, headed by Field Marshal Prabhas Charusthira, Deputy Prime Minister, to draft such a constitution, but soon it appeared that this government measure did not satisfy the so-called "demand for a constitution" group, organized by the Secretary-General of the National Student Centre of Thailand. This group included a few former members of the National Assembly, government officials, university lecturers and students, politicians and entertainers. At first the drafting committee fixed a period of three years for the completion of a permanent constitution, but in view of the opposition by the public, and the newspapers it was reduced to one year. Even then, this did not meet with the wishes of the "demand for a constitution" group, 25 members of which proceeded to organize a protest meeting at the World War One Volunteers' Monument near Thammasat University on October 6, 1973, and to distribute leaflets urging support for a movement aimed at the early promulgation of a permanent constitution.

Considering that such a meeting contravened a National Executive Council decree, forbidding the gathering of more than five people for political purposes, the police swooped down on the group and arrested 13 activists including both lecturers and students who hailed from Thammasat and Ramkamhaeng Universities plus a few politicians. This police action brought about a huge rally at Thammasat University which quickly snowballed its forces, since it was supported by the National Student Centre of Thailand, joined by students from other universities, vocational colleges, and high schools not only in the metropolitan area, but also from other provinces such as students from the Teachers' College at Bangsaen, Chon Buri, and also from Chiang Mai and Khon Kaen universities. The rally escalated into a colossal protest march estimated to comprise opproximately 100,000 students along Rajdamnern Avenue, passing in front of the Public Relations Department and the Democracy Monument and reaching the Phanfah Bridge opposite the Metropolitan Police Headquarters. The result was that a confrontation, accompanied by bloodshed, between soldiers and students, exploded on October 14, 1973, which His Majesty the King aptly described as the "Day of Great Sorrow," involving a loss of 69 lives, and the wounded numbered more than 800. In addition, four buildings were burnt down, namely, the Bangkok Co-operative Store, the National Lottery Office, the Office to Follow Up Government Work and the Metropolitan Police Headquarters.

Although Field Marshal Thanom Kittikachorn was absolutely determined to quell the student uprising, he did not achieve the result aimed at, most probably due to the fact that the army under him in his capacity as the Supreme Commander of the Armed Forces ceased to be a military monolith. Obsessed with the futility of his action in controlling the situation of the country, he submitted, on the "Day of Great Sorrow," his resignation to His Majesty the King, which was accepted, and on the following day, the trio-Field Marshal Thanom Kittikachorn, Field Marshal Prabhas Charusthira, and Colonel Narong Kittikachorn, a son of Thanom Kittikachorn who played a part in endeavouring to crush the student uprising, departed by plane from Bangkok for a foreign stay so as to find peace and safety.

In the evening of October 14, the King issued a royal proclamation, appointing Mr. Sanya Dharmasakdi as Prime Minister. Without much ado, he made haste to bring the country back to normalcy. At 11.15 p.m. he spoke to the public over the broadcasting and television networks that there would be a constitution and elections within six months, which satisfied not only the students in particular but also the people in general. Two days later law and order returned to Bangkok, causing much relief to the silent majority.

Born in 1907, Sanya Dharmasakdi studied Law and became a Thai barrister-at-law as well as an English barrister-at-law. He joined the Ministry of Justice where he rose to be the Chief Judge of the Supreme Court before the mandatory retirement age of 60. On his assumption of the premiership, he relinquished membership in the King's Privy Council and the rectorship of Thammasat University.

He proceeded to promote unity not only in the government circle but also among the students and the public, as is witnessed by the fact that out of 27 members of his Cabinet, 14 had served in the Cabinet of Field Marshal Thanom Kittikachorn and that a legal pardon was proclaimed, absolving those who had transgressed the law in the student uprising.

In the execution of his main task to produce a permanent constitution to satisfy the wishes of the people, he took the following measures, the first of which was the dissolution of the National Legislative Assembly. By Royal Command, then, a National Convention was established, having as its sole function the election of a new National Legislative Assembly on December 10, 1973.

The National Convention comprised 2,347 members, including armed forces officers, police officers, government officials, provincial governors, district officers, tambon or commune and village headmen, bankers, merchants, journalists, writers, representatives of professional groups, etc. One noteworthy point that should be borne in mind is the fact that the members were both men and women, most of whom belonged to the middle age group, the idea being to secure as wide and pervading public opinion as possible. The King himself performed the opening ceremony of the National Convention, on December 18, 1973. Under the chairmanship of His Royal Highness Prince Wan Waithyakorn, Krommuen Naradhip Bongsprapandh, former Deputy Prime Minister, it finished its assignment quickly and elected the new National Legislative Assembly from its own members. With Momraj-wongse Kukrit Promoj as its president, the National Legislative Assembly which was composed of 299 members began, on March 7, 1974, its deliberations of the draft constitution, submitted by a small compact committee which had been set up by the Sanya Government in order to accelerate the completion of this momentous piece of legislation. On August 15, 1974, it passed the draft constitution by an overwhelming vote of 280 against 6. With the royal signature affixed to it, the tenth constitution went into force on October 7, 1974. In the meantime, the Government had been intermittently encountering great difficulties in the smooth administration of the country. Taking undue advantage of full freedom, granted by the Government for the purpose of promoting democracy, the students, workers and farmers had formed themselves into centres, groups and unions without police registration, which was in fact contrary to the law. They claimed that they worked for social justice. Some teachers' college students submitted a demand for the elevation of their institutions to a degree granting one, but being unable to reach an accomodation with them, the Minister of Education, Abhai Chandavimol, resigned from the Government and was followed by the Prime Minister, Sanya Dhamasakdi on May 21, 1974. However, the National Legislative Assembly, which had placed confidence in the Prime Minister, overwhelmingly voted him back into office a few days later. Apparently sympathizing with the plight of the workers who were suffering from the high cost of living, originating from the oil crisis started by the Organization of Petroleum Exporting Countries, the Government continued to boost their daily minimum daily wage of 12 baht to 16 baht which then rose to 20 baht and finally to 25 baht (approximatety US $ 1.20). Some hotels and factories could not afford to pay even this modest wage at once, since their enormous expenses were continually rising. The farmers also agitated for assistance from the Government to palliate their lot, as some of them were in debt, and others had no land to cultivate or could not sell their crops at a profitable price.

At the same time, the Communists stepped up their activities, which, thanks to the armed forces and police, were curbed and contained in the remote and inaccessible districts with fair results. Egged on by the students, the workers and farmers held protest rallies, demonstrations, marches against the Government. One regrettable feature was that some twenty Buddhist monks participated in one of these marches in Bangkok in order to seek justice for the recovery of the farmers' land, but their action was immediately disapproved by the Grand Buddhist Council.

The Government moved forward with the preparations of a general election in accordance with the 1974 constitution, although it had been plagued by protest rallies, demonstrations and marches which were successfully contained solved in the end.

Some main provisions of the constitution deserve mention here.

1. The form of government is a constitutional monarchy with the King as Head of the State.

2. He has a Privy Council of 15 members as his advisory body.

3. Not only a prince but also a princess who is a King's daughter, may succeed to the throne, subject to the approval of the National Assembly. This is indeed an innovation, introduced into the constitution for the first time, and supporting the equal status of women.

4. The National Assembly consists of the Senate and the House of Representatives. The terms of office for a senator and a member of the House of Representatives are six and four years respectively.

5. The minimum age for a senator is 35, while that for a member of the House of Representatives is 25. The former is appointed by the King, while the latter is elected by the people, both male and female, whose minimum age is 20.

6. The Thai people enjoy the same rights as in any full-fledged democracy such as religious freedom, freedom of speech and freedom of the press.

7. The Council of Ministers is charged with the responsibility of government.

8. The leader of the largest party in the House of Representatives which is not in power will be officially appointed the leader of His Majesty's opposition. This is another innovation.

The general election was held on January 26, 1975, in which 22 parties vied for seats. The Democratic party which had announced its socalled liberal policy won 72 seats, while 45, 28, 19, 18, and 14 seats went to Social Justice, the Chart Thai (Thai Nation), the Social Agricultural, the Social Action, and the Social Nationalist parties respectively. The Democrat leader, M.R. Seni Pramoj, therefore, formed his cabinet, but for various reasons, he failed to secure the confidence vote of the House of Representatives. The difficult task of forming a cabinet then devolved on M.R. Kukrit Pramoj, his younger brother, who is the leader of the Social Action party.

Through his extremely skilful and clever negotiatious, M.R. Kukrit Pramoj successfully tackled his task, and, at the age of 64, he became Prime Minister on March 14, 1975, enjoying the confidence of the House of Representatives. He referred to his Government as a coalition one, composed of four main parties, namely, his own party, the Social Justice, the Thai Nation, the Social Nationalist parties plus ten small parties.

M.R. Kukrit Pramoj is, in fact, the first Thai Prime Minister who made a direct study of Politics at Oxford University, where he graduated with a B.A. degree with honours in Philosophy, Politics and Economics or Modern Greats. After holding an important post at the Bank of Thailand for a few years, he decided to take up a political career in which he has engaged in journalism and banking up till now. He was once a Democrat and a Deputy Minister of Commerce in the Pibulsonggram Government in 1948.

In his statement of policy to the House of Representatives, he set down the following targets for his government to achieve :-

1. The political target: To eliminate what might have developed into a class struggle for the sake of national unity and stability.

2. The economic target: To make efforts to get rid of poverty among those whose monthly income is less than 1,000 baht through the creation of employment for them within five years.

3. The social target : To narrow down the gap between the rich and the poor and to arrange social welfare for the poor by providing free hospital treatment, free bus rides, and low cost housing.

4. The administrative target: To effect the decentralization of the administration to the provincial or changwat level and to develop the local administration by a tambon or commune council.

5. The military target: To strengthen the armed forces for the performance of their duties to maintain national independence and sovereignty by themselves.

6. The foreign relations target : To conduct an independent foreign policy through the inauguration of friendly relations with countries which reveal a good intention to Thailand, irrespective of their political ideologies and systems of government by focussing special attention on such a super power as the People's Republic of China and the Indo-Chinese countries. Cordial negotiations would be opened for the withdrawal of all foreign troopes from Thai soil within one year.

It is a matter of regret to note that the student uprising and its unfavourable consequences such as protest rallies against the socalled exploitation of the Thai people by foreign companies, and factory and hotel strikes to press their demand for a better pay had adversely affected the implementation of the Third Economic and Social Plan B.E. 2515-2519 (1972-1976), especially in connection with foreign investment. In 1975, the total amount of approved investment reached only 1950 million baht, compared to 9,220 million baht in 1974, and 26, 232 million baht in 1973. In addition, 62 projects of investment with a capital of 2,091 million baht were withdrawn. This gloomy situation was attributed to the following factors : The worldwide economic and financial turmoil due to the oil price rise ; worldwide recession; the political changes in Indo-China originating from the fall of Phnompenh to the Khmer Rouge on April 17, the capture of Saigon by the North Vietnamese troops on April 30, and the establishment of the People's Democratic Republic of Laos by the Pathet Lao on December 2, 1975; Government instability ; and labour problems. At the beginning of 1976, foreign and local investment has declined to a critical level. The Board of Investment has forecast a grim future for Thailand's economy with disturbing social implications, unless the Government makes a major effort to re-establish confidence in the country and halts the potentially disastrous slump in foreign and local investment. Is this a fair price for excessive freedom, initiated by the Sanya Government and upheld by the Kukrit Government in the name of democracy?

M.R. Kukrit Pramoj should deserve credit for the attainment of some of his targets, especially in the field of foreign affairs. He strengthened Thailand's cordial relations with the member states of the Association of Southeast Asian Nations (ASEAN) by his visits to Malaysia from June 9-11 , to Indonesia from June 11-14, the Philippines from July 21-24, and Singapore from July 24-27, 1975. He has been the first Thai Prime Minister to visit, from June 30-July 6, 1975, the People's Republic of China where he met the Communist leader Mao Tse-tung, and Prime Minister Chou En-lai in Peking with a result that a statement was signed on July 1, announcing the opening of diplomatic relations between the Kingdom of Thailand and the People's Republic of China, on July 1, 1975.

As time went on, the Prime Minister began to be plagued by all sorts of demand, put forward by his supporters in the House of Representatives, such as a seat in the Cabinet, to such to an unbelievable extent that he could no longer tolerate them. He therefore dissolved the House on January 12, 1976, and ordered a new general election to be held on April 4, 1976.

The general election took place as scheduled, in which members of 19 parties were elected. The four large parties, namely, the Democratic (114 members), the Thai Nation (56), the Social Justice (28), and the Social Nationalist (8) Parties, which constituted the large majority in the House of Representatives, joined forces to form a new government with M.R. Seni Pramoj the leader of the Democratic Party, as Prime Minister, on April 20, 1976.

The outgoing Prime Minister, M.R. Kukrit Pramoj, claimed in his farewell speech to the public that he had achieved most of the targets in his government policy. It is too early yet to form an opinion about this matter. Only time will tell. Suffice it is to say that the people sincerely and ardently hope that M.R. Seni Pramoj will energetically lead the country along the path of peace, prosperity and stability, since his intellectual and legal abilities, coupled with vast political experience, have equipped him well for the post.

His government policy may be summarised as follows:

1. The urgent policy.

The Government will take urgent action in expediting the solution of the important problems presently facing the people throughout the country. These are aid to farmers, correction of the high cost of living conditions, maintenance of law and order, suppression of corruption, local administration and the extension of electric service to rural areas.

2. The long term policy.

The Government will uphold the Nation, the Religion and the Monarchy in accordance with the democratic form of government, while strengthening the armed forces for the defence of the monarchy, national independence, security and national interests.

The Government will pursue an independent foreign policy on the basis of mutual friendship and non-interference in the internal affairs of Thailand, especially with countries in the Indo-Chinese peninsula.

The Government will undertake a reform of the economy for the sake of creating social justice and benefit to the country by respecting individual rights to possess property. It will also reform the system of taxation, undertake the role of operating public utilities and other activities for the benefit of the people, and promote internal and foreign trade as well as local and foreign industrial investment.

In the field of education, the Government will carry out reforms so as to harmonise with social and economic conditions. For instance, aid will be given to poor but able students. Emphasis will be placed on agricultural and industrial disciplines.

With regard to the public welfare, the health services will be expanded to cover all the districts of the Kingdom. Free medical treatment will be arranged for the poor. Housing will be constructed to meet public requirements.

The Government will reform its administration, so that officials will genuinely serve the people. Freedom of the judiciary in the execution of its duties will also be respected.

On April 30, 1976, M.R. Seni Pramoj won a resounding victory for his government policy in the House of Representatives by a vote of 212 to 5. It is, therefore, generally hoped that this will provide a firm and solid support for his Government to fulfill its term of office according to the constitution of 1974.

In conclusion, it is a matter of real contentment to record that whatever may happen to Thailand, the people will always look up hopefully to His Majesty King Bhumibol Adulyadej as the symbol of unity. Since his return from Switzerland to Bangkok to reign over the people in December 1951, following the death of the Regent, Prince Rangsit of Jainat, he has easily proved himself to be a shining example of what a good and great monarch should be in accordance with Thai tradition. Discarding his layman's garb, he entered the monkhood from October 22, 1956 to November 5, 1956, thus securing a profound knowledge of both theoretical and practical Buddhism. From June 1960 to January 1961, he made a world tour, paying state visits to the United States of America, Great Britain, West Germany, France, Italy, Switzerland, Denmark, Norway, Sweden, the Netherlands, Belgium, Luxemburg, Portugal, and Spain, thereby strengthening the already existing ties of friendship and stimulating wide interest in Thailand. After his brilliant success in military science at Dultroon College in Australia, His Royal Highness Prince Vajiralongkorn who is his only son is now the Crown Prine of Thailand. The King always regards the well-being of the people as of prime concern to him, for he has up till now, visited them practically all over the Kingdom. Long may he reign over the people.

# BIBLIOGRAPHY

## BOOKS

*An Account of Ayutthaya by Khun Luang Wat Pradu Rongtham.* Royal Library Edition. Bangkok, 1970. (คำให้การขุนหลวงวัดประดู่โรงธรรม ฉบับหอหลวง)

*An Account of the Krungkao People.* Bangkok, 1924. (คำให้การชาวกรุงเก่า)

Anuman Rajadhon, Phya. *History of the Customs Duties.* Bangkok, 1939. (ตำนานศุลกากร)

........ *The Thai Nation.* Bangkok, 1940. (เรื่องของชาติไทย)

Bidhayalaph, Krom Muen (H.H.Prince Dhani Nivat). *The Restoration of Culture by Rama I.* Bangkok, 1957. (เรื่องพระบาทสมเด็จพระพุทธยอดฟ้าจุฬาโลกทรงฟื้นฟูวัฒนธรรม)

*Biography of Field Marshal Sarit Thanarat by the Army.* Bangkok, 1964. (อนุสรณ์ ฯพณฯ จอมพลสฤษฎิ์ ธนะรัชต์ กองทัพบกจัดพิมพ์)

*Collected Correspondence of King Chulalongkorn Concerning the Administration of the Kingdom, Part 3 Section 1.* Bangkok, 1970. (ประชุมพระราชหัตถเลขาพระบาทสมเด็จพระจุลจอม-เกล้าเจ้าอยู่หัวที่ทรงบริหารราชการแผ่นดิน ภาค ๓ ตอน ๑ ระหว่าง พุทธศักราช ๒๔๓๔ ถึง พุทธศักราช ๒๔๔๓)

*Collected History Part 62 "Western Envoys to Bangkok."* Bangkok, 1937. (ประชุมพงศาวดาร ภาคที่ ๖๒ เรื่องทูตฝรั่งสมัยกรุงรัตนโกสินทร์)

*Collected Writings in Honour of Major General H.R.H. Prince Wan Waithayakorn, Krom Muen Naradhip Bongsprapandh.* Bangkok, 1963. (ประชุมนิพนธ์เพื่อถวายพระเกียรติแด่พลตรี พระเจ้าวรวงศ์เธอ กรมหมื่นนราธิปพงศ์ประพันธ์)

*Constitution of the Kingdom of Thailand, enacted on June 20, B.E. 2511 (A.D. 1968).* Bangkok, 1970. (รัฐธรรมนูญแห่งราชอาณาจักรไทย พุทธศักราช ๒๕๑๑)

Damrong Rajanubhab, H.R.H. Prince. *Biography of King Naresuan the Great.* Bangkok, 1960. (พระประวัติสมเด็จพระนเรศวรมหาราช)

........ *History of the Reign of Rama V* (First part). Bangkok, 1950. (พระราชพงศาวดารรัชกาลที่ ๕ ตอนต้น)

........ *Lecture on the Ancient Government of Siam.* Bangkok, 1927. (ลักษณะการปกครองของประเทศสยามแต่โบราณ)

........ *Lectures on Siamese History.* Bangkok, 1924. (บรรยายพงศาวดารสยาม เล่ม ๑)

........ *Story of Pra Ruang.* Bangkok, 1946. (เรื่องพระร่วง)

........ *The Thais Fight the Burmese.* Bangkok, 1932. (เรื่องไทยรบพม่า)

Direk Jayanam. *Thailand and the Second World War.* Bangkok, 1967.
(ไทยกับสงครามโลกครั้งที่สอง)

*Essays on Rama V (Chulalongkorn).* Bangkok, 1952. (ประกวดเรียงความเฉลิมพระเกียรติคุณพระ
บาทสมเด็จพระปรมินทรมหาจุฬาลงกรณ์ พระจุลจอมเกล้าเจ้าอยู่หัว)

*History of Sukhothai Part I.* Bangkok, 1955. (ประวัติศาสตร์สุโขทัยภาค ๑)

*History of the Thai Commerce.* Bangkok, 1943. (วัฒนธรรมไทยเรื่องประวัติการค้าขายของไทย)

*History of the Thai Ministry of Education.* Bangkok: Teachers' Council Press, 1964.
(ประวัติกระทรวงศึกษาธิการ)

*Inscriptions of the Kingdom of Nanchao B.E. 1309.* Printed by the Committee in charge of
publishing historical, cultural and archaeological documents.
(จารึกอาณาจักรน่านเจ้า พ.ศ. ๑๓๐๙)

*Judgments of the Court of Appeal and the Supreme Court on the Death of Rama VIII.* Bangkok, 1955. (คำพิพากษาศาลอุทธรณ์ ศาลฎีกา คดีประทุษร้ายต่อพระบาทสมเด็จพระปรเมนทรมหาอานันท-
มหิดล รัชกาลที่ ๘)

*Judgment of the Criminal Court on the Death of Rama VIII.* Bangkok, 1951.
(คำพิพากษาคดีประทุษร้ายต่อพระบาทสมเด็จพระปรเมนทรมหาอานันทมหิดล รัชกาลที่ ๘)

Khuang Abhaiwongse. *My Life.* Bangkok, 1968. (ชีวิตของข้าพเจ้า)

Laelamsastri, Luang, Chunhakasikorn, Luang, and Withayawut, Khun. *History of Siam.*
Bangkok, 1947. (ประวัติศาสตร์ไทยสำหรับนักเรียนมัธยม ๔-๕-๖ และเตรียมอุดมศึกษา)

Likhit Hoontrakul. *History of the Relations Between the Thais and the Chinese.* Bangkok,
1966. (ประวัติการสัมพันธ์ระหว่างชาติไทยกับชาติจีน)

Manoon Borisut. *The Thai Council of Ministers.* Bangkok, 1963.
(เรื่องคณะรัฐมนตรี)

*Memorandum on the Work of the Government of Field Marshal P. Pibulsonggram B.E. 2491–
2499 (1948–1956).* (บันทึกผลงานของรัฐบาลจอมพล ป. พิบูลสงคราม ระหว่าง พ.ศ. ๒๔๙๑-๒๔๙๙)

Naradhip Bongsprapandh, Krom Muen (H.R.H. Prince Wan Waithyakorn). *Diplomatic
History of Thailand.* Bangkok, 1958. (ประวัติการทูตของไทย)
......... Article on "Siam." *Journal of the Research Society of Thailand.* (Bangkok) Thai
edition. No. 3 August, 2488 (A.D. 1945).
*National Economic Development Plan B.E. 2504–2509 (1961–1966).* Bangkok, 1960.
(แผนพัฒนาการเศรษฐกิจแห่งชาติระยะเวลา พ.ศ. ๒๕๐๔ ถึง พ.ศ. ๒๕๐๖ และ ถึง พ.ศ. ๒๕๐๙)

Pin Malakul, M.L. *Education under Prince Dhani.* Bangkok, 1969.
(การศึกษาสมัยที่มหาอำมาตย์เอกพระวรวงศ์เธอพระองค์เจ้าธานีนิวัติทรงเป็นเสนาบดีกระทรวงธรรมการ)
Prajakitkorachak, Phya. *History of Yonok.* Bangkok, 1907. (พงศาวดารโยนก)
Prasert, Luang. *History of Siam.* Bangkok, 1943. (พระราชพงศาวดารฉบับหลวงประเสริฐ)
Prayad Buranasiri. *A Summary of the Second National Economic and Social Development*

194

*Plan B.E. 2510–2514 (1967–1971)*. Bangkok, 2510. (สรุปสาระสำคัญแผนพัฒนาการเศรษฐกิจ
และสังคมแห่งชาติฉบับที่ ๒ (๒๕๑๐–๒๕๑๔)

*Present Day Thailand*. Bangkok, 1940. (ไทยในปัจจุบัน)

*A Public Development Programme for Thailand*. Bangkok, 1960. (โครงการพัฒนาเศรษฐกิจ)

*The Return of Some Territories to Thailand*. Bangkok, 1941. (ประเทศไทยเรื่องการได้ดินแดนคืน)

Rong Syamananda. *History of the Thai Ministry of Education*. Bangkok, 1952.
(ประวัติกระทรวงศึกษาธิการ)

*Royal Ceremonies and Activities during King Bhumibol's Monkhood, October-November B.E.
2499 (A.D. 1956)*. Bangkok, 1970. (พระราชพิธีและพระราชกิจในการทรงผนวช ตุลาคม–
พฤศจิกายน ๒๔๙๙)

*Royal History of Siam*. Royal Autograph Edition. Bangkok, 1938.
(พระราชพงศาวดารฉบับพระราชหัตถเลขา)

*The Royal House of Chakri*. Bangkok, 1969. (ราชสกุลวงศ์)

Sa-nguan Leksakun. *Reform Work in Rama V's Reign*. Bangkok, 1963.
(งานปฏิรูปในรัชกาลที่ ๕)

Seni Pramoj, M.R. *Thai Laws in the Ayutthaya Period*. Bangkok, 1967. (กฎหมายสมัยอยุธยา)

*Siam from Ancient to Present Times*. Bangkok, 1927. (หนังสือสยามตั้งแต่ยุคดึกดำบรรพ์ถึงสมัย
ปัจจุบัน)

Siri Premchit. *Thai History during the Democratic Period of Thirty Years*. *Bangkok*, 1962.
(ประวัติศาสตร์ไทยในระบอบประชาธิปไตย ๓๐ ปี)

Songsri Arch-Arun. *Extra-Territoriality in Rama VI's Reign*. Bangkok, 1963.
(การแก้ไขสนธิสัญญาว่าด้วยสิทธิสภาพนอกอาณาเขตกับประเทศมหาอำนาจในรัชสมัยพระบาทสมเด็จพระมง-
กุฎเกล้าเจ้าอยู่หัว)

*Statements of Policy by Governments of Thailand since 1932*. Bangkok. (Typescript)
(นโยบายของคณะรัฐบาลต่าง ๆ ตั้งแต่ พ.ศ. ๒๔๗๕ เป็นต้นมา)

Sukhum Naipradit, Luang. *My Story in Brief*. Bangkok, 1967.
(หนังสือบันทึกเรื่องของข้าพเจ้าโดยย่อ)

*Thailand during the Period of National Reconstruction*. Bangkok, 1941.
(ไทยในสมัยสร้างชาติที่ระลึกงานฉลองวันชาติ ๒๔๘๔)

Tipakornwong, Chao Phya. *History of the Reign of Rama I*. Bangkok, 1935.
(พระราชพงศาวดารรัชกาลที่ ๑)

......... *History of the Reign of Rama II*. Bangkok, 1961.
(พระราชพงศาวดารรัชกาลที่ ๒)

......... *History of the Reign of Rama III*. Bangkok, 1938.
(พระราชพงศาวดารรัชกาลที่ ๓)

......... *History of the Reign of Rama IV*. Bangkok, 1934.
(พระราชพงศาวดารรัชกาลที่ ๔)

Vajiravudh, King. *A Tour of the City of Sukhothai*. Bangkok, 1928.
(เรื่องเที่ยวเมืองพระร่วง)

Vichitmatra, Khun. *Thai Background*. Bangkok, 1934. (หลักไทย)

Vichitvadhakarn, Luang. *Research Work on Thai Peoples*. Bangkok, 1961.
(งานค้นคว้าเรื่องชนชาติไทย)

......... *Universal History*. Bangkok, 1950. 5 vols.
(ประวัติศาสตร์สากล)

Varapakpibul, Pra. *Lectures on the Legal History of Thailand*. Bangkok, 1953.
(คำบรรยายประวัติศาสตร์กฎหมายไทย)


**IN ENGLISH**


Anuman Rajadhon, Phya. *The Cultures of Thailand*. Thailand Cultural Series No.2. 2nd
ed. Bangkok: National Culture Institute, 1953.

*Aspects and Facets of Thailand*. Bangkok: Public Relations Department, 1959.


Bidyalabh, Krom Muen (H.H. Prince Dhani Nivat). *An Outline of Siamese Cultural History*.
Bangkok: Prachandra Press, 1954.

*Bilateral Treaties and Agreements between Thailand and Foreign Countries and International
Organizations. Volume I: 1617-1869*. Bangkok: Treaty and Legal Department,
Ministry of Foreign Affairs, 1968.

*Bilateral Treaties and Agreements between Thailand and Foreign Countries and International
Organizations. Volume II: 1970-1910*. Bangkok: Treaty and Legal Department,
Ministry of Foreign Affairs, 1969.

Bowring, Sir John. *The Kingdom and People of Siam*. London: Parker, 1857. 2 vols.

*British and Foreign State Papers*. Volume 112, pp. 76-77.


Cady, John F. *Southeast Asia: Its Historical Development*. New York: McGraw-Hill, 1964.

Chula Chakrabongse, H.R.H. Prince. *Lords of Life*. London: Redman Ltd., 1960.

*Chulalongkorn University Announcement B.E. 2512-2513 (1969-1970)*. Bangkok, 1969.

*The Complete Journal of Townsend Harris*. New York, 1930.

Crawfurd, John. *Journal of an Embassy from the Governor-General of India to the Courts of
Siam and Cochin China*. London: Colburn, 1830.

Crosby, Sir Josiah. *Siam: the Crossroad*. London: Oxford University Press, 1945.


Darling, Frank C. *Thailand and the United States*. Washington, D.C.: Public Affairs
Press, 1965.

De Campos, Joaquim. *Early Portuguese Accounts of Thailand*. Journal of the Siam Society,
31, Pt. 1(1940), 1-27.

De La Loubère. *A New Historical Relation of the Kingdom of Siam*. London: Printed by
F.L. for Tho. Horne at the Royal Exchange, Francis Saunders at the New Exchange,
and Tho. Bennet at the Half-Moon in St. Pauls Church-Yard, 1693.

Dodd, D. William Clifton. *The Tai Race*. Cedar Rapids, Iowa, Torch Press, 1923.


*English Translation of the First Stone Inscription of the Sukhotai Period*, 1292.

Fifield, Russell H. *The Diplomacy of Southeast Asia*. 1945-1958. New York: Harper, 1958.

Goodrich, L. Carrington. *A History of the Chinese People*. New York, 1958.
Grim, S. *Thailand in the Light of Official Chinese Historiography*.
A Chapter in the History of the Ming Dynasty by S. Grimm. Journal of Siam Soeiety XLIX, Pt. 1 (July 1961), 1-20.
Griswold, A.B. *King Mongkut of Siam*. New York: the Asia Society, 1961.

Hall, D.G.E. *A History of South-East Asia*, London: Macmillan, 1955.
Harvey, G.E. *History of Burma*. London: Longmans, 1929.
Htin Aung Maung. *A History of Burma*. New York and London: Columbia University Press, 1967.
Hutchinson, E.W. *Adventurers in Siam in the Seventeenth Century*. London: the Royal Asiatic Society, 1940.

Ingram, James C. *Economic Change in Thailand since 1850*, Stanford: Stanford University Press, 1955.
Insor, D. *Thailand: A Political, Social, and Economic Analysis*. London: G. Allen and Unwin, 1963.

Landon, Kenneth P. *Siam in Transition*. Chicago: University of Chicago Press, 1939.
Le May, Reginald. *The Coinage of Siam*, 2nd ed. Bangkok: the Siam Society, 1961.

Nathabanja, Luang. *Extraterritoriality in Siam*. Bangkok: Bangkok Daily Mail, 1924.
Nuechterlein, Donald E. *Thailand and the Struggle for South-East Asia*. Ithaca: Cornell University Press, 1965.

Pieris, P.E. *Religious Intercourse between Ceylon and Siam in the Eighteenth Century*. Bangkok: Siam Observer Office, 1908.
Prachoom Chomchai. *Chulalongkorn the Great*. Tokyo: Centre for East Asian Cultural Studies, 1965.

Reeve, W.D. *Public Administration in Siam*. London: Royal Institute of International Affairs, 1951.
*Report of the Superintendent of Siamese Government Students in Great Britain for the Period April 1929 to March 1930 B.E. 2472*. Edinburgh: the Darien Press, 1931.

Sarasas, Pra. *My Country Thailand*. Bangkok: Chatra Press, 1956.
Sayre, Francis Bowes. *Glad Adventure*. New York: Macmillan, 1957.
Seidenfaden, Major Erik. *The Thai Peoples*. Bangkok: the Siam Society, 1958.
Silcock, T.H., ed. *Thailand: Social and Economic Studies in Development*. Canberra: Australian National University Press, 1967.
Siwasariyanon, Wit. *Trends and Highlights of Thai Literature*. In *Aspects and Facets of Thailand*. Bangkok: Public Relations Department, 1959.
Smith, Malcolm. *A Physician at the Court of Siam*. London: Country Life, 1946.
Smith, Ronald Bishop. *Siam or the History of the Thais from the Earliest Times to 1569 A.D.*

Maryland: Decatur Press, 1966.
......... *Siam or the History of the Thais from 1569 A.D. to 1824 A.D.* Maryland: Decatur Press, 1967.
Spinks, Charles Nelson. *The Ceramic Wares of Siam.* Bangkok: the Siam Society, 1965.

*Thailand Official Year Book 1968.* Bangkok, 1968.
*Thailand, Past and Present.* Bangkok: Thai Watana Panich, 1957.
Thompson, Virginia. *Thailand: the New Siam.* New York: Paragon Book Reprint Corporation, 1967.

Vella, Walter F. *Siam under Rama III, 1824-1851.* New York : Augustin Incorporated Publishing, 1957.

Wales, H.G. Quaritch. *Ancient Siamese Government and Administration.* London: Bernard Quaritch, Ltd., 1934.
Wiens, Herald J. *China's March Towards the Tropics.* Connecticut: Shoestring Press, 1954.
Wenk, Klaus. *The Restoration of Thailand under Rama I.* 1782-1809. Tucson: University of Arizona Press, 1963.
Wood, W.A.R. *Consul in Paradise.* London: Souvenir Press, 1965.
......... *A History of Siam from the Earliest Times to the Year A.D. 1781. with, a Supplement Dealing with More Recent Events.* Bangkok: Siam Barnakich, 1933.

Xumsai, M.L. Manich. *History of Laos.* Bangkok: Chalermnit, 1967.

**IN FRENCH**

Aymonier, Etienne. *Le Siam Ancien.* Paris: Imprimerie Nationale, 1903.

Coedès, George. *Les Etats Hinduisés d' Indochine et d' Indonésie.* Paris: E. De Boccard, 1948.

Fistié, Pierre. *L' Evolution de la Thaïlande.* Paris:Armand Colin, 1967.

Pallegoix, Mgr. *Description du Royaume Thaï ou Siam.* Paris: La Mission de Siam, 1854.
Plion-Bernier, Raymond. *Fêtes et Cérémonies de Thaïlande.* Bangkok: Assumption Press, 1969.

Suvanij, Pensri. *Les Relations entre la France et la Thaïlande (Siam) au XIX siècle d' après les Archives des Affaires Etrangères.* Bangkok: Librarie Chalermnit, 1962.

198

**PERIODICALS**

Bulletin of the Faculty of Arts, Chulalongkorn University. Bangkok, 1964. In Thai. (อักษรศาสตร์)

Bulletin of History, Documents and Archaeology. Bangkok, 1969. In Thai. (แถลงงาน ประวัติศาสตร์ เอกสารโบราณคดี)

Bulletin of the National Assembly of Thailand. Bangkok, 1963. In Thai. (ข่าวรัฐสภาสาร)

Bulletin of Silpakorn. Bangkok, 1967, 1968. In Thai. (นิตยสารศิลปากร)

Journal of Siam Society. Bangkok, 1967, 1968.

Royal Gazette of Thailand. Bangkok, 1917, 1932. In Thai. (ราชกิจจานุเบกษา)

# INDEX